W9-DCG-416

DATE DUE

GAYLORD

PRINTED IN U.S.A.

One Voice and Many

One Voice and Many

Modern Poets in Dialogue

Beth Ellen Roberts

DELAWARE

Newark: University of Delaware Press

Associated University Presses
2010 Eastpark Boulevard
Cranbury, NJ 08512

The paper used in this publication meets the requirements of the American National Standard for Permanence of Paper for Printed Library Materials Z39.48-1984.

Library of Congress Cataloging-in-Publication Data

Roberts, Beth Ellen, 1963–
    One voice and many : modern poets in dialogue / Beth Ellen Roberts.
       p.   cm.
    Includes bibliographical references and index.
    ISBN 0-87413-907-4 (alk. paper)
    1. English poetry—20th century—History and criticism.   2. Modernism (Literature)—English speaking countries.   3. American poetry—20th century—History and criticism.   4. Body and soul in literature.   5. One (The One in philosophy)   6. Philosophy in literature.   7. Many (Philosophy) I. Title.
    PR605.M63R63   2006
    821'.9109384—dc22   2005019243

Contents

Acknowledgments

I WOULD LIKE TO THANK THE EDITORS OF THE UNIVERSITY OF DELAware Press, especially Donald Mell. The book was produced with guidance and support from: Barry Ahearn, Suzanne del Gizzo, Christine Ferguson, Ellen Burton Harrington, E. Kay Harris, Michael Kuczynski, Cynthia Lowenthal, Donald Pizer, Christopher Ricks, and Molly Travis. A portion of the chapter on Robert Frost was presented as a paper at a symposium sponsored by the Leslie Center for the Humanities at Dartmouth College, and I am greateful for the feedback I received from the Frost scholars there. The Tulane University Graduate School and the University of Southern Mississippi provided financial support.

I am also grateful for permission to publish excerpts from:

THE AGE OF ANXIETY by W.H. Auden, copyright 1947 by W.H. Auden and renewed 1975 by Monroe K. Spears and William Meredith, executors of the Estate of W.H. Auden. Used by permission of Random House, Inc.

"A Never Naught Song," "Build Soil," "West-Running Brook," and "The Literate farmer and the Planet Venus" from THE POETRY OF ROBERT FROST edited by Edward Connery Lathem. Copyright 1936, 1942, 1956, 1962 by Robert Frost, copyright 1964, 1970 by Lesley Frost Ballantine, copyright 1928, 1969 by Henry Holt and Company. Reprinted by permission of Henry Holt and Company, LLC.

"An Eclogue for Christmas," "Eclogue By a Five-Barred Gate," "Eclogue From Iceland," "Eclogue Between the Motherless," and "Plurality" from THE COLLECTED POEMS OF LOUIS MACNEICE edited by E. R. Dodds. Copyright 1966 by the estate of Louis MacNeice, 1967 by the Oxford University Press. Reproduced by permission of David Higham Associates.

Abbreviations for Primary Works

CP	Auden, W. H. *Collected Poems*. Ed. Edward Mendelson. New York: Random House, 1976.
CW	Auden, W. H. *The Complete Works of W. H. Auden*. Vol. 2: *Prose: 1939–1948*. Ed. Edward Mendelson. Princeton: Princeton University Press, 2002.
DH	Auden, W. H. *The Dyer's Hand and Other Essays*. New York: Random House, 1962.
E&I	Yeats, W. B. *Essays and Introductions*. New York: MacMillan, 1961.
FA	Auden, W. H. *Forewords and Afterwords by Auden*. Ed. Edward Mendelson. New York: Random House, 1973.
KE	Eliot, T. S. *Knowledge and Experience in the Philosophy of F. H. Bradley*. New York: Farrar, Straus, 1964.
Life	Hardy, Thomas. *The Life and Work of Thomas Hardy*. Ed. Michael Millgate. Athens, GA: University of Georgia Press, 1985.
Memoirs	Yeats, W. B. *Memoirs*. Ed. Denis Donoghue. New York: MacMillan, 1972.
MP	MacNeice, Louis. *Modern Poetry: A Personal Essay*. 1938. New York: Haskell House Publishers, 1969.
PW	Hardy, Thomas. *Thomas Hardy's Personal Writings*. Ed. Harold Orel. London: MacMillan, 1967.
PWBY	MacNeice, Louis. *The Poetry of W. B. Yeats*. 1941. New York: Oxford University Press, 1969.
SE	Eliot, T. S. *Selected Essays 1917–1932*. New York: Harcourt, Brace, 1932.
SF	MacNeice, Louis. *The Strings Are False: An Unfinished Autobiography*. Ed. E. R. Dodds. London: Faber and Faber, 1965.
SL	Frost, Robert. *Selected Letters of Robert Frost*. Ed. Lawrance Thompson. New York: Holt, Rinehart and Winston, 1964.
SLC	MacNeice, Louis. *Selected Literary Criticism of Louis MacNeice*. Ed. Alan Heuser. Oxford: Clarendon Press, 1987.
SP	Frost, Robert. *Selected Prose of Robert Frost*. Ed. Hyde Cox

and Edward Connery Latham. New York: Holt, Rinehart and Winston, 1966.

Vision   Yeats, W. B. *A Vision*. 1937. N.p.: Collier Books, 1970.

VMP   Eliot, T. S. *The Varieties of Metaphysical Poetry*. Ed. Ronald Schuchard. New York: Harcourt, Brace & Co., 1993.

One Voice and Many

1
Introduction

If you know whether a man is a decided monist or a decided pluralist, you perhaps know more about the rest of his opinions than if you give him any other name ending in ist. To believe in the one or in the many, that is the classification with the maximum number of consequences.
—William James, *Pragmatism*

Both the One and the Many as well as man's relation to them must forever elude final formulation.
—Irving Babbitt, *The Masters of Modern French Criticism*

The relationship between form and matter is like a marriage; matter must find itself in form and form must find itself in matter.
—Louis MacNeice, *The Poetry of W. B. Yeats*

IN HIS STUDY OF W. B. YEATS, LOUIS MACNEICE TAKES A STRONG STAND on the relationship between content and form in poetry: "It is an outrage to a poem to think of it as such-and-such matter plus such-and-such form, or even as a matter put into form. Form must not be thought of as a series of rigid moulds" (*PWBY*, 19). "Artistic form," he continues, "is more than a mere method or convenience or discipline or, of course, décor." Furthermore, he argues, content and form interpenetrate in a manner analogous to the relationship between body and soul: "Just as one cannot, by the furthest analysis, completely deformalize matter, so one cannot completely desubstantialize form. . . . Artists use form not merely to express some alien matter but because form itself is a spiritual principle which calls for expression in matter." As a compound of "form" and "matter," a poem, according to Mac-Neice represents "a complex unity, that is, complex *but* a unity (or a unity *but* complex)" (22). Just as a marriage exists as a unity

13

that contains two individuals, a poem is a unity in which content and form co-inhere but maintain their individual characteristics. By defining a poem as a "complex unity," MacNeice situates questions regarding the nature of poetry squarely within one of the most compelling debates of the first half of the twentieth century, that of the problem of the One and the Many.

From the late nineteenth century through the beginning of the twentieth, the problem of the relationship between unity and plurality, between the world and the individual, occupied the minds, lectures, and writings of the most eminent philosophers of both Europe and America. For Irving Babbitt, the "question of the One and the Many, on which all the other main aspects of our modern thought finally converge"[1] had such primacy that "all other philosophical problems are insignificant in comparison."[2] In the chapter of *Pragmatism* called "The One and the Many," William James declares that he considers this paradox "the most central of all philosophic problems"[3] and concludes that the pragmatist "must equally abjure absolute monism and absolute pluralism."[4] Most of his contemporaries agree that the real problem of the One and the Many lies in the paradoxical simultaneity of the two. As Bertrand Russell describes this difficulty in *The Problems of Philosophy*, "According to our temperaments, we shall prefer the contemplation of the one or of the other. The one we do not prefer will probably seem to us a pale shadow of the one we prefer, and hardly worthy to be regarded as in any sense real. But the truth is that both have the same claim on our impartial attention, both are real, and both are important to the metaphysician. Indeed no sooner have we distinguished the two worlds than it becomes necessary to consider their relations."[5] The fact that, as Babbitt states it, "Both the One and the Many as well as man's relation to them must forever elude final formulation,"[6] engendered a heated debate. Josiah Royce found it so disturbing that F. H. Bradley's ontological theory "undertakes to render wholly impossible . . . any explicit and detailed reconciliation of the One and the Many, or any positive theory of how Individuals find their place in the Absolute,"[7] that Royce added an essay called "The One, the Many, and the Infinite," in which he defends the concept of the "Infinite Multitude,"[8] to the 1900 edition of *The World and the Individual*.

The One/Many problem has concerned philosophers since

long before the twentieth century; according to the *Cambridge Dictionary of Philosophy*, "early Greek metaphysics revolved around the problem of the one and the many," and it was "the central question for pre-Socratic philosophers."[9] Among the pre-Socratics,

> [t]hose who answered "one," the monists, ascribed to all things a single nature such as water, air, or oneness itself. They appear not to have been troubled by the notion that numerically many things would have this one nature. The pluralists, on the other hand, distinguished many principles or many types of principles, though they also maintained the unity of each principle. Some monists understood the unity of all things as a denial of motion, and some pluralists advanced their view as a way of refuting this denial. . . . In the modern period the dispute between monists and pluralists centered on the question whether mind and matter constitute one or two substances and, if one, what its nature is.[10]

Modern thinkers, however, apply this terminology more widely than is suggested by the *Cambridge Dictionary*, and an understanding of the possible variations on conceptions of the relationship between the One and the Many, as well as the ways in which these relate to variations in dialogue forms, requires a further exploration of the problem. What the *Cambridge Dictionary* conveys most clearly is that possibilities for understanding the terms "One" and "Many," and, therefore, the possible relationships between the two, abound. Confusion is inevitable. Two general divisions exist for each of the terms: the unity implied by the "One" may be either immanent or transcendent, and the multiplicity implied by the "Many" may be either dualistic or pluralistic. Further confusion results from the fact that a Neoplatonic belief in a transcendent unity requires the creation of certain dualistic philosophies, so that such dualisms actually imply a belief in a One,[11] and some types of monism, such as materialism, result in a perception of disunity. This means that monism and unity, and pluralism and multiplicity, might or might not coincide.

As the *Cambridge Dictionary* notes, monistic philosophies date back at least as far as the pre-Socratics; a belief that "all is one," a type of substantial monism, is attributed by Plato to Parmenides. As one, being necessarily must be indivisible and therefore unchangeable and eternal. Parmenides' and all other visions of the One exclude the temporal, or division of eternity. Because the material world is manifestly divisible and changeable, Plato and others posit a transcendent spiritual realm of unity, separate and superior to the physical world. This leads to a body/soul duality in which the eternal, unextended soul represents the One descended into this world, a spirit which, when released from the body will reascend to the One. In Christian thought, that unity is God, the realm of the soul is in God's heaven, and, in the particular case of the Incarnation, the descent of the One into bodily form is that of God himself. In Neoplatonic systems, such of those of Plotinus or kabbalist mysticism, the One exists simultaneously as a nongenerative, indivisible being and as a series of emanations that emerge from that being and descend into the material world. In systems in which the unity is transcendent, the relationship between an individual person and the One has no bearing on the relationship of one individual to another individual, nor on the relationship of the individual to the material world. Relationships between individuals, however, and/or relationships between individuals and nature become necessary for unity in most conceptions of an immanent One, such as those found in pantheism, Buddhism, Hinduism, Bergsonism, and so on. Human society then becomes important, and the focus moves to community rather than the individual.

Different ideas of the Many also come with their own sets of variants and associated factors. When the "Many" takes the form of a pluralism such as that of Democritus, no transcendent unity can exist, and, therefore, no absolute truth. Time exists as a succession of points. The nature of the world is one of flux in which change is continual. Individuals may create temporary, partial bonds, but do not truly participate in any One. Dualism would seem to be by definition on the side of the Many, but as we have seen in the case of body/soul dualism, such a split does not necessarily preclude a belief in any given type of unity. When the One/Many takes the form of a dualism in which the question is whether mind and matter are identical, the duality may precipitate a number of different answers. Descartes' distinction between extended substance and thinking substance privileges the Many, but also endows the soul with characteristics of the One, including immateriality and immortality. Certain types of idealism favor the One, others the Many. Absolute idealism, in which a mind outside of the world creates that world, is a form of a transcendent One. Personal idealism, on the other hand, in which the minds of individuals constitute the world, is clearly on the side of the Many. Also, certain types of materialism, such as those of Hobbes, Marx, and modern scientists, which suggest that mind arises out of the matter of the brain, although technically monistic, deny any sort of unity other than that of substance.

In the early twentieth century, philosophers began to superimpose this problem on all of the major problems of the day, in science, psychology, theology, and even literary criticism. The dissemination of these ideas is in large part attributable to the charisma of Henri Bergson, whose theories were so wildly popular that his lectures became social events at which admirers showered him with flowers as if he were a stage idol; in just two years, the British press published more than two hundred articles about him, and all of his books were translated into English between 1910 and 1912.[12] In *Creative Evolution*, Bergson applies the One/Many problem to the science of biology, suggesting that if "the distinctive feature of the organized body is that it grows and changes without ceasing, as indeed the most superficial observation testifies, there would be nothing astonishing in the fact that it was *one* in the first instance, and afterwards *many*. The reproduction of unicellular organisms consists in just this— the living being divides into two halves, of which each is a complete individual."[13] He goes on to extrapolate from the cellular level to that of the individual, stating that the self constitutes "a unity that is multiple and a multiplicity that is one; but unity and multiplicity are only views of my personality taken by an understanding that directs its categories at me. . . . Such is my inner life, and such also is life in general."[14] Jung's principle of the four faculties of the personality has its origin in this Bergsonian concept, and Bergson's thinking anticipated paradoxes in physics, such as the particle-wave theory of light, which assert the simultaneity of One and Many.

In literary criticism, the One/Many problem serves as a paradigm for critics like Babbitt and George Santayana. In *The Masters of Modern French Criticism*, Babbitt justifies this con-

junction of philosophy and criticism: "For, to inquire whether
the critic can judge, and if so by what standards, is only a form
of the more general inquiry whether the philosopher can
discover any unifying principle to oppose mere flux and relativity."[15] He credits Bergson and James with performing a "substantial service to philosophy in thus turning its attention to what
Plato would have called the problem of the One and the
Many."[16] Santayana begins his *Three Philosophical Poets* with
praise for the interaction of the One and the Many in Lucretius's
De Rerum Natura. It is the simultaneity of the two, he claims,
that leads to "a very great thought, perhaps the greatest thought
that mankind has ever hit upon, and which was the chief inspiration of Lucretius. It is that all we observe about us, and ourselves also, may be so many passing forms of a permanent
substance."[17] All philosophies, he argues, no matter the forms
they assume, exist to establish some sort of unity to allow us to
deal with the "the same vicissitudes of good and evil," which
mark the paradoxically permanent mutability of life.

In criticism, as in other fields, the model of the One/Many paradox was expanded to encompass a number of related dualities.
Perhaps the best-known literary application of the problem appears in T. S. Eliot's "Tradition and the Individual Talent,"
which asserts a reciprocal relationship between individual poets
and the whole of tradition and culture. His lamentation of the
"dissociation of sensibility" in "The Metaphysical Poets" is also
grounded in a desire to fuse feeling and thought in the state of
immediate experience; in his dissertation, Eliot relates the feel-
ing/thought duality with the subject/object and unity/multiplic-
ity pairs among those united in the condition of immediate
experience (*KE*, 18–19). James Smith, in a 1933 essay in *Scrutiny*,
makes a more explicit connection between metaphysical poetry
and the philosophical question, submitting a definition of such
poetry: "It is, that verse properly called metaphysical is that to
which the impulse is given by an overwhelming concern with
metaphysical problems; with problems either deriving from, or
closely resembling in the nature of their difficulty, the problem
of the Many and the One."[18] Smith associates a number of dichotomies beyond the question of monism versus pluralism
with this problem:

For whether the problems discussed by metaphysics in its long history are or are not derived from that of the Many and the One, they resemble it in the nature of their difficulty, and they are restricted in number. At times the individual has fought against, and depended upon, its fellow individual, much as multiplicity unity; or the individual has fought against the universal; or against the universe, or against God. Or the here-now has risen up against its natural ally the then-there, and both have risen up against eternity. Or the spirit, partaking of the universal, has had nothing to do with the flesh; and the flesh, primed with the certainty of the here-now has dismissed the spirit as a fable. And so on.[19]

Smith was by no means alone in grouping these questions together; numerous writers of the early twentieth century employ the One/Many problem as a means of exploring various types of relationships between unity and plurality, not just the philosophical implications, in their poetry and prose, including essays, letters, diaries, and other writings. A chart of characteristics generally associated with the One and the Many appears below:

ONE	**MANY**
Unity	Multiplicity
Monism	Pluralism
Eternal, atemporal, history	Ephemeral, temporal, present
Soul	Body
Faith, intuition	Science, reason
World, society	Individual
Absolute truth	Relativism
Stasis	Flux
Classicism	Romanticism
Content (by analogy with the soul)	Form (by analogy with the body)

Eliot, in his Clark lectures on metaphysical poetry, declared, "Surely the thinking of the poet should be no more than transposing into poetry the thought of the time which he selects as important to him" (*VMP*, 223–24). For the modernists, the transposition into poetry of a philosophy that envisions a simultaneity of One and Many suggested the need not only for an avowal of that idea in poetry, but also as the establishment of a relationship between content and form. T. E. Hulme, who was early in his career an adherent of James and Bergson,[20] advocated the use of free verse as appropriate to the manifestation of a modern pluralistic philosophy. In his "Lecture on Modern Poetry," he associates the formality of classical poetry with the "hypostasized ideas of Plato" and a desire "to create a static fixity" against a "universal flux which frightened them"; since society no longer believes in "absolute truth," he says, modern poets must do away with regular meter.[21] Michael Levenson painstakingly traces the convergence of two opposing currents of thought in his 1982 book, *A Genealogy of Modernism*, contending that the development of modern poetic form involved "a doctrinal struggle waged often between mutually excluding extremes" in which "apostles of freedom contended with guardians of order, realists with abstractionists, sceptics with dogmatists, subjectivists with anti-humanists" that converge finally in Eliot.[22] According to this view, decided pluralists vied with decided monists for control of the modernist agenda, with no interchange occurring between the two camps.

The problem with such a division is that allegiances to pluralistic and monistic philosophies tended to shift, sometimes from one side to the other, sometimes between competing versions of pluralism or monism. Robert Frost begins his career as an adherent of Jamesian pragmatic pluralism and ends as a theist. Louis MacNeice starts out as an Absolute Idealist and winds up ridiculing all Idealism in a poem titled "Plurality." Eliot seeks unity throughout his career, but moves from Bradleyan Idealism to Anglo-Catholicism. What remained constant was an interest in the paradox of the universal and the particular. Not surprisingly, the poets who studied in the Harvard philosophy department that was home to Royce, James, Babbitt and Santayana, including Eliot, Frost, and Wallace Stevens, incorporated frequent explicit and implicit explorations of the problem of the One and the Many into their poetry.[23]

Because various philosophies of the One and the Many found their ways into literary theory, aesthetics, psychology, theology, and even popular culture, modern writers who did not study philosophy at Harvard also devoted their energies to investigations of the problem, from the very beginning of the century to its midpoint. In his source study, *The Shaping of "The Dynasts,"*

Walter F. Wright traces the influence of Arthur Schopenhauer and Eduard von Hartmann on Thomas Hardy's philosophical development and recognizes that *The Dynasts* is "a poem that attempts to symbolize both the monistic Will and the plural phenomena."[24] W. H. Auden claimed to share a similar "world and sensibility" with Hardy, whom he called his "first master" (*DH*, 38), and he immersed himself in Jung's psychology and the theology of Søren Kierkegaard and Reinhold Niebuhr, whose ideas of the relationship between one and many he examines in poems such as *For the Time Being*, *The Sea and the Mirror*, and *The Age of Anxiety*.[25]

Levenson identifies *The Waste Land* as the first formal equivalent to the recognition of a paradoxical relationship between unity and plurality: "[T]he poetic solution is continuous with the philosophic solution: individual experiences, individual personalities are not impenetrable. They are distinct, but not wholly so. Like the points of view described in the dissertation, the fragments in *The Waste Land* merge with one another, pass into one another."[26] While Levenson is correct about the correlation between the form of the poem and Eliot's belief that multiplicity and unity depend only on one's point view, Eliot was neither the first poet to explore the relationship of One and Many, nor was *The Waste Land* the first poem to exhibit a form appropriate to such an exploration. Eliot's use of multiple voices in *The Waste Land* represents not a radical break with conventional form, but a refinement of the ancient and well-established tradition of dialogue poetry. Eliot himself experimented with variations on dialogue forms from the very beginning of his career, and throughout the first half of the twentieth century, poets used dialogue forms extensively to represent links between aspects of the One/Many problem, including those between the individual and the world, between body and soul, and between faith and reason. Poems written in dialogue forms, that is, poetry in which lines are attributed to more than one voice, inevitably recapitulate the question of the relationships between One and Many, because such poems must be understood both as the products of the one voice of the poet and of the multiple voices of the poem's designated speakers.

In the first half of the twentieth century, dialogue forms enjoyed a tremendous popularity, among poets if not among readers. In its first ten years (1912–21), *Poetry* not only published numerous dialogue poems, but actively encouraged their production. Of the regular prizes, including the Levinson prize, awarded by *Poetry* in its first decade, eight went to dialogue poems.[27] In 1916, the magazine offered a hundred-dollar prize for the best verse drama submitted, a prize won by a young poet named Wallace Stevens. *Poetry* was not the only publication in which dialogue poetry appeared; the four editions of *Georgian Poetry* contain an average of three dialogue poems each, and a number of book-length dramatic poems appeared as well.[28] Poets from across the philosophical spectrum produced adaptations of the conventional dialogue forms, which include eclogues, ballads, dialogues of body and soul, and dramatic verse.

Not only do dialogue forms represent the paradox of the One and the Many in the presence of multiple voices derived from the one voice of the poet, these forms also allow the poet to represent different types of monistic and pluralistic philosophies through the manipulation of the distances inherent in dialogue poetry. Each poet's depictions of the relationships between individuals is informed by his understanding of the relationship between One and Many. While readers of dialogue poetry remain aware of the one voice behind the many speakers, pure dialogue forms—those without any narrative or other type of unifying voice—naturally tend toward a sense of plurality. The more that one believes that multiplicity predominates over unity, the less one believes in connections between individuals. As a means of representing the gaps between people, dialogue poetry has an advantage over lyric and narrative forms in that it contains three inherent types of distance, one more than the other forms. In lyric or narrative poetry, distances exist between the poet and the poem, and between the poem and the reader, but dialogue poetry also includes the distance between speakers.

Edward Mendelson claims that "[a]mong the historical crises faced, and in part invented, by modernism was a breakdown in what might be called the symbolic contract, the common frame of reference and expectation that joins a poet with a finite audience, and joins both with the subjects of his poems."[29] His acknowledgment that the "breakdown" in the relationships between poet, poem, and reader was "in part invented" by the modernists falls short of recognizing that poets have a great deal of control over these gaps. In dialogue poems that explicitly or implicitly address the One/Many paradox, a number of modern poets manipulate the distances inherent in the traditional dialogue forms in order to reconcile those forms with the philosophies expressed in the poems. For Auden, adaptation of forms is necessary in order to negotiate between an overly rigid conformity and chaotic multiplicity: "A work of art, like a life, can fail in two different ways: either, in terror of admitting that there is any chaos, it takes refuge in some arbitrary conscious order it has acquired ready-made from others or thought up itself on the spur of the moment, some order which, because it ignores the chaos that exists, can do nothing with it but suppress it; or, lacking the courage and the faith to believe that it is possible and a duty to bring the chaos to order, it contents itself with a purely passive idolization of the flux," (*CW*, 125). "In poetry," he claims, "the first attitude leads to a lifeless academic rhetoric"; the second leads to "the formless, the vague, the nonsensical." A successful marriage of form and content requires a willingness to stay within the bounds of form without allowing the form to distort the content.

The distance between the speakers in written dialogue includes the physical distance on the page, emotional distance (emphasized by the presentation of purely external characteristics), political or philosophical distance (especially in debate poems), and the distance created by difficulties in comprehension of one another's thoughts as represented imperfectly by language. In general, the greater the distance between the speakers, the greater the distance between poet and reader, since the poet's underlying message can be concealed among competing voices and because the reader has difficulty relating to more than one speaker at a time. The more speakers involved in the dialogue, the less chance that their viewpoints can be synthesized by either poet or reader. Poets may also increase the distance between themselves and the poem by adopting a persona, by avoiding the inclusion of any personal information, and by maintaining an air of objectivity through the abstention from commentary on the proceedings. Dialogue poetry features an inherently greater distance between reader and poem than that of lyric or narrative forms as the result of an "eavesdropping" effect because the speakers direct their lines to each other, not to the reader. The lack of an invitation to join or to listen in on the conversation may evoke a feeling of unease, alienation, or even guilt in the reader, which increases the sense of distance. The poet may impose an even greater distance between the reader and the poem by making the poem less approachable through the use of arcane diction or allusions, offensive language or material, or confusing syntax.

Perhaps because dialogue poetry frequently alienates (or bores) readers as a result of the distance it establishes between reader and poem, little critical attention has been paid to it. Despite a history that dates back to classical times and its immense popularity in the early twentieth century, forms of dialogue poetry have been either taken for granted, or, more often, ignored. None of the poets who have written dialogue poetry seem to have articulated their reasons for doing so, and critics who examine dialogue poems by specific poets rarely take notice of the form, focusing only on content. Prose dialogues, however, have attracted several theorists, and the relationship between these forms and the question of unity versus multiplicity has been noted. Michael Prince describes the applicability of dialogue to the representation of a tension between the One and the Many: "Dialogue did nothing less than replicate the fundamental problems of modern philosophy in fictional form. It represented the stages of analytical method—division, analysis, synthesis, and composition—in philosophical fictions. Dialogue portrayed a mind capable of enacting division, of breaking wholes (received truths) down into disparate parts, yet capable also of recovering coherence through the free use of reason. Dialogue dramatized one being made two, and two being made again one."[30] The "fundamental problems of modern philosophy" to which Prince refers, those of the eighteenth century, are essentially the same as those of the early twentieth century—questions as to the ways in which the individual relates to the whole—and dialogue forms serve the same purpose in both eras.

Prince traces two incompatible strains of prose dialogue, one dialectic, resulting in the synthesis of opposing viewpoints, and the other dialogic, in which no unity is possible. He associates the two diametrically opposed situations with those of comedy and tragedy: "The opposition between these two conceptions might be likened to the difference between comedy and tragedy.

In comedy initial divisions among characters often reach a happy reconciliation, usually a marriage of some sort. In tragedy, divisions threaten never to be healed. If dialogue embodies transcendental dialectic, then its structure can be called comedic. If, however, dialogue enacts the possibility of impasse, then it resembles tragedy."[31] The comedic type is typified by religious dialogue in which two speakers appear to debate, but in which the outcome is preordained to verify the existence of a transcendent One. As Prince suggests, "This authority, the transcendent third or *criterium veritatis*, both permitted human agents to reason their way towards divinity and was in turn confirmed by the success of their deliberations."[32] Such dialogues, he claims, "*conventionally* (as an embodiment of metaphysical dialectic) subordinated the many to the one."[33] When the validity of the transcendent One comes under attack, or becomes dependent on the reasonings of the Many, the coherence of the individual speakers dissolves, and the dialogue becomes tragic. Prince traces the rise of such prose dialogues in eighteenth-century England and associates them with an increasing dramatization—in effect, further individuating the speakers—which he credits with the eventual appearance of the novel.[34] Conventional poetic dialogue forms also encompass a range along the scale from One to Many, from dialectic to dialogue.

The poetic equivalent of the religious prose dialogue is the dialogue (or debate) of body and soul, a didactic and allegorical form which had attained a certain popularity by the beginning of the fourteenth century. Rosalie Osmond, in her comprehensive study, *Mutual Accusation: Seventeenth-Century Body and Soul Dialogues in Their Literary and Theological Context*, provides a history of the form and describes its variants. The body/soul duality presupposes a transcendent third that unites the two, making the debate of body and soul, among the conventional dialogue forms, the most predisposed to unity. It is true that the unity between the components of the self, which are, as Osmond says, "essential to one another and yet incompatible,"[35] suffers from a continual impulse to fly apart. Osmond cites Plotinus from the *Enneads* to explain the nature of the relationship: "But when two distinct things become one in an artificial unity, there is a probable source of pain to them in the mere fact that they were inapt to partnership. . . . Then the essential duality becomes also a unity, but a unity standing midway between what the lower was and what it cannot absorb, and therefore a troubled unity."[36] This troubled unity is exemplified by form of the debate of body and soul in which the voices, which we know to be subordinate to the Neoplatonic One, remain stubbornly discrete.

However, any dialogue that portrays the essential construction of dualism implies the possibility of integration. Prince associates the misapprehension of the etymology of "dialogue" as "di-logos" with the idea that "the division of the *logos* is always in principle reversible, from many to two, from two to one" and proposes that "the *logos*, conceived as absolute unity, permits itself to be divided for the sake of human comprehension, with the proviso that division remain all the time a propaedeutic to the recovery of the whole."[37] Roman Jakobson argues that the debate of body and soul is a species of lyric since the two speakers "are presented in the form of two metonymies related to the same object, therefore synonymous—the man with respect to the soul and the same man with respect to the body. Both are objectivized, independent being is attributed to both, which is a typical actualization of synonyms."[38] Jakobson goes too far in making the body and soul equivalent; even though each relates to a single man, they represent irreconcilable opponents battling within him. Nevertheless, the dialogue of body and soul does engender a fairly strong sense of unity.

Another, more ancient form of dialogue poetry, the eclogue, also generally consists of the opposition of two incompatible viewpoints; but, lacking the presence of a truly transcendent third, the eclogue holds less potential for unity. The eclogue originated, according to W. W. Greg, in the fifth-century BCE. when Theocritus adapted the Sicilian peasant tradition of the singing contest into poetry.[39] The singing contest, which, in classical and Renaissance eclogues, usually takes place between a city dweller and a farmer or peasant, conventionally takes place in a *locus amoenus* (pleasant place) and in a golden age. Frequently, the contest is overseen by a judge, usually imagined as the poet, who offers a prize for the winning contestant. Whereas the debate of body and soul (generally thought to have been derived from Virgil's seventh eclogue) takes place between opponents who, though incompatible, are inextricably linked together, the eclogue features disputants who remain distinct individuals. The contest format, with its selection of a winner and bestowal of a prize, ensures that no dialectic occurs, and therefore no synthesis. While the poet or judge stands outside the debate, he cannot transcend it and must elect one side or the other. In his introduction to *The Idylls of Theocritus*, Robert Wells suggests that the eclogue derives from the inability of the Alexandrian poets, Theocritus among them, to locate authority for any absolute truth:

> Their own temperaments and the conditions of the age, with its huge shifts and uncertainties, brought them up against the question of whether a full, direct confrontation with a great subject was possible any longer in poetry. They seem to have felt that they had no way of judging human experience, of knowing whether actions and emotions were trivial or profound, and to have been forced to the conclusion that their art, if it was to keep its integrity, must necessarily be limited in its scope. What the limits were to be was the subject of much debate. In the absence of other fixed points, their poetry is intent on making an absolute value of the words themselves. . . . In tone, on the other hand, it is habitually elusive and ambiguous; it refuses to allow itself to be judged just as it refuses to pass judgement.[40]

The *New Princeton Encyclopedia of Poetry and Poetics* traces the etymology of the word "eclogue," from the Greek *eklegein* (to choose), to the fact that it "originally denoted a selection, i.e., a notable passage from a work or a choice poem;"[41] but *eklegein* might also imply a choice between a multiplicity of viewpoints, which Wells suggests was prevalent among the poets.

The eclogue and debate of body and soul represent one line of dialogue poetry; the other strain, the dramatic, is developed through the ballad and the verse drama, and of these, the ballad is more inclined to unity. Not all ballads employ dialogue, but many folk ballads are made up entirely of dialogue. The *Princeton Encyclopedia* lists three characteristics of the ballad: 1) "Ballads focus on a single crucial episode," 2) "Ballads are dramatic. . . . Protagonists are allowed to speak for themselves, which means that dialogue bulks large," 3) "Ballads are impersonal. The narrator seldom allows his or her own attitude toward the events to intrude."[42] The focus on a single episode gives the ballad an inherent unity not present in the longer verse drama and ensures that the number of speakers is small, usually only two. Furthermore, when there are two speakers, one of them generally acts either as narrator or as an interlocutor who prompts the other in the telling of the story, as in "Lord Randal" ("O where ha' ye been, Lord Randal my son?"). The presence of the ballad singer, even when only implied in a written version, forces the reader's attention to the single voice behind the multiple speakers of the verse, especially when the ballad has narration. The impersonal nature of the narration suggests that the narrator represents a transcendent One, and The *Princeton Encyclopedia* emphasizes this aspect of the narrator's role: "There may be an "I" in a ballad, but the singer does not forget his or her position as the representative of the public voice. Bias there is in ballads, of course, but it is the bias of a party, community, or nation, not an individual's subjective point of view."[43] Because the listener or reader presumably belongs to the same party, community, or nation as the singer and speakers, the ballad can transmit the values of an immanent, as well as a transcendent, unity.

The ability of dramatic poetry to represent the struggle of an individual to discover some equilibrium with unity in a fragmented world and within a fragmented self made it a favorite of the Romantic poets. Dramas like Shelley's *Prometheus Unbound* and Byron's *Manfred*, according to Alan Richardson, work by "fusing the objective portrayal of action with the subjective lyrical voice,"[44] and Richardson points out that Romantic dramas typically concern not only the clash of dichotomous oppositions, but also "their equally violent interpenetration."[45] Although modernist critics generally condemned the Romantics as practitioners of an extravagant individualism, Romanticism is differentiated from the ardent pluralism of postmodernism by its quest to discover some sort of One, whether in nature or in the spiritual realm, and the relationship of the individual to that unity. Even Eliot concedes in "The Metaphysical Poets," that, "in one or two passages" of Romantic poetry, "there are traces of a struggle toward unification of sensibility" (*SE*, 248), and such a tendency is evident in Coleridge's designation of the imagination as an "esemplastic" power in the *Biographia Literaria*.[46] Nevertheless, the importance placed by the Romantics on the individual makes dramatic verse a particularly appropriate form for the mimesis of such a philosophy,[47] since drama typically tends more toward multiplicity than do any of the other conventional dialogue forms.

The exigencies of plot and characterization in dramatic poetry both contribute toward a greater representation of plurality than can be found in the other types of dialogue poetry. Plot relies on transformation, and Prince identifies the true etymology of "dialogue" with the type of dialogue found in dramatic verse: "*Dia* means passage, transition, movement, with no limitation upon the number of voices sharing in the *logos*. The important point here is that emphasis shifts from the *logos* to the activity it enjoins among thinking subjects, finally irreducible one to the other. Thus, another definition of dialogue simply referred to any verbal interaction among two or more voices, leading to no necessary resolution."[48] Passage, transition, movement—all modes of change without which there can be no drama and all antithetical to the eternal, static One. Many dramas also juggle multiple plots, so that the action is fractured and depicts more than one path of mutability. Even if the poet observes the classical unities of time, place and action, the drama still relies on transformation. Adding to the drama's effectiveness in representing multiplicity is the differentiation of the speakers, who are "fleshed out" and given individual motivations, mannerisms, and identities. Dramatic poetry allows for less individuation of the speakers than does prose drama when characters all speak in the same meter; but compared to other types of dialogue poetry, dramatic verse allows for the greatest variety in voice. Obviously, the poet has a great deal of latitude in the development of character—he may invoke unity by making the characters stereotypical or allegorical, or he may distinguish them by having the characters speak in different rhythms and meters. As Prince points out, dramatic dialogue may result in unity, as in comedy, or may conclude in disunity, as in tragedy.[49] Even when the mode is comic, dramatic verse tends more toward multiplicity than toward unity, if for no other reason than the fact that it involves a greater number of speakers than do other types of dialogue poetry, which makes recognition of the one underlying voice of the poet more difficult.

As in all literary criticism, this study has as its basis a search for unity—an underlying pattern, order, an overarching idea—and it finds a common ground in a philosophical problem that was at the center of a cultural phenomenon, and in the intersection of this idea with a concurrent literary aesthetic. But plurality appears in the unique ways in which each poet developed his philosophy, in the ways in which each interprets the problem of the One and the Many, and in the particular ways in which each adapts dialogue forms to match his ideas. Each of the poets examined here—Hardy, Auden, Eliot, Yeats, Frost, and Mac-Neice—is connected in some way: Auden and MacNeice were close friends; Eliot served as an editor to both while at Faber; Eliot and Frost both studied (though a decade apart) philosophy at Harvard; MacNeice claims Eliot and Yeats as his major influences; Frost and Auden were both greatly influenced by Hardy.[50] Each of them, and consequently, each of the poems, is a product not only of the culture of the time, but also of their personal circumstances, including their educations, families, and friends. Their work is a negotiation between the prevailing thought of their time and their own individual experiences, and that tension is particularly visible in their dialogue poems, where the complex unity of content and form amplifies the poets' understandings of the problem of the One and the Many. As this is not a comprehensive study, I cannot claim that all dialogue poems written by modern poets are concerned primarily with the problem of the One and the Many or that they all exhibit the same type of "marriage" between content and form when they do, but all of the poems that I have looked at have fit this pattern.

In his introduction to his study of Yeats, MacNeice writes, "Poetry nowadays appears to need defending. I would not attempt however to defend poetry itself; that poetry is good seems to me axiomatic; if you do not accept this axiom, we have no common ground for argument" (*PWBY*, 17). For many critics today, it seems that the idea that poetry is bad is axiomatic; poetic form is viewed as an aesthetic and not historical concern, and poetry is regarded as detached from social and cultural reality. I am not going to attempt to defend poetry either, nor am I going to argue its moral value. But I will argue that a poetry that advocates the recognition of a tension between the temporal and the atemporal deserves to have that tension recognized, and I am reading these poems as a complex of the historical and the aesthetic. MacNeice comments that "it seems to me to be helpful to know who Yeats was, who were his friends, what were his literary influences, political opinions, and social prejudices. These things were not the cause of his poetry but they were among its conditions" (23). Since I am looking at form as a product of those conditions, I also find it helpful to examine the poets' influences and opinions. Each chapter begins with a summary of the poets' positions on the problem of the One and the Many drawn from essays, diaries, letters, class notes, and any other prose writings in which they work out their philosophies. From there, I read the relevant poems to demonstrate how those influences and opinions manifest themselves in the content of the poetry. Finally, I examine the ways in which the poets' manipulations of the conventional dialogue forms reflect the positions manifested in the content.

In chapter 1, I contrast Auden's *The Age of Anxiety* with Hardy's *The Dynasts*. Both of these prosimetric dramas concern the question of unity in a time of war, a time of apparent disunity. These two works span the first half of the twentieth century, and *The Age of Anxiety* (1947), written in the aftermath of World War II, might be seen as a reply to *The Dynasts* (1900–1908). The chapter explores the ways in which both poets make extensive use of prose stage directions and the chapter compares the differences in form evident in those stage directions that allow them to mirror respectively Hardy's de facto pluralism and Auden's insistence on the possibility of a relationship between an individual and society and between the individual and a transcendent God. Despite Hardy's insistence that the philosophy of *The Dynasts* is monistic, that of an immanent unity derived from Schopenhauer, both the content and form of the work display pluralistic tendencies. The addition of prose stage directions should, theoretically, lessen the overall distance between poet and reader inherent in dramatic verse; however, Hardy's refusal to provide any insight into the speaker's minds, commentary on the action, or his own connections to some of the characters allow him to maintain his own distance from the poem. His use of the present tense and the lack of temporal references and/or continuity from one scene to another in the stage directions do not provide the reader with any assistance in synthesizing the disparate components of the epic drama. In *The Age of Anxiety*, Auden's use of kabbalistic imagery and of Jung's theory of the four faculties of the personality both reflect his belief in the possibility of a coincidence of Many and One, even if temporary, and his stage directions make use of narration, commentary, insight into the characters' thoughts, and double voicing to narrow the gaps between reader, poem, and poet even more than would be possible with conventional stage directions.

Chapter 2 considers the differences between two modifications of the debate of body and soul, Eliot's "The Love Song of J. Alfred Prufrock" and Yeats's "Ego Dominus Tuus." Yeats wrote his dialogue only months after the publication of "Prufrock," and if not a direct response to Eliot's poem, "Ego Dominus Tuus" at least engages the same questions. Yeat's antinomial philosophy, as described in *A Vision*, is reviewed, and the chapter traces Eliot's interest in uniting One and Many during the period in which he wrote, and later published, the poem, including the early influence of Bergson and his dissertation on F. H. Bradley. The chapter examines features of both poems common to the conventional debate form and proposes that in "The Love Song of J. Alfred Prufrock" Eliot produced a modified dialogue that may be read simultaneously as a dramatic monologue and as a debate of body and soul, as a representation of a personality which is both subjective and objective at once in the unity of immediate experience. As a poem that may be read either as a dramatic monologue or as a dialogue, depending on the reader's point of view, the form of the poem reflects its desire to overcome any radical split between body and soul, subject and object. Separating the soul from the body temporarily (in *ecstasis*) is one of the goals of mystical rituals such as those practiced by Yeats's companions in the Order of the Golden Dawn, and Eliot's portrayal of Prufrock echoes some of Yeats's descriptions of his experiences as a mystically inclined young man. Yeats's later theory of the antiself requires that both halves of the dichotomy remain always separate, but reaching toward unity, directly opposite of Eliot's unity always on the verge of splitting; the form of "Ego Dominus Tuus" reflects this vision of a divided unity.

Chapter 3 examines Frost's use of small amounts of narration in his adaptations of the dialogue ballad form in *North of Boston* as a way to "transcend the strife method," to overcome the opposition of dualities. The chapter traces Frost's early philosophical development and the influence of James on his early conception of an interpersonal One and a desire to find a bridge between the One and the Many. *North of Boston* dialogues such as "Death of the Hired Man," "The Mountain," "The Generations of Men," and "Home Burial" stage debates between opposing sides of the One/Many question, which are held in tension by the narrator. The narrator also establishes a relationship with the reader that is absent in Frost's later dialogues, written when he had changed his views from the idea of a Jamesian interpersonal unity to that of a transcendent One. The chapter compares the earlier and later poems, particularly "Build Soil" and the two masques, *A Masque of Mercy* and *A Masque of Reason*, and demonstrates how this change in philosophy results in a change in Frost's use of dialogue forms.

Chapter 4 argues that MacNeice's four eclogues, "An Eclogue for Christmas," "Eclogue by a Five-Barred Gate," "Eclogue from Iceland," and "Eclogue between the Motherless," appeared at a transition point in the poet's philosophy when he moved from a belief in a transcendent One to a denial of any unity but that of an ephemeral interpersonal connection. All four poems concern the search for a relationship between self and world, but in none of them has any of the speakers actually found any such communion. Accordingly, the chapter demonstrates, the dialogues make no use of any unifying voice, but each of the eclogues is shown to be composed of a debate between aspects of the poet's own self. Subtle differences in the four eclogues reflect the evolution of MacNeice's philosophy as he moves toward pluralism and an incipient postmodernism.

2

"Looking at Life From a Very Great Height": Hardy's *The Dynasts* and Auden's *The Age of Anxiety*

ASIDE FROM THE PULITZER PRIZE COMMITTEE, HARDLY ANYONE considered W. H. Auden's *The Age of Anxiety* worth reading at the time of its publication. Most reviewers then, and many critics now, considered the poem nearly unreadable, pointing to the distance at which it keeps the reader as its main fault. In one of the kinder reviews, the *Times Literary Supplement* (*TLS*) reviewer finds that "[t]he reader is left admiring but unmoved, as though all the time he were watching a brilliant public exhibition which was intended as a display of versatility rather than the result of any deep-seated conviction" and that "[t]he reader is at once the neglected guest outside the circle."[1] Randall Jarrell had no reservations about releasing some venom, calling *The Age of Anxiety* "the worst thing Auden has written since 'The Dance of Death.'"[2] The reviewer in the *Spectator* suggests that the best way to read the book would be "on benzedrine or some equally enlightening drug"[3] and judges that the poem "is not merely obscure; it is preposterous and baffling."[4] David Bromwich calls *The Age of Anxiety* "a long dull forced amusement,"[5] and Richard Hoggart claims that despite some "bright aperçus," much of *The Age of Anxiety* is "perverse" and "much batters at the reader."[6] Herbert Greenberg's assessment is tempered by mild admiration; however, he admits, "it is difficult to evaluate justly because many of its effects do not simply fail—they alienate."[7] Given that the poem focuses on a shared mystical experience between four strangers in a New York bar and advocates the necessity of communion between individuals as a prerequisite for communion with God, this perceived inhospitality to the reader is at odds with Auden's ostensible purpose.

The volley of abuse fired at *The Age of Anxiety* echoes the criticism aimed at an earlier dramatic poem much admired by Auden, Thomas Hardy's *The Dynasts*. After the publication of the first part of the poem in 1904, Hardy was shocked by the reviews, writing that they were "useless as guides, the critics seeming to be puzzled—a thing I did not expect."[8] The *TLS* reviewer focused his spleen on the poem's form: "It is well to say at once that this is not the book we desired or expected. Why should Thomas Hardy, a master of prose narrative, have chosen to hamper himself with the dramatic form? Why should the poet who can interpret nature, idyllic or tragic, with perfect sympathy, yet too strict a conscience ever to make her the puppet of his plot, now relegate her to stage directions?"[9] A. B. Walkley's review, which particularly infuriated Hardy, appeared in *TLS* a few weeks later, on January 29, 1904.[10] Walkley, like the first reviewer, attacks the very idea of a play for mental performance, wittily suggesting that "[s]ome plays may be read, just as *faute de mieux*, shoe-leather may be used as an article of diet instead of as a protection for the feet."[11] Walkley recognizes the difficulties precipitated by the discontinuities inherent in the drama and thoroughly castigates Hardy for placing the burden for integrating the parts of the drama on the reader: "Unfortunately, the 'gaps' in a closet-play, being just those parts of a play which cannot be expressed in dialogue, are its vital parts."[12] Despite the poem's claims of an immanent unity connecting all of humanity, the people depicted in *The Dynasts* fail to relate to each other, to the author or to the reader.

The dramatic form so roundly denounced by critics of *The Dynasts* was, significantly, one of the aspects of the poem that Auden most admired and one that he copied in *The Age of Anxiety*. As Anthony Hecht notes, "*The Age of Anxiety* does not fit easily into what preceded or what followed it, with which it seems stylistically at odds—a kind of daring, and not wholly successful, experiment."[13] The poem stands out from the others most obviously due to its meter and diction, but it also differs in form from Auden's other dramatic poems of the time, including *Paid on Both Sides*, *For the Time Being*, and *The Sea and the Mirror*. Of these, only *The Age of Anxiety* contains extensive prose stage directions, suggesting that Auden had a specific reason for including them in this work, and it is not unreasonable

to suppose that he intended to recall the prose passages of *Th
Dynasts* that he so admired. Auden, who once declared, "M
first master was Thomas Hardy" (*DH*, 38), credits Hardy's use o
stage directions with the ability to bring about an accord be
tween the individual and society: "What I valued most in Hardy
then, as I still do, was his hawk's vision, his way of looking a
life from a very great height, as in the stage directions of *Th
Dynasts*, or the opening chapter of *Return of the Native*. To se
the individual life related not only to the local social life of it
time, but to the whole of human history, life on the earth, th
stars, gives one both humility and self-confidence."[14] *The Age o
Anxiety*, like Hardy's poem, is set in a world at war, at a tim
when the relationships between individuals and society are par
ticularly in need of reconciliation and when the relation of th
individual to the One represented by history (or fate or God) i
particularly in question.[15]

Although *The Age of Anxiety* and *The Dynasts* share an inter
est in the relationship between the individual and the world, th
two poets' interpretations of the problem of the One and th
Many differ, and so do the ways in which they adapt the dramat
icform to those understandings. As Edward Mendelson observes
Auden "retained from Hardy the vast historical perspectives o
The Dynasts, its conjunction of great aeons and distances with
minute local detail, and put it to different use. Where Hard
stood ironically aloof from a brute mechanistic history, Auder
saw an obligation to bring knowledge to the service of responsi
bility."[16] Despite Hardy's depiction of a Schopenhauerean im
manent unity in *The Dynasts*, his insistence on the inability o
individuals to recognize their place in the One tips the balanc
strongly toward pluralism, and his stage directions link him
only weakly to both the text and the reader. Auden concurs with
Hardy's assessment that most individuals have no apprehensior
of any connection between themselves and others, or betweer
themselves and the spiritual world; but, unlike Hardy, he sug
gests that individuals, by finding unity within themselves, ir
the form of an integrated personality, may achieve a connectior
with a transcendent God.

In accordance with his belief in the possibility of communion
Auden employs the stage directions of *The Age of Anxiety* to ti
him as closely as possible to both the text and the reader. Whil

Hardy's stage directions make use of the present tense, confining the reader's perceptions to the present and providing no continuity of time or place, Auden's stage directions are mostly in the past tense, which not only provides continuity, but also places the poet and the reader together in the same time frame. Hardy's stage directions are exclusively descriptive, avoiding evaluation, while Auden's narrator draws conclusions about the speeches and actions of the characters. Hardy avoids personal identification with his characters, to the extent of concealing the fact that one of the characters is his own ancestor, while Auden makes his characters readily identifiable as aspects of his own personality. Hardy strictly refrains from revealing any knowledge of his character's internal thoughts, while Auden describes their inmost thoughts and emotions. Where Hardy's prose passages differ in diction and tone from the voices of his characters, Auden's narrator shares with his characters their alliterative speech patterns. Hardy's stage directions impose distance; Auden's create intimacy. Yet the link that Auden creates between himself, in the voice of the stage directions, and the reader cannot overcome the gaps between the reader and the other speakers of the poem.

In his seminal source study, *The Shaping of "The Dynasts,"* Walter F. Wright warns that "[w]e must keep in mind that Hardy wavered between alternatives in his search for a cosmic view."[17] Indeed, Hardy's position on questions related to the One and the Many varies so markedly that any one of his pronouncements must be taken with a grain of salt, and his vacillations are too numerous to examine here in detail. Wright's book provides the best examples of Hardy's various philosophical influences and stances, but an assortment of his positions follows. At times, he emphasizes the union of apparently distinct elements, declaring that "[i]f it be possible to compress into a sentence all that a man learns between 20 & 40, it is that all things merge in one another—good into evil, generosity into justice, religion into politics, the year into the ages, the world into the universe" (*Life*, 114). Elsewhere, he appears to prefer a middle way, stating forthrightly that "[r]ationalists err as far in one direction as Revelationists or Mystics in the other; as far in the direction of logicality as their opponents away from it" (358).[18] Each of these

statements indicates a desire to find a position that balances fac
ets of the One and the Many, yet they appear among numerou
indications that Hardy favored one side or the other.

At times, he disavows a middle way, as when he admits to
"mistrust of metaphysic" precisely *because* "it is a sort of bas
tard, begotten of science upon theology—or, in another form,
halfway house between Deism & Materialism."[19] As far as th
One goes, Hardy rejects transcendent unity out of hand, declar
ing, "I have been looking for God 50 years, and I think that if h
had existed I should have discovered him" (*Life*, 234). On th
other hand, he frequently expresses the belief that some sort o
unity underlies the universe, and he suggests that "[i]t would b
an amusing fact, if it were not one that leads to such bitter strife
that the conception of First Cause which the theist calls 'God
and the conception of the same that the so-styled atheist call
'no-God,' are nowadays almost exactly identical" (326). At th
same time, he locates an immanent unity in the material: "Mar
kind, in fact, may be, and possibly will be, viewed as members o
one corporeal frame" (235). However, he expresses an apparentl
pluralistic viewpoint elsewhere, emphasizing the disunity be
tween individuals.[20]

When he comes out in favor of unity, Hardy is inconsisten
as to whether it represents monism or dualism.[21] In addition t
Hardy's claims in the preface to *The Dynasts* as to its monisti
viewpoint, several other pieces of evidence exist that he actuall
did subscribe to monism. In an 1892 letter, admitting his inter
est in the Psychical Society, he warns that he "cannot find an
irrefutable evidence, in the mass offered, of spiritual action apar
from corporeal."[22] Wright describes Hardy's reaction to a 190
review of Ernst Haeckel's *Concepts of Monism* in which the re
viewer denies the validity of monism by averring that "It is in
large measure based on assumptions as to the unity of mind +
matter, the functional relationship of the soul to the body + th
mind to the brain, that are accepted by no man of science or psy
chologist of the first rank;" Hardy's response, according t
Wright: "!".[23] Hardy's apparent dismissal of the reviewer's asser
tion accords with his denunciation of Henri Bergson, on th
grounds that Bergsonism is "only our old friend Dualism in
new suit of clothes" (*Life*, 400).[24]

On the other hand, Hardy himself often makes frankly dualis

tic statements. People, he proposes, may be separated "into the mentally unquickened, mechanical, soulless; and the living, throbbing, suffering, vital. In other words into souls and machines, ether and clay" (*Life*, 192), and at a concert, he claims, "I saw Souls outside Bodies" (209).[25] Hardy never managed to resolve any of these inconsistencies or to formulate a coherent philosophy, though, by the time he wrote *The Dynasts*, he apparently thought that he had done so. As Wright demonstrates, the fragmentary and contradictory nature of Hardy's borrowings from various philosophers was unimportant to him because he was engaged primarily in the search for an answer to the question of the source of human suffering, not in metaphysics per se.

Unlike Hardy, who never found evidence for the existence of God, Auden recanted his earlier denial of religion and embraced Christianity in 1940. Although he recognizes that plurality, resulting in isolation and solipsism, dominates our world, he finds in religion, and particularly in Christianity, a unity that counteracts alienation. Civilization, he claims, came about only when men embraced an absolute—"the One, the Unknowable, the Unconditional," and it was the Christian church that "was able to relate the universal and the particular, the spiritual and the material, and made the technical advance of civilization possible."[26] He considers both monism and dualism heretical.[27] For Auden, the One and the Many are joined and held in tension in the Christ figure, a symbol of a symbiotic relationship between God and Man. In *For the Time Being*, which he completed two years before he began *The Age of Anxiety*, Simeon voices this belief, as he announces:

> Because in Him the Word is united to the Flesh without loss of perfection. Reason is redeemed from incestuous fixation on her own Logic, for the One and the Many are simultaneously revealed as real. So that we may no longer, with the Barbarians, deny the Unity, asserting that there are as many gods as there are creatures, nor, with the philosophers deny the Multiplicity, asserting that God is One who has no need of friends and is indifferent to a World of Time and Quantity and Horror which He did not create, nor with Israel, may we limit the coherence of the One and the Many to a special case, asserting that God is only concerned with and of concern to that People out of all that He created He has chosen for His own. (*CP*, 300)

For Auden, the coexistence of the One and the Many as a mutual dependence between God and Man represents an ideal relationship necessary for the attainment of paradise.[28] In a chart presented to a class at Swarthmore in 1943, he names this condition a "differentiated unity."[29] On the side of the chart labeled "Hell of the Pure Deed," he identifies "order" as "monist unity," while he situates "dissociated multiplicity" on the side labeled "Hell of the Pure Word." [30] The "differentiated unity" that appears in the middle maintains its character as One, while allowing for the variant characteristics associated with the Many. That he does not posit a "unified plurality" indicates the superiority of unity in his scheme; man belongs in a relationship with God, but does not equal him.

Where Hardy, following Schopenhauer, expects only a few enlightened individuals, artists like himself, to recognize their places in an immanent unity that controls their fates, Auden trusts that God is accessible to everyone. Although he respected and was slightly inclined toward the *via negativa*,[31] the negative way which encourages asceticism and withdrawal, Auden's vision of Christianity included the perfection of society as whole, not himself alone. He delayed public revelation that he had been greatly influenced by Kierkegaard's insistence on the relationship between the individual and the absolute because Kierkegaard did not provide Auden with a model for communal access to such a One.[32] Communism had failed as a means for producing a just society, and he now believed that the ideal of an "open society" would acknowledge not only "logical necessity," but also that only "acts of faith" make possible the exercise of free will.[33] In *The Prolific and the Devourer*, Auden claims that "[a]ll the striving of life is a striving to transcend duality, and establish unity or freedom. The Will, the Unconscious, is this desire to be free. . . . We are not free to will not to be free" (*CW* 411). Progress, he says, consists of a successful struggle to overcome duality, either between "[t]he Whole and its parts, or one part of the whole and another" (424–25).

In the chart that he presented at Swarthmore, the middle way, the path which leads to paradise, has as its "relations between selves," the "neighborliness" of such a society, and that neighborliness proceeds from the free acts of individuals who achieve "self-realization." Under the heading "requiredness," in the chart is the "subjective," which leads to "grace," which in turn leads to "Agape." Auden claimed to have experienced in 1933 a vision of Agape, which, in addition to its experience of the love of God, includes the love of one's fellow man, and in that moment he felt that he truly loved his neighbor as himself (*FA*, 69–70). In his conception of the middle way between One and Many, then, he leans toward a One that is transcendent, but accessible only through inter- and intrapersonal unities.

In *The Dynasts* and *The Age of Anxiety*, Hardy and Auden recognize that the vast majority of people live their lives in isolation, not perceiving their ties to each other or to the world around them; the two poets differ in their understandings of the unknown unity and in their ideas of the means and consequences of learning one's relationship to this unity. In *The Dynasts*, the people of Europe, although they do not know it, are mere puppets in their wars as individuals and as nations, puppets maneuvered blindly by the Immanent Will. At the beginning of *The Age of Anxiety*, four alienated New Yorkers have failed to recognize God as their salvation, because they have not found unity within themselves or with their neighbors. For Hardy, the recognition of a deterministic unity results only in further separation. Only Napoleon, in *The Dynasts*, receives any intimation of his place in the One, and the result is his consequent disastrous disregard of the lives of the Many. Where Napoleon acquires his sense of the unity passively after having it whispered to him by a spirit, the two characters in *The Age of Anxiety* who achieve some understanding of their relationship to the transcendent God do so through their own volition, through inner soul-searching and through communing with other individuals; and the result, if not happiness, is at least a sense of purpose.

Throughout *The Dynasts*, Hardy continually emphasizes the inability of the men and women of Europe, from the monarchy to the common soldiers and camp followers, to know anything outside of their immediate situations, anything outside of the here and now. During wartime, this failure is particularly evident. At the Battle of Borodino, the Spirit of the Years depicts the combatants as *"mindless minions"* who act in *"mechanized enchantment"* (III, I,v,4–5), and the Spirit of the Pities later refers to humanity as *"pale pathetic peoples"* who *"still plod on / Through hoodwinkings."* (III, IV, iv,135–36). Hardy rarely permits the armies access to certain intelligence, and when the military receives good information, it fails to recognize it as such. He devotes consecutive scenes to the Russian and French speculations as to the other's plans at Austerlitz (I,VI, ii and iii). Mistaken rejections of good intelligence also abound: at Ulm, Jellachich discounts the report of a French deserter as to the movement of British troops (I, IV, iii,108–14), and at Salamanca, the British, having learned from the wives of two officers that the Spanish have left the fort to the French, fail to heed the information and allow the French to escape (III, I, ii and iii).

This inability of individuals to locate their places in the whole is not restricted to the chaos of battle. Many of the nonmilitary scenes also consist of bewildered people blindly attempting to puzzle out the course of events. Political policy debates inevitably entail competing forecasts of future events, none of which may prove correct, and Hardy frames *The Dynasts* with two such scenes. In one of the work's first scenes, Pitt, Sheridan, and others participate in the 1805 House of Commons debate over the Militia Act, a debate in which the participants make *"their admonishments little conceiving how / Scarlet the scroll that the years will unwind!"* (I, I, iii,24–25). Confusion reigns at all levels of society—while the wealthy attempt to sort out the latest events from newspaper and courier accounts, including the "fashionable crowd" at "the house of a lady of quality" who discuss the treaty between Russia and France (I, I, v), the ladies in Berlin who try to discern the truth in the news of the occupation of their city (II, I, v and vi), and the crowd at Vauxhall learning of Austria's falling-out with France (III, II, iv). The simple folk credit wild rumors such as Napoleon's diet of human babies (I, II, v,71–96) and a plan to burn the captive emperor on Durnover Green (III,V,vi,19–26). Not one of the participants has the first idea of how he or she fits into the overall scheme of things, a scheme laid out by the unknowing and unknown Immanent Will that controls them all.

The characters in *The Age of Anxiety*, unlike those of *The Dynasts*, control, through their own volition, the degree to which they participate in any unity. At the beginning of the poem, they have no conception of this possibility; they seek solace from the disunity of the war by retreating from others. "Modern society," wrote Auden in a 1941 essay, "is a differentiated society in disorder, the result of our ignoring the relations between its different elements" (CW, 102).[34] According to the opening comments by the narrator, the bar in which the four meet offers "a choice of physiological aids to the imagination whereby each may appropriate it for his or her private world" (3), and a refuge from the "universal disorder of the world outside" (4). The characters are Malin, a medical officer in the Canadian Air Force; Emble, a young sailor; Quant, a widower and clerk in a shipping office; and Rosetta, a buyer for a department store, and each sits in the bar while engrossed in private fantasy. For most of the Prologue, the characters do not address one another out loud; their "speeches" consist of their *unspoken* thoughts. Quant observes himself in a mirror and asks himself why "he was still so interested in that tired old widower" (4); Malin attempts to forget his present as a medical officer in the Canadian Air Force; "trying to recapture the old atmosphere of laboratory and lecture hall," he regresses into memories of his youth (5). Rosetta escapes into "her favorite day-dream," in which she inhabits the type of charming British country village featured in murder mysteries (5). And vain Emble observes the others observing him, "slightly contemptuous when he caught an admiring glance, and slightly piqued when he did not" (6). Each longs to find some unity; they long to find some Eden, a "primitive pact with pure feeling," and they are "for ever expecting / Night after night the Nameless One" (10). As they sit alone, passively waiting for some imaginary beatific god to rescue them, however, they become only more isolated from their fellow men: "[T]heir vision shrinks / As their dreams darken; with dulling voice / Each calls across a colder water" (11). In Auden's world, this passive dreaming of the One leads to no better consequences than it does in Hardy's; only a positive movement toward unity can bring more unity.

Auden emphasizes the solipsism of each of the characters at the outset of *The Age of Anxiety* not only through the presentation of their thoughts, but also by preventing them from engaging in real dialogue when they finally speak. Never in the entire poem does any one character address any one of the others by name. In a contemporary review, Delmore Schwartz notes that

"*The Age of Anxiety* simulates narrative, drama, and philosophical dialogue. In actuality, it is hardly more than a suite of expo-
sitions, alternately discursive, allegorical, and lyrical," and he
observes that, "the eloquent dialectic inherent in the use of dialogue comes to almost nothing because each character often
speaks as if he had not heard what the previous character said."[35]
Dialectic, however, is not inherent in dialogue, as Michael
Prince demonstrates; dialogue is as capable of depicting irresolv-
able disunity as of representing the reconciliation of views (1–
20).[36] Auden makes full use of this capability in *The Age of
Anxiety*. As Schwartz suggests, the characters speak in alterna-
tion, but do not communicate. The first lines in which the characters supposedly address each other demonstrate what he is
talking about:

> ROSETTA
> spoke first: Numbers and nightmares have news value.
>
> Then
> MALIN: A crime has occurred, accusing all.
>
> Then
> QUANT: The world needs a wash and a week's rest.
>
> (17)

Emble then launches into a long lecture rather than a discussion:

> To which
> EMBLE said: Better this than barbarian misrule.
>   History tells more often than not
>   Of wickedness with will, wisdom but
>   An interjection without a verb,
>   And the godless growing like green cedars
>   On righteous ruins. The reticent earth,
>   Exposed by the spade, speaks its warning
>   With successive layers of sacked temples
>   And dead civilians . . .
>
> (18)

This type of minimal connection between the speeches of the
characters continues; when Malin directly addresses the others,
asking where they shall direct their discussion, the others reply
elliptically:

But EMBLE
objected: Muster no monsters, I'll meeken my own.

So did
ROSETTA: You may wish till you waste, I'll want here.

So did
QUANT: Too blank the blink of these blind heavens.
                                                    (22–23)

None of these responses acknowledges the previous speaker in any recognizable way, and the distorted syntax and unlikely diction further impede communication; the characters have not yet found a way to achieve communion with one another.

Many critics interpret the incomprehensibility of the "dialogue" as a poetic failure, failing to recognize that Auden intends this type of speech to be mimetic of the gaps between individuals. Mendelson attributes to Auden "a technique of writing about the darkest possible subjects in a tone that deceived real or imaginary enemies,"[37] a technique Mendelson claims Auden derived from Robert Frost; if Auden intended for critics to detest the style of the dialogue, he succeeded. Schwartz, who asserts that the storyline of the poem is "muffed," attributes the lack of communication between the characters to some deficiency on Auden's part,[38] and Greenberg suspects the baroque style of the verse to be a self-indulgent whim, complaining that, "Auden seems easily distracted into entertaining himself."[39] Auden himself denounces critics like Schwartz and Greenberg when he grumbles about "the kind of critic . . . to whom when he condemns a work or a passage, the possibility never occurs that its author may have foreseen exactly what he is going to say" (DH, 8). In a letter to Theodore Spencer, he confirms that the incomprehensibility of the "dialogue" is a deliberate attempt to represent the characters' aversion to revealing their true selves: "Re the 'made-up' feeling of some of the verse, I've probably failed to do what I wanted which is a difficult thing, namely to devise a rhetoric which would reveal the great vice of our age which is that we are all not only 'actors' but know that we are (re-duplicate Hamlets) and that it is only at moments, in spite of ourselves, and when we least expect it that our real feelings break through."[40] Instead of failing to convey the lack of communion between people, Auden probably does too good a job of it, preventing the reader from relating to any of the four characters through most of *The Age of Anxiety*.

Mendelson asserts that in Auden's later poetry, Auden "treats the gulf between language and world" as a difficulty, but one that does not preclude communication or the recognition of "a physical and ethical world whose order and events are not only verbal ones."[41] Between his early poetry, in which the gap between language and world cannot be bridged, and later poems like *The Age of Anxiety*, according to Mendelson, "Auden moves from a world *without* choice to a world *with* choice"; in this new conception of the world, "differences are overcome by mutual forgiveness and responsibility."[42] Communication becomes an act of volition. At the end of the poem, once Rosetta and Malin recognize their places in the One, they distinguish themselves by speaking coherently, substituting lucid speeches for the gibberish of much of the rest of the book, while Emble lies passed out and Quant continues to babble (Babel). Had the difficulty of most of the verse resulted from a failure to communicate on Auden's part, Rosetta and Malin would continue to spout nonsense.

Both *The Dynasts* and *The Age of Anxiety* show evidence of some effort to find a tension point between unity and plurality, but Hardy's method requires the reader to swing back and forth between the spiritual and the material, setting it at odds with his stated monistic philosophy, and making the form effectively pluralistic. The distance he needs in order to achieve any perception of the One, what Auden called his "hawk's vision," his way of "looking at life from a very great height," Hardy accomplishes by splitting *The Dynasts* into two viewpoints—the material world of the individual and the overworld of the spirits, which is also occupied by the artist/narrator. Oddly, in the Preface, Hardy declares that "[t]he wide acceptance of the Monistic theory of the Universe forbade, in this twentieth century, the importation of Divine personages from any antique Mythology as ready-made sources or channels of Causation, even in verse" (50–54), an unlikely statement given that the double perspective of the epic represents a frankly dualistic system, in which the material concerns itself with the Many, the present and the here, while the spirit world partakes of the One, the eternal and all space.

This dualism conflicts with Hardy's numerous statements as to the Schopenhauerean monistic philosophy of *The Dynasts*, but it allows him to explore the tension between the One and the Many. Wright notes that "the concept of a single Immanent Will does not free Hardy from the sensation of life as the outward expression of an inherent conflict of plural forces," and that Hardy's "need for a reconciliation" results in "tension in a poem that attempts to symbolize both the monistic Will and the plural phenomena."[43] In practice, not even what Wright refers to as the abstract logic of the Overworld remains fully free of "plural phenomena"; not even the spirits who inhabit the higher plane possess an omniscient vision. Their vantage point above the earth and their ability to range across space and time allow them a wider perspective than that of humanity, but one that is still limited. Not only do the spirits lack infinite vision, not even the Immanent Will knows what it wreaks on the unknowing world.

Although the Spirit of the Years insists that the Will is an immanent One, and describes it explicitly as such, the spirit world appears outside of it enough to observe it, and therefore must be effectively distinct from it. From the very great height of the Overworld, the spirits reveal, as in a diorama,[44] the influence of the unconscious unity of the Will on an apparently pluralistic world:

> SPIRIT OF THE YEARS
> *These are the Prime Volitions,—fibrils, veins,*
> *Will-tissues, nerves, and pulses of the Cause,*
> *That heave throughout the Earth's compositure.*
> *Their sum is like the lobule of a Brain*
> *Evolving always that it wots not of;*
> *A Brain whose procedure may but be discerned*
> *By phantom eyes like ours; the while unguessed*
> *Of those it stirs, who (even as ye do) dream*
> *Their motions free, their orderings supreme;*
> *Each life apart from each, with power to mete*
> *Its own day's measures; balanced, self-complete;*
> *Though they subsist but atoms of the One*
> *Labouring through all, divisible from none.*
>   (Fore Scene, 161–81)

The spirit insists on the unconscious nature of the Immanent Will, comparing its workings to that of "*a knitter drowsed, / Whose fingers play in skilled unmindfulness*," a knitter who "*has woven with an absent heed / Since life first was; and ever so will weave*" (37–40). This ignorance of its own effects suggests a greater discontinuity between the Will and the world it weaves than that of the apparent plurality Hardy wishes to convey. If the people know nothing of the Will that controls them, the disunity is illusory; when the Will knows no more of the people than they do of it, the gap seems more substantial. Even the spirits are uncertain of the true nature of the Will. The Spirit of the Years does not know the Will's unconsciousness for a fact: it reports that some believe that Man's sinfulness caused the Will to abandon this world in disgust, but that the Spirit does not believe the story (Fore Scene, 20–29). Even as the Spirit asserts that no evidence exists that the Will ever exerted any conscious sway over the earth, he qualifies his assertion in an apostrophe, equivocating that, "*such is my thinking*" (36). Since the One must be boundless, the liminality of the spirits' awareness reinforces the pluralistic tendencies of *The Dynasts*.

Hardy's mistrust of unity in *The Dynasts* extends to the idea that knowing, or at least suspecting, one's place in the larger scheme may have dire consequences. Only Napoleon among the humans eventually realizes that he acts on "Some force within me, battling mine intent" (II, I,viii,201) and, in dialogue with several spirits at the end of the epic, he declares that "I have ever known / That such a will I passively obeyed" (III, VII, ix, 9–10). As Katherine Kearney Maynard puts it: "[T]hough Napoleon correctly recognizes that his life is part of a larger force, he fails to understand the true significance of this relationship: that he shares an indestructible physical bond to others."[45] Maynard, who does not consider the question of unity and plurality explicitly, seems surprised that recognition of one's place in the Will could fail to reinforce one's knowledge of the unity of man; if Hardy's vision in *The Dynasts* were truly monistic, that expectation should hold true. However, Hardy sees knowledge of the determinism of the One as an opportunity to shirk responsibility for the other individuals who make up mankind.[46] When confronted before Waterloo by a nightmare vision of the corpses of his soldiers, Napoleon demands to know, "Why, why should this reproach be dealt me now? / Why hold me my own master, if I be / Ruled by the pitiless Planet of Destiny?" (III, IV, iii,83–85). Hardy makes no answer as to why or how anyone should be held responsible under these circumstances, leaving us to think that we are better off not perceiving the One, that it is better to retain the illusion of individual free will.[47]

In *The Age of Anxiety*, free will is no illusion, the volition of the individual can lead to knowledge of the One, and the One and the Many achieve a much greater coherence than they do in *The Dynasts*. Auden indicates that the poem concerns this tension through the words, "Anxiety" and "Baroque" in the title, both of which hold a special significance for him in regard to this middle position. The temporary unity achieved by the characters in the bar also indicates a balance between One and Many. While in *The Dynasts*, the perception by human beings of the machinations of an unknowing unity leads to dissolution of whatever tentative bonds may exist between individuals, in *The Age of Anxiety*, the establishment of relationships among individuals, along with the cultivation of an integrated self, leads to the recognition of a transcendent unity, in the form of the Judeo-Christian God. The poem portrays both interpersonal and intrapersonal unities, both temporary, among four strangers. At the same time, these four people symbolize four aspects of the self as they, for a short time, become as one. The communion that the characters achieve through their drunken collective dream, even though short-lived, demonstrates the possibility of both the social and psychic wholeness. This condition endures past the fantasy, as demonstrated by Rosetta and Malin, whose speeches at the end of the poem sum up respectively the Jewish and Christian conceptions of a relationship to God and to one's fellow man. Since none of these relationships hold together permanently, they always occupy some position between the Many and the One. Another indication of the desire to embrace the One and the Many coincidentally appears in Auden's use of kabbalistic symbolism in the image of the body as landscape, which serves here to emphasize the union of body and soul.

The complete title of the poem, *The Age of Anxiety: A Baroque Eclogue*, makes two gestures toward the middle way between the One and the Many. In the chart that he presented at Swarthmore, Auden locates "anxiety," under the category of

"sin" in the middle column, the column belonging to "differentiated unity." On either side of this column, sin under the condition of monistic unity is described as "sensuality," and sin under
the condition of multiplicity is defined as "pride." The word
"baroque" also has significance in the search for a middle way.
In the same Swarthmore seminar, Auden had defined the baroque as "the counter-reformation's theatrical use of *matter*
against the abstract and *earnest* thinking of the Reformers"
(Auden's emphasis).[48] While the emphasis on the baroque might
therefore appear to favor the material, the key word in Auden's
definition is "against"; he sets matter in opposition to the ideal,
in tension with it, not in place of it. The greatest coincidence of
the One and the Many in *The Age of Anxiety* appears in "The
Seven Stages," and Auden associated the baroque with at least a
portion of this section. The year before he published the entirety
of *The Age of Anxiety*, he submitted one of the lyrics from "The
Seven Stages" titled "Baroque" to the magazine *Christianity
and Crisis*, referring to the song as "a counter-Reformationary
number."[49]

The most obvious of the unities explored by Auden in *The Age
of Anxiety* is that of the social interaction among individuals.
On the concrete level of the allegory, in which four individual
people with four individual lives meet one night in a bar, the
unity among the characters takes place in response to both an
abstract religious phenomenon, the night of All Souls, which
unites particulars, and to the radio, which particularizes the abstract. The action takes place on All Souls Night, the observance
of which, according to one of Auden's favorite theologians at the
time, Eugen Rosenstock-Huessy, "established the solidarity of
all souls from the beginning of the world to the end of time."[50]
On the night of All Souls, all of the individuals of each particular
time and space join together in the eternal. On this night, the
four characters are jolted out of their reveries by the intrusion of
the radio: "But now the radio, suddenly breaking in with its
banal noises upon their separate senses of themselves, by compelling them to pay attention to a common world of great
slaughter and much sorrow, began, without their knowledge, to
draw these four strangers closer to each other" (11). The radio
establishes that individual lives like those of the drunks in the
bar, not only the fates of entire armies and nations, are at stake:

"*Lucky charm / Saves sniper*"; "*Rochester barber / Fools foes*"; "*Doomed sailors / Play poker*" (11, 12). Auden once noted that propaganda's effects come about because of the ability to "change what was an abstract relation into a personal relation,"[51] and the radio announcements do just that, allowing the individual characters to recognize their commonality.

The other necessary unity in the poem is that of psychic integration. On the symbolic level of *The Age of Anxiety*, the four characters represent four discrete aspects of the self that combine to function as one. A number of critics have shown that these four characters represent the four faculties of the self as described in Jung's 1939 book, *The Integration of the Personality*, with Malin representing Thought; Emble, Sensation; Quant, Intuition; and Rosetta, Feeling. When, just before "The Seven Stages," they unite in their shared vision, they become symbolically a completely integrated personality: "For it can happen, if circumstances are other wise propitious, that members of a group in this condition establish a rapport in which communication of thoughts and feelings is so accurate and instantaneous, that they appear to function as a single organism" (57). Hecht points out that the four aspects of the self, according to tradition, "were once perfectly united in the person of Adam before the Fall; but Original Sin separated them and unbalanced their harmony."[52] Reuniting the four faculties, then, would be necessary in order to reunite the self to a unity of purpose with God. This concept of a fourfold division of personality that must be integrated, and that may be represented by assigning the characteristics of each faculty to separate characters, appears in a number of Auden's works, including *The Ascent of F6*, "For the Time Being," and *The Orators*, besides *The Age of Anxiety*.[53]

Anthony Hecht notes that Auden "was particularly given to moralizing landscapes, and using them in symbolic ways, as Hardy did,"[54] and "The Seven Stages" is strikingly similar to one of Hardy's landscape symbols. In *The Dynasts*, Hardy describes Europe as "a prone and emaciated figure, the Alps shaping like a backbone, and the branching mountain-chains like ribs, the peninsular plateau of Spain forming a head" (Fore Scene, 1–3), an image that has no significance beyond the material; it recalls his suggestion in the *Life* that "Mankind, in fact, may be, and possibly will be, viewed as members of one corporeal frame" (235). At the end of "The Seven Ages," the narrator introduces the image of a landscape in bodily form: "So it was now as they sought that state of prehistoric happiness which, by human beings, can only be imagined in terms of a landscape bearing a symbolic resemblance to the human body" (57). As the key unifying experience of the characters' shared vision, the voyage across the symbolic body in "The Seven Stages" represents both interpersonal and psychic integration, and, on an esoteric level, a coherence of body and soul.

Auden's image partakes of the spiritual as well as the material. To his student Alan Ansen, Auden explained that the symbolism of "The Seven Stages" derives from kabbalah mysticism, declaring, "It's all done in the Zohar."[55] To anyone familiar with kabbbala, "The Seven Stages" represents a poetry not of the body alone, but of the body and spirit together, and of the relationship between the One and the Many. The kabbalistic system of the *Zohar* consists of a Neoplatonic mysticism in which the ten divine emanations, or *sefirot*, represent the aspects of God perceptible in the world, as opposed to the *Ein-Sof*, which is God's hidden nature. According to Gershom Scholem, the One and the Many of these two concepts exist simultaneously: "The hidden God in the aspect of *Ein-Sof* and the God manifested in the emanation of *Sefirot* are one and the same, viewed from two different angles."[56] The process of emanation produces the *olam ha-yichud*, or "world of unification," which is simultaneous with and opposed to the *olam ha-perud*, or "world of separation."[57] In other words, unification and separation exist in tandem. The title of the section, "The Seven Stages," also indicates Auden's familiarity with the concept of *sefirot*; one of the euphemisms for the *sefirot* is *madregot*, which means "stages."[58] Scholem also uses the word "stages" in his explanation of the process from unity to plurality: "On the model of the neoplatonic hierarchy, according to which the transition from the one to the many was accomplished through the stages of intellect, universal soul, and nature, many kabbalists . . . thought of the *Sefirot* as also comprising these stages."[59] In "The Seven Stages," because Auden's characters begin from the many and return to the many, they take a slightly different route, one that begins with soul, moves up to intellect, and returns down to nature.[60]

After the last stage, Rosetta, Quant, Emble, and Malin awake

from their unified vision, the details of which they have forgot-
ten. Only after this shared vision of unity do Rosetta and Malin
accede to their places in the One and, unlike Hardy's pessimistic
vision of the abandonment of human bonds upon such a recognition, Auden's philosophy finds these two strengthening their
ties to their communities. For Rosetta, this means acknowledging that she cannot escape her Judaism, the entire history of her
people, or its One God. In her soliloquy, she sets aside her fantasies of the English country life and acknowledges that however
many gentile lovers she might take, she can never shed the reality of her heritage: "I shan't find shelter, I shan't be at peace /
Till I really take your restless hands, / My poor fat father" (126).
In an allusion to a midrash that envisions that all of Israel, even
those not yet born, were present when Moses presented his people with the Law at Mt. Sinai, a story congruent with the cele-
bration of All Souls, Rosetta recognizes that the connection
remains: "Moses will scold if / We're not all there for the next
meeting / At some brackish well or broken arch" (126–27). She
emphasizes this sense of the eternal and the present collapsed
together, of the One and the Many simultaneously, when she be-
moans the fact that "Time is our trade, to be tense our gift"
(124). To be in the present tense, particularly in the present of
the Holocaust is such an unwelcome "gift," that Rosetta has,
until this moment, attempted to escape her part in the unity of
the Jews.

Yet Rosetta does, as Simeon says of the House of Israel, "limit
the coherence of the One and the Many to a special case"; she
specifically rejects the gentile world in her soliloquy, beginning
with her mock bridegroom, Emble, because she perceives that
she does not have absolute freedom to choose; she recognizes
that she has been chosen.[61] In her speech, Rosetta makes evident
that the cessation of her solipsistic fantasies stems from her
newfound acceptance of the inevitability of her place in the One
of her race. She somewhat resentfully lectures the sleeping
Emble on his ability as a gentile to choose whether to believe or
not:

You're too late to believe. Your lie is showing,
Your creed is creased. But have Christian luck,
Your Jesus has wept; you may joke now,

> Be spick and span, spell out the bumptious
> Morals on monuments, mind your poise
> And take up your cues, attract Who's-Who,
> Ignore What's-Not. Niceness is all and
> The rest bores. I'm too rude a question.
>
> (124

In her soliloquy, she realizes that being chosen, she cannot choose:

> He won't alter
> Nor fake one fact. Though I fly to Wall Street
> Or Publisher's Row, or pass out, or
> Submerge in music, or marry well,
> Marooned on riches, He'll be right there
> With His Eye upon me. Should I hide away
> My secret sins in consulting rooms,
> My fears are before Him; He'll find all,
> Ignore nothing. He'll never let me
> Conceal from Him the semi-detached
> Brick villa in Laburnum Crescent,
> The poky parlor, the pink bows on
> The landing-curtains, or the lawn-mower
> That wouldn't work, for He won't pretend to
> Forget how I began, nor grant belief
> In the mythical scenes I make up
> Of a home like theirs, the Innocent Place where
> His Law can't look, the leaves are so thick.
>
> (125–26)

So cohesive is the unity of the Jews, for Auden, that, although they might attempt to escape, or might be separated, they can never escape their identity.

At the end of her speech, however, Rosetta does not just stop running from her place in the One, she embraces it. She acknowledges that the current state of her people, particularly in the wake of the diaspora and in the shadow of the Holocaust only a few years past, appears to be a dissociated multiplicity, but is really a differentiated unity. She relates this situation to the kabbalistic story of the breaking of the vessels, in which the Divine unity was shattered when only the first three *sefirot* managed to contain its light, and the remaining emanations in

the line of descent to the material broke; the resulting divine
sparks scattered and became imprisoned in matter:

> We'll point for Him,
> Be as obvious always if He won't show
> To threaten their thinking in their way,
> Nor His strong arm that stood no nonsense,
> Fly, let's face it, to defend us now
> When bruised or broiled our bodies our chucked
> Like cracked crocks onto kitchen middens
> In the time He takes.
>
> (125)

Yet, in the face of disunity and the apparent absence of God, she
unites herself with all other Jews across time and space and affirms the unity of that same God as she completes her soliloquy
by reciting in Hebrew the *Shema*, in Auden's transliteration:
"Sh'ma' Yisra'el, / ª'donai 'ᵉlohenu, 'ªdonai 'echad" (Hear, O Israel, the Lord is our God, the Lord is One) (127). Even in a time
of war, in a time of unique horror, in which both God and social
bonds seem to be absent, she affirms the One.

In the Epilogue, the Christian Malin's acknowledgment of the
universality of the coherence of the One and the Many comes
not as an affirmation, but as a rejection of the individuals who
fail to recognize the connection between themselves, others,
and God. His own understanding, he says, came as "only the
flash / Of negative knowledge," as it must, because the One cannot be apprehended through the application of logic:

> For the new locus is never
> Hidden inside the old one
> Where Reason could rout it out,
> Nor guarded by dragons in distant
> Mountains where Imagination
> Could explore it; the place of birth
> Is too obvious and near to notice,
> Some dull dogpatch a stone's throw
> Outside the walls, reserved
> For the eyes of faith to find.
>
> (135)

Mankind, slave to the present, to time, to the material world
cannot conceive of the eternal and the spiritual, and of the di-

vine link between the two worlds, in which, according to Simeon, "the One and the Many are simultaneously revealed as real":

> We're quite in the dark: we do not
> Know the connection between
> The clock we are bound to obey
> And the miracle we must not despair of.

(134)

Malin realizes that not only do we not recognize our place in the One, we revel in materialism and multiplicity:

> for plainly it is not
> To the Cross or to Clarté or to Common Sense
> Our passions pray but to primitive totems
> As absurd as they are savage; science or no science,
> It is Bacchus or the Great Boyg or Baal-Peor,
> Fortune's Ferris-wheel or the physical sound
> Of our own names which they actually adore as their
> Ground and goal. Yet the grossest of our dreams is
> No worse than our worship which for the most part
> Is so much galimatias to get out of
> Knowing our neighbor, all the needs and conceits of
> The poor muddled maddened mundane animal
> Who is hostess to us all [. . .]

(136)

In this speech, he also rejects a worship of the One which celebrates only the transcendent unity, and not also the immanent unity between men. Without agape, no true communion with the One is complete.

In Hardy's philosophy, only a very few people apprehend the One, and then only if fate wills it; for Auden, each person has the capacity to find his connection to God, but most choose not to love either themselves or their neighbors, precluding any relationship to the eternal, and "in choosing how many / And how much they will love, our minds insist on / Their own disorder as their own punishment" (137). Stuck in the material world, he says, we want to belong to the One, as "Temporals pleading for eternal life with / The infinite impetus of anxious spirits, / Finite in fact yet refusing to be real." In our state of anxiety, we desire to experience unity and multiplicity concurrently, but we stubbornly refuse to look inside ourselves in order to approach the source of such a state, "unwilling to say Yes / to the Self-So which is the same at all times, / That Always-Opposite which is the whole subject / Of our not-knowing" (137). As in *The Dynasts*, people "wait unawares for His World to come" (138), but they need not. By limiting and quantifying our own relationships with ourselves and others, ties for which we actually have limitless potential, Auden says, we deny ourselves the consolation of the order found in unity.

Both Hardy and Auden make extensive use of prose stage directions, or *didascalia*, so much so that *The Dynasts* and *The Age of Anxiety* both have prosimetric, not purely poetic forms, and they adapt those stage directions so that their forms echo the philosophy of each of the works, reflecting Hardy's de facto multiplicity and Auden's preference for unity. Hardy's unvarying use of the present tense in *The Dynasts* not only mimics the disjunctions in time associated with plurality, it also prohibits the special relationship between narrator and reader that results from the sharing of a temporality. Auden generally makes use of this phenomenon to create a sense of intimacy with the reader in *The Age of Anxiety*, but turns to the present tense in "The Seven Stages," so that both poet and reader share the experience of the characters in that section. The two poets' descriptions of the material world also reflect their differences; Hardy restricts description in his didascalia to phenomena available to the senses, while Auden's narrator avoids the concrete in favor of the abstract. The narrator of *The Age of Anxiety* has access to, and shares with the reader, the characters' innermost thoughts and feelings, while *The Dynasts* is restricted to exteriors only.

Edward Mendelson asserts that "[i]n the aftermath of romanticism, the community of knowledge between characters and their authors broke down"; the artist, "perceiving more than other men" then "lost hope of communicating with them."[62] After "signs of increasing distance of the artist from his subject" throughout the Victorian era, he claims, Hardy's position in *The Dynasts* represents the "final separation."[63] Hardy achieves distance between himself and the poem by differentiating the voice of the stage directions from the voices of the characters through diction and tone, by disavowing responsibility for its content, and by downplaying his biographical connections to the story. Where Hardy retreats from connections with *The Dynasts*, the voice of Auden's narrator, which will be identified with that of the poet, asserts its closeness to the characters through similarities in diction and through double-voicing techniques, as well as through access to their interior thoughts. Auden also saturates *The Age of Anxiety* with elements of his own biographical and philosophical background.

Both *The Age of Anxiety* and *The Dynasts* contain all four of the types of stage directions identified by Michael Issarachoff in his book *Discourse as Performance*. Issarachoff categorizes the didascalia found in all types of dramatic writing, both closet dramas and plays meant for performance. These categories include extratextual didascalia—discourses on subjects other than the play (such as the Preface to *The Dynasts*);[64] technical didascalia—lighting, etc.; and normal didascalia—indications of settings, speakers, etc.[65] Issarachoff also identifies stage directions that he labels "autonomous didascalia," those "manifestly intended for reading; [which] are in fact spurious stage directions, not meant to guide stage presentation."[66] In dramatic poems, all of the "stage directions" must be considered to be autonomous didascalia; however, extended descriptions or narrative such as those found in *The Age of Anxiety* and *The Dynasts* imply a much greater relationship between poet and reader than do imitations of "normal" didascalia that identify the speakers and furnish brief descriptions of the setting.

Hardy's use of the present tense and his restriction of the stage directions to objective description give the didascalia the appearance of instructions from the poet/playwright, which, in a playscript, most readers interpret as outside the text. In the case of technical and normal didascalia, it makes no sense to attribute these notes to any personage but the author. Issarachoff, for example, contends that "it is essential to realize that stage directions constitute nonfictive utterance, in contrast to the fictive utterance of the dialogue,"[67] and asserts that "while in the novel, just as in poetry, the author can conceal his presence by allowing the *I* to refer to someone else," in dramatic writing, "his voice is always present, albeit in a minor key, in the didascalia."[68] Most critics agree that stage directions provide some relationship between the reader and the text, but do not necessarily identify the voice present with that of the author. In her essay, "Reading Modern Drama: Voice in the Didascaliae," Mary Witt also implies that the stage directions create a direct relationship between author and reader: "A voice in the didascaliae speaks to an implied reader. . . . We don't need to eavesdrop;" however, she cautions, "It remains to be shown whose and what voice is speaking."[69] The blatant factitiousness of the stage directions in *The Age of Anxiety* means that a practiced reader is unlikely to identify the voice of the didascalia with the poet himself, but he might well interpret the voice as that of a persona adopted by the poet.

Assuming that the voice of the stage directions is that of the poet, the tense in which the didascalia appears affects the closeness of the relationship between author and reader. When the stage directions appear in present tense, as do the normal didascalia in a play meant for performance, author and reader experience time on the same scale as do the characters, and there is no sense of any continuity. The reader moves forward in time jumping from one speaker to another as the dialogue progresses. But when written in the past tense, stage directions turn the dramatic dialogue into reported speech, as in narration typical of fiction, a technique that demonstrates a belief in the connectedness of points in time. Clearly, the drama is not being played out within earshot of the reader; the action has already occurred, and the reader and author share a temporal dimension. From that temporal perspective, the action of each scene constitutes a single occurrence in which each speaker contributes to the whole.

Hardy's stage directions in *The Dynasts* remain resolutely in the present tense, to the extent of the exclusion of all time references, a technique that causes the reader to experience an unsettling disjunction in time. Some of Hardy's fidelity to the present tense stems from his adoption of dramatic conventions; for the most part, the normal didascalia in *The Dynasts* mimic the didascalia in playscripts meant for performance, such as the instructions in the opening scenes: "Enter the Ancient Spirit" (Fore Scene), "He unpacks a case of pistols" (I, I, i,70), "Exit horseman" (I, I, i,82), and so on. But Hardy also employs the

present tense exclusively in his extensive, explicitly autonomous didascalia, particularly in his descriptions of settings and
in short prose passages labeled "Dumb Shows." The "Dumb
Show" passages contain descriptions of actions occurring either
prior to or concurrent with the scene, extensive movements impossible on any stage. The first "Dumb Show" appears in part
first, act first, scene IV, and begins: "Moving in this scene are
countless companies of soldiery, engaged in a drill-practice of
embarking and disembarking, and of hoisting horses into the
vessels and landing them again. Vehicles bearing provisions of
many sorts load and unload before the temporary warehouses.
Further off, on the open land, bodies of troops are at field drill.
Other bodies of soldiers, half stripped and encrusted with mud,
are labouring as navvies in repairing the excavations" (17–23).
Writing the passage in the present tense implies that the author
experiences the scene at the same moment as the reader and has
time neither for analysis nor for reflection; in the instant, one
has time only for the processing of sensory information. By es-
chewing the past tense in *The Dynasts*, he transfers the analytical position from himself to the reader. Now, not only does he
no longer have access to the characters' interior thoughts, but
his job is complete as soon as he finishes writing, while that of
the reader has only begun.

When poet and reader can look back in time, the past tense
allows them a certain amount of distance from which to perceive the unity of what might have once seemed to be disparate
events. Hardy expresses the belief in distance as desirable for the
appreciation of unity in his poem "Self-Unconscious" in which
the speaker declares, "O it would have been good / Could he
then have stood / At a clear-eyed distance, and conned the
whole."[70] In *The Dynasts*, however, when Hardy uses the present tense, he disposes of the temporal distance between the narrator's retrospective view and the experiences of the characters,
and he makes no effort to close up the rifts in time within the
drama. The spirits may claim to possess all time in a single moment; but in their verse, they exist just as much in the present
as do the humans or earth or as does the narrator. Where, in the
novels, Hardy's use of the past tense reconciles his perspective
with that of the reader—they both look back over the continuity
of history from the same point in time—in *The Dynasts*, narra-

tor, characters, and reader each individually have the experience of "from moment to moment moving toward the future."

By refusing to supply the reader with dates or other temporal references, Hardy further emphasizes the multiplicity of the individual points in time represented by each scene. The descriptions of the settings, from the height of the spirit world, encompass vast spatial realms and display a whole made up out of individuals, but they have no connection in time to any of the other scenes. Other than the opening directions for part first, act first, scene I, in which he indicates the time as "a fine day in March 1805," Hardy rarely give any clues as to the date of the scene or the passage of time between scenes. The Dumb Show from part first, act first, scene IV demonstrates the immensity of the vision shared by the narrator and reader, but, its only temporal reference is a description of the dawn:

> The morning breaks, with early sunlight. The French Army of Invasion is disclosed. On the hills on either side of the town and behind appear large military camps formed of timber huts. Lower down are other camps of more or less permanent kind, the whole affording accommodation for one hundred and fifty thousand men.
>
> South of the town is an extensive basin surrounded by quays, the heaps of fresh soil around showing it to be a recent excavation from the banks of the Liane. The basin is crowded with the flotilla, consisting of hundreds of vessels of sundry kinds: flat-bottomed brigs with guns and two masts; boats of one mast, carrying each an artillery waggon, two guns, and a two-stalled horse-box; transports with three low masts; and long narrow pinnaces arranged for many oars.
>
> Timber, saw-mills, and new-cut planks spread in profusion around, and many of the town residences are seen adapted for warehouses and infirmaries. (1–16)

The description resembles a static landscape painting, in which no time passes. Although the action covers ten years, none of the stage directions after the first indicates the year, and only forty-nine of the one hundred and sixteen scenes have any sort of temporal indication at all, mostly consisting of terse directions such as "July," "a winter midnight," "summer evening," and so on. The effect is to maintain the reader's senses always in the present, leaving him unanchored in time, with no reassuring touchstones in the past, no knowledge of the future, and no sense of the continuity of time. The absence of dating is so disconcerting that editor Samuel Hynes provides an appendix to *The Dynasts* with a chart showing approximate dates and times of each of the scenes (part third, appendix A).

While Hardy's use of the present tense indicates a prevalence of the Many, Auden's limited use of the present tense in *The Age of Anxiety* emphasizes a tension between the One and the Many. In accordance with Auden's preference for the One, the vast majority of the stage directions appear in the past tense; even the "normal" didascalia introducing the characters' speeches indicate not only the speakers' names, but also, in a deviation from a conventional playscript, that the speeches occurred in the past, in other words, "Quant was thinking" (7), "Malin thought" (12), and "Rosetta spoke first" (17). Most of the autonomous stage directions also appear in the past tense as narration, as when after the radio breaks into their individual thoughts, the narrator says, "they could no longer keep these thoughts to themselves, but turning towards each other on their high wooden stools, became acquainted" (17). However, when the four characters enter into their mystical vision in "The Seven Stages," all of the stage directions, normal and autonomous, switch to the present tense. The prose introduction begins, "At first all is dark and each walks alone," and the first indications of speech are: "Quant is the first to see anything. He says: ..." and "Now Rosetta perceives clearly and says: ..." (61). As soon as this mass hypnosis or mutual dream ends, the narrator reverts to past-tense narration: "Saying this, they woke up and recognized where they sat and who they were" (99). The effect of the present tense during the vision is to include both the reader and narrator in the mystical union and journey into which the characters have entered, as in a midrash to which Rosetta alludes where all Jews throughout time attend the giving of the Law at Sinai. Basically, when the four speakers are distinct from one another, the narrator balances their multiplicity with the unity implied by the past tense; when the four characters become united, he balances their union with the plurality implied by the present tense. At the very end of *The Age of Anxiety*, however, the narrator reports of Malin that "he returned to duty, reclaimed by the actual world where time is real and in which, therefore, poetry can take no interest" (138), and in this observation, Auden acknowledges that temporality reigns in our daily lives, where it cannot be countered by the manipulations of a poet.

The other variations from the past tense in *The Age of Anxiety* occur in the prose sections that might be considered extratextual didascalia, in which the narrator seems to speak directly to the reader, and the use of the present tense in these passages promotes the idea of unity in two different ways. For one thing, the present tense here reinforces the sense that the poet and reader share a time frame distanced from the temporality of the story; when a narrator addresses a reader, he creates the illusion of contemporaneity between the two. Auden also uses the present tense to make assertions of universal and eternal truths, as in the opening pages when the narrator declares: "When the historical process breaks down and armies organize with their embossed debates the ensuing void which they can never consecrate, when necessity is associated with horror and freedom with boredom, then it looks good to the bar business" (3). He does this again at the end of "The Seven Ages," when he explains the unifying properties of alcohol: "For it can happen, if circumstances are otherwise propitious, that members of a group in this condition establish a rapport in which communication of thoughts and feelings is so accurate and instantaneous, that they appear to function as a single organism" (57). In order to make a statement universal, we must use the present tense; for example, we say "war is hell," because to say "war was hell" or "war will be hell" is to particularize and limit the statement. Auden's use of the present tense in these stage directions, therefore, differs from Hardy's in *The Dynasts*, because Hardy's present-tense didascalia describe only particulars.

Hardy also limits his stage directions in their descriptions of the material world to details that may be sensed by the organs of the body, to the senses which are associated with the Many. A number of critics have concentrated on the visual nature of the prose sections of *The Dynasts*. Bonamy Dobrée, for instance, comments that, "In default of keeping the ear occupied and delighted, which Hardy rarely does . . . , he arranged that the eye of the imagination should be kept continually at work."[71] If Hardy fails to keep the ear delighted through his poetry, he at least offers descriptions of auditory details, as in this introduction to

Pitt's speech before the House: "During the momentary pause before he speaks the House assumes an attentive stillness, in which can be heard the rustling of the trees without, a horn from an early coach, and the voice of the watch crying the hour" (I, I, iii, following l. 85). In several scenes, he even provides musical notation to supplement his prose descriptions (III, II, iv and III,VI, ii).

Not only does Hardy confine his accounts to descriptions of the material world, he also consistently employs stage directions to limit the reader's views of individual scenes, throwing the reader into the restricted sensory world of characters who cannot know their places in the whole. Susan Dean points out that a number of scenes are peopled with sentinels and generals with field glasses attempting to see distant sights, and she observes that "[r]eading alongside these straining protagonists, with the drama's point of view consistently burdened with the limitations that mortal senses labor under, is an exercise in sympathy."[72] The sympathy generated, if any, stems from the limitations on the individual's knowledge of his place in the universe. Frequently, Hardy forces such sympathy on the reader by imposing on him physical barriers to sight in the stage directions that mirror those experienced by the characters: "The Show presently dims and becomes broken, till only its flashes and gleams are visible. Anon a curtain of cloud closes over it" (I,I,iv); "A moving stratum of summer cloud beneath the point of view covers up the spectacle like an awning" (II,II,iii); "The room darkens, and ends the scene" (III,III,i). These limitations emphasize that even the view from the narrator's and reader's perspective does not afford an unbounded view of the whole, that none of us can truly perceive the unity underlying our world.

The lack of sensory detail in the didascalia of *The Age of Anxiety* results not from any limitation of the narrator's or reader's perceptions, but from a refusal to focus on the material world. Auden, in his essay "Practiced Topophile," regrets his inability "to attempt . . . poetry which requires a strong visual imagination."[73] However, only the narrator, not the characters in *The Age of Anxiety*, demonstrates any lack of "visual imagination." On the contrary, the four characters provide vivid sensory descriptions, as when Quant describes his boyhood:

Secret meetings at the slaughter-house
With nickels and knives, initiations
Behind the billboards. Then the hammerpond looked
So green and grim, yet graciously its dank
Water made us welcome—once in, we
Swam without swearing. The smelting mill
We broke into had a big chimney
And huge engines; holding our breath, we
Lighted matches and looked at the gears,
The cruel cogwheels, the crank's absolute
Veto on pleasure.
. . . .
    Heavy like us
Sank the gas-tanks—it was supper time.
In hot houses helpless babies and
Telephones gabbled untidy cries,
And on embankments black with burnt grass
Shambling freight-trains were shunted away
Past crimson clouds.

                                       (30–31)

His pun on "crank" and "absolute" underscores the boys' attraction to the material; the Absolute, transcendent unity, requires one to reject sensuality for morality—only a "crank," an eccentric, crazy, or crotchety person would do so in their opinions. In contrast to the sensory detail of these memories, the narrator's description of Quant's reminiscences emphasizes the abstract: "[F]rom time to time, images, some highly-colored, some violent, would enter unexpectedly and incomprehensibly into his dreams" (4). Even in "The Seven Stages," when the characters travel across the symbolic landscape, he leaves the description largely to the characters. The narrator, in one of his most detailed visuals, says, "And so, on a treeless watershed, at the tumbledown Mariners Tavern (which is miles inland) the four assemble, having completed the first stage of the journey. They look about them, and everything seems somehow familiar," while Emble describes vividly "the sawtooth range / Our nickel and copper come from," and where "A brown blur of buildings marks / Some sacred or secular town" (66). Through their use of sensory details, Auden sets the characters' baroque descriptions of the material against the narrator's abstractions, to the One implied by formlessness, creating a balance between them, but giving the greater authority to the narrator who relates the tale.

The prose stage directions in *The Dynasts* and in *The Age of Anxiety* also reflect Hardy's and Auden's differing philosophies of the One and the Many in the techniques used to modify the distances between the prose voice of the didascalia and those of the characters. Hardy's focus on the material world requires him to maintain a strict objectivity, not only in regard to nature, but in regard to the characters also. The dramatic form inherently lends itself to the display of external characteristics only; it generally has no mechanism for the examination of internal thoughts and feelings—paradoxically, the common bonds which unite people—and Hardy adheres to this convention. Auden, however, breaks from dramatic convention by telling us what the characters think and by analyzing their motivations. He emphasizes the connection between the psyches of the characters and that of the narrator through the use of Bakhtinian double-voicing techniques normally found in the novel. Even the diction and tone adopted by the voices of the prose stage directions in the two works demonstrate the differences in distance—Hardy's prose appears in a voice distinct from those of the characters of *The Dynasts*, while Auden's prose echoes some of the unique patterns of speech employed by the four speakers in *The Age of Anxiety*.

Auden's exploration of the interior thoughts of his characters is striking in comparison to Hardy's focus on exteriors. Even when Hardy makes some note of emotional states, he does so only in regard to a large group of people, in order to set a scene, not to explore any interior or spiritual motivations. For example, in part second, act 1, Scene III, he describes the state of the citizenry as being "in an excited and anxious mood." Later in the same scene, he notes that "some young officers in a frolic of defiance halt, draw their swords and whet them on the steps of the FRENCH AMBASSADOR'S residence as they pass." When Napoleon falls asleep, then wakes from a nightmare vision—"A horrible dream has gripped me—horrible! / I saw before me Lannes—just as he looked / that day at Aspern: mutilated, bleeding!"—the stage directions make no mention of his terror. The preceding prose notes that as his cavalry struggles at Waterloo, "over the bodies of those previously left there, and amid horses wandering about without riders, or crying as they lie with entrails trailing or limbs broken," that "Napoleon falls into a drowsy stupefaction as he looks on near the farm of Rossomme, till he nods in momentary sleep" (III, VII, vi, 1–3). In the normal didascalia indicating that Napoleon is the speaker, a parenthetical note declares that he is "starting up" from his sleep, not that he is "terrified" or "horrified" or "in fear."

In contrast, Auden's opening prose section provides a detailed psychological analysis of Emble's motivations for his promiscuity: "In certain cases—his was one—this general unease of youth is only aggravated by what would appear to alleviate it, a grace of person which grants them, without effort on their part, a succession of sexual triumphs. For then the longing for success, the doubt of ever being able to achieve the kinds of success which have to be earned, and the certainty of being able to have at this moment a kind which does not, play dangerously into each other's hands" (6). And at the beginning of "The Masque," the narrator analyzes the motivations of all four of the characters:

> Had they been perfectly honest with themselves, they would have had to admit that they were tired and wanted to go home alone to bed. That they were not was in part due, of course, to vanity, the fear of getting too old to want fun or too ugly to get it, but also to unselfishness, the fear of spoiling the fun for others. Besides, only animals who are below civilization and the angels who are beyond it can be sincere. Human beings are, necessarily, actors who cannot become something before they have first pretended to be it; and they can be divided, not into the hypocritical and the sincere, but into the sane who know they are acting and the mad who do not. (109)

As Auden reminds us that his characters exist between the pure materiality of the animals and the pure spirituality of the angels, that they have concerns that are both individual and communal, that they balance between plurality and unity; the fact that the narrator has access to their thoughts emphasizes the balance between interiority and exteriority as well.

In addition to creating this tension between the narrator and the speakers through access to their emotions and thoughts, Auden also creates a balance between the One narrator and the Many characters through the use of a type of dialogism described by Bakhtin in his "Discourse in the Novel" as a "hybrid construction." Bakhtin defines this "hybrid construction" as "an utterance which belongs, by its grammatical . . . and compositional markers, to a single speaker, but that actually contains mixed within its two utterances, two speech manners, two styles, two 'languages,' two semantic and axiological belief systems."[74] According to Bakhtin, such dialogism may come in the form of "character zones," which are "formed from the fragments of character speech . . . , from scattered words and sayings belonging to someone else's speech, from those invasions into authorial speech of others' expressive indicators (ellipsis, questions, exclamations)."[75] Auden makes use of this species of double-voicing in the Prologue, in the descriptions of the characters. For instance, the narrator tells us that Quant, as he looks in the mirror, wonders "why he was still so interested in that *tired old widower* who would never be more than a clerk in a shipping office near the Battery" (my emphasis) (4). At minimum, the words "tired old widower" represent the incorporation of Quant's own words into the narrator's speech. Auden makes his greatest use of the double-voicing technique in his introduction of Rosetta, where the narrator integrates her own plaintive questions into his own description:

> Lighting a cigarette, ROSETTA, too ignored her surroundings but with less ease. Yes, she made lots of money—she was a buyer for a big department store and did it very well—and that was a great deal, for, like anyone who has ever been so, she had a sensible horror of being poor. Yes, America was the best place on earth to come to if you had to earn your living, but did it have to be so big and empty and noisy and messy? Why could she not have been rich? Yes, though she was not as young as she looked, there were plenty of men who either were deceived or preferred a girl who might be experienced—which indeed she was. But why were the men one liked not the sort who proposed marriage and the men who proposed marriage not the sort one liked? (5)

When, as Bakhtin suggests, the characters' words appear to be "encroaching in one way or another upon the author's voice,"[76] infiltrating the "author's" prose, the character and narrator enter into a reciprocal relationship in which both voices are present, but neither is distinct; they are simultaneously one and many in the stage directions even more than in the verse dialogue.

Hardy, on the other hand, keeps the voice of the stage directions in *The Dynasts* strictly distinct from those of the characters, using variations in diction and tone to maintain a distance between them and himself. Through the use of different dictions appropriate to the various classes of the characters, he insures that each remains discrete. At the highest level, the Spirits deliver their speeches in an elevated and educated language ("*Nothing appears of shape to indicate / That cognizance has marshalled things terrene*" [Fore Scene, 34–35]), as acknowledged by Hardy: "The Spirits do, indeed (owing perhaps to the evil example set by scientists & philosophers) seem to prefer words from the Greek to simpler ones."[77] The Spirits' diction, in other words, aligns them with the objective observers of the world, which is indeed their place in *The Dynasts*. Among the humans, the upper classes generally speak a stilted blank verse in a stereotypically poetic diction, as in Napoleon's speech to his troops before the invasion of Russia:

> Then let us forthwith stride the Niemen flood,
> Let us bear war into her great gaunt land,
> And spread our glory there as otherwhere,
> So that a stable peace shall stultify
> The evil seed-bearing that Russian wiles
> Have nourished upon Europe's choked affairs
> These fifty years!
>
> (III,I,i,18–24)

To distinguish them as members of the lower classes, the Wessex farmers, the soldiers, and the camp followers speak mostly in prose dialect; a spectator on Rainbow barrow discusses the possibility of the kidnapping of King George: "Lard, Lard, if 'a were nabbed, it wouldn't make a deal of difference! We should have nobody to zing to, and play single-stick to, and grin at through horse-collars, that's true. . . . But we should rub along some way, goodnow" (I, II, iv,32–36).[78] The voice of the didascalia, to distinguish itself from the characters, both Spirit and human, avoids both elevated and low diction, settling on a journalistic tone instead. The First of the Dumb Shows epitomizes the forthright diction of this voice: "Moving in this scene are countless companies of soldiery, engaged in a drill-practice of embarking and disembarking, and of hoisting horses into the vessels and landing them again. Vehicles bearing provisions of many sorts load and unload before the temporary warehouses. Further off, on the open land, bodies of troops are at field-drill. Other bodies of soldiers, half stripped and encrusted with mud, are labouring as navvies in repairing the excavations" (I, I, iv,17–23). The diction and tone of the didascalia, in conjunction with the physical remove of the point of view, serve to create the impression of a passive observer who merely records the scenes that appear before him and who has no emotional connection to the actors of the drama.

The emotional connection between the voice of the didascalia and the characters in *The Age of Anxiety*, on the other hand, is emphasized by Auden through the use of alliteration and diction that, in attenuated forms, echo those of the four speakers. The use of alliteration (and/or consonance) appears frequently in the stage directions, as in the opening paragraphs where the narrator speaks of "an unprejudiced space in which nothing particular ever happens, . . . whereby each may appropriate it for his or her private world of repentant felicitous forms, heavy expensive objects or avenging flames and floods" (my emphasis) (3). At other times, Auden wrenches the syntax of the narrator to approximate the meter of the verse: "Matter and manner set their teeth on edge, especially Malin's" (22). The narrator's diction, although not as extravagant and unlikely as the high, latinate, baroque diction of the speakers ("fioritura" [13]; "amoeboid" [15]; "farouche" [20]), nonetheless consists of a multisyllabic and slightly elevated vocabulary. Prior to the "felicitous forms" in the first lines of narration, he describes "embossed debates" that lead to "the ensuing void which they can never consecrate" (3). As in the use of hybrid constructions that incorporate expressions belonging to the characters into the narrator's speech, these appropriations of their speech patterns also serve to create a partial merger between the two speakers, as well as between the prose and the verse.

The distance between the poet and the poem provides another indicator of each of the poets' positions on the problem of the relationship between the One and the Many. In *The Dynasts*, Hardy's use of prose stage directions that emulate those of conventional verse dramas lends the impression that those didascalia constitute a direct communication from the poet to the reader. However, he takes pains to distance himself from the content of the work by attributing all of its ideas to the characters and disavowing those ideas in the prose sections, by professing his reliance on history instead of art, and by concealing his personal associations with the story. Auden takes the opposite approach, creating a prose voice that is conspicuously factitious, but that makes pronouncements of philosophy that must be attributed to the poet. The baroque style of *The Age of Anxiety* proclaims it to be a work of art, the invention of the poet, and Auden includes a number of thinly disguised references to his own life. In the balance between distance and nearness of the poet to the poem then, Hardy tends much more to distance, which is appropriate to an apparently pluralistic world where people cannot know their connections to one another. Auden's predilection for closeness conforms to his idea of a world in which people may overcome the distances between them.

Despite the illusion that the didascalia of *The Dynasts* represent Hardy's own voice, their lack of insight and analysis makes Hardy seem disturbingly distant from the work. Kenneth Millard points out that "*The Dynasts* is notable for the dispersal of its authorial voice through the medium of stage directions, dumb shows, and various Spirit voices. Rather than a central governing omniscient persona, the poem has a variety of commenting phantoms."[79] He attributes Hardy's "pains to disguise authorial intention" to a reluctance to submit himself to the same type of criticism he encountered after the publications of *Tess of the D'Urbervilles* and *Jude the Obscure*,[80] a reasonable surmise, but not wholly satisfactory. Millard recognizes the unresolved nature of the debate between the various spirits as "the reason for the poem's impression of being remote and inaccessible," an impression that results from the fact that "the reader is given no clear and reliable directions."[81] The reader gets no sense of the unity of the work, of its overall meaning or purpose, and has no more understanding of the whole than do the characters themselves, because Hardy, who is standing outside the work and who could provide an overview, refuses to do so. Dean concedes that the "apparent absence of Hardy's voice" contributes to the failure of *The Dynasts* to engage its readers,[82] but she also considers Hardy's "reticence and reserve" and "silent, non-committal registering,"[83] as a generous gift of freedom to the reader—"an indication of this author's objectivity that he would share his powers with us, and that he should even, in his artful, art-concealing way, set us ahead of himself," leaving the reader free to interpret as he sees fit.[84] Whether or not this freedom might be interpreted as "generous" is up for debate, particularly given Hardy's less than charitable attitude in the Preface toward the reader who fails to envision the whole: "[T]he subject is familiar to all; and foreknowledge is assumed to fill in the junctions required to combine the scenes into an artistic unity. Should the mental spectator be unwilling or unable to do this, a historical presentment on an intermittent plan, in which the *dramatis personae* number some hundreds, exclusive of crowds and armies, becomes in his individual case unsuitable." (78–84). The fault in such cases, he implies, belongs to an obstinate or dimwitted philistine, and may in no way be attributed to the author. In any event, whether it is liberating or tyrannical, Hardy's relegation of responsibility to each individual reader for the integration of the whole is consistent with the apparent pluralism of *The Dynasts*.

Hardy also attempts to distance himself from the philosophy expressed by the Spirits, not only by placing all such discussion in their mouths and banishing it from the didascalia and by making all of their speeches tentative, but also by an explicit statement. In the Preface, he denigrates the Spirits as "intended to be taken by the reader for what they may be worth as contrivances of the fancy merely" and demurs that "[t]heir doctrines are but tentative, and are advanced with little eye to a clear metaphysic, or systematized philosophy warranted to lift 'the burthen of the mystery' of this unintelligible world" (44–47). Not only does he avoid acknowledging the ideas as his own by writing "*[t]heir* doctrines" rather than "*my* doctrines," but he also avoids responsibility through the use of the passive voice, making it unclear as to precisely by whom the doctrines "are advanced." Through these equivocations, Hardy does not quite deny that the ideas belong to him, but he stops short of averring their truth. After the publication of Part First, he carried his denial of responsibility for its philosophy into his famous dispute with reviewer A. B. Walkley in the *Times Literary Supplement*. In the course of his diatribe against Walkley, he also asserts vehemently and somewhat disingenuously that the philosophy is not unique to himself, but concurs with universal Christian tenets: "The philosophy of "The Dynasts," under various titles and phases, is almost as old as civilization. Its fundamental principle, under the name of Predestination, was preached by St. Paul. "Being predestinated"—says the author of the Epistle to the Ephesians, "Being predestinated according to the purpose of Him who worketh all things after the counsel of His own will"; and much more to the same effect, the only difference being that externality is assumed by the Apostle rather than immanence."[85] Perhaps realizing that the difference between transcendence and immanence represents more than the trifle he suggests, Hardy then reiterates his assertion from the Preface that the ideas are only tentative.

Another means by which Hardy distances himself from the characters involves his avowed "tolerable fidelity" to the facts of his subject matter, minimizing his input as an artist: "Whenever any evidence of the words really spoken or written by the characters in their various situations was attainable, as close a paraphrase has been aimed at as was compatible with the form chosen. And in all cases outside oral tradition, accessible scenery, and existing relics, my indebtedness for detail to the abundant pages of the historian, the biographer, and the journalist, English and Foreign, has been, of course, continuous (Preface, 31–39). Where Auden advertises through extravagant diction and surrealistic plot that *The Age of Anxiety* represents Art with a capital "A" and the product of his own vivid imagination, Hardy sets himself up as nothing but a transcriber of historical facts, distancing himself from responsibility for the selection and organization of those facts. As with his repudiation of responsibility for the philosophy of *The Dynasts*, he reiterated his denial of aesthetic selection in several forums. In a letter, Hardy asks, "Had I, when I knew the exact words, or at least sentiments, uttered by a character, any right to change them into more complicated thoughts, or into what Wordsworth called 'poetic diction,' for the sake of heightening the drama?"[86] He immediately answers his own query in the negative, reasoning that he has no "right" to make changes, "the date of action not being remote enough to warrant it, for one reason." In the next two lines, he imagines that Shakespeare must have considered the same issue when writing *Henry VIII* and wonders whether it bothered the Bard to have fiddled with such recent history. Given that Shakespeare obviously had no problem with dramatizing events that had occurred approximately seventy years prior to his version of them, Hardy's supposed reluctance to meddle with events preceding his own time by nearly a century seems disingenuous.

Throughout *The Dynasts*, Hardy also distances himself by minimizing biographical identification with the work by declining to impart any of his recognizable personal characteristics to the characters and also by the omission of key personal information from the Preface. He does include a number of Wessex scenes in *The Dynasts* that link the author of this epic-drama to the author of *Tess* and *The Mayor of Casterbridge*, but he presents in those scenes only the most rustic characters, none of whom could be confused with the poet personally. None of the Wessex scenes includes any characters, like Jude, who could be identified in any way with Hardy.[87] When it comes to the one character with whom he has undeniable personal associations, he is at pains to mask the relationship. In the Preface, he offers as one of the reasons for his interest in the Napoleonic wars the fact that he was familiar with "the village which was the birthplace of Nelson's flag-captain at Trafalgar" (16–17). He fails to mention that the captain of the *Victory*, namely one Captain Thomas Hardy, was a distant relation of the poet himself. Although Thomas Hardy the writer claimed not to know precisely the manner in which he was related to Thomas Hardy the naval officer, he knew that some relationship did indeed exist (*Life*, 351–52). Not only does he fail to fully acknowledge the role his ancestor played in the conception of *The Dynasts*, he includes the captain in only two scenes—those which depict the battle of Trafalgar. The lengths to which he goes to obscure what would seem to be the perfectly innocuous, or even admirable, fact of his relationship to the antecedent Hardy, suggests that his purpose in establishing such a distance between himself and the text derives from artistic as much as personal reasons.

Auden, on the other hand, infuses *The Age of Anxiety* with

attributes of his own personality, his own interests, and his friends and acquaintances. His adoption of the Jungian scheme of the four faculties allows Auden to explore the facets of his own personality. Having once declared that "[t]o present artistically a human personality in its full depth, its inner dialectic, its self-disclosure and self-concealment, through the medium of a single character is almost impossible" (*DH*, 110), he distributes himself across the four speakers. Even prior to identification of the characters with Jung's system, critics recognized the four speakers as components of the author's own psyche. In his review of *The Age of Anxiety* for the *Nation*, Randall Jarrell complained that while "[m]ost of '*The Age of Anxiety*' is supposed to be thought or said by four different characters," in fact, "they are only four chairs in which Auden takes turns sitting."[88] Similarly, the *TLS* reviewer asserted that "it is impossible not to read into Mr. Auden's American dialogues his own *déraciné*, nostalgic predicament, the subconscious need for explanation which has developed into a neurosis, his own abdication from the issues of the heart."[89]

A number of elements of Auden's "nostalgic predicament," his outsider status, and his acquaintances appear in *The Age of Anxiety*. He sets the poem in New York City, his home since having emigrated there from England in 1939. Auden's homosexuality appears in the poem in various ways through each of the male characters: Emble plays on his attractiveness to both sexes (6); Malin recognizes Emble's vanity and admits his own attraction to the younger man, saying, "Girlishly glad that my glance is not chaste, / He wants me to want what he would refuse" (86); and, in the Epilogue, Quant refers to himself as "Miss *ME*" and "Tinklebell" (135). Auden barely disguises that the character of Rosetta is based on Rhoda Jaffe, the Jewish woman with whom Auden carried on a heterosexual affair, a woman who, as Auden was writing *The Age of Anxiety*, was considering a position as a department store buyer—in the same line of work as Rosetta.[90] Malin has also been identified as based on a real person. Mendelson, who considers Malin to be "Auden's straightforward self-portrait,"[91] identifies the source for the character's exoteric attributes as John Thompson, a British psychoanalyst and medical officer who defended homosexuals from prosecution by courts-martial.[92] Both Rosetta's and Malin's psychic journeys reflect aspects of Auden's own road to religious conversion. Rosetta's discovery of her Judaism reflects not Rhoda's, but Auden's own interest in Jewish practice, mysticism, and even language. In the end, he found his desired tension between the One and the Many within Christianity, as does Malin in the Epilogue.

While both Hardy and Auden produced through the use of dialogue a mimesis of the disunity among humanity, both sought to balance the plurality they illustrated with a unifying voice in the didascalia. Neither of them, however, succeeded in creating enough of a link between drama and reader to produce a pleasurable reading experience; both *The Dynasts* and *The Age of Anxiety* have been criticized for their alienating effects. Hardy, in particular, was surprised by the failure of readers to fill in the gaps in his epic-drama. Before publication of the first volume of *The Dynasts*, he had congratulated himself on the approachability of the work, writing in a letter that he anticipated that his drama would be "as readable as a novel, owing to certain arrangements in its construction."[93] Since the only difference between *The Dynasts* and a conventional drama, other than its length—which would not make it more readable—consists of its lengthy prose descriptions, those "certain arrangements" must refer to the didascalia. For his part, Hardy refuses to admit any fault in the form, which leads him to blame the poor reception of the book on a rejection of its "monistic" philosophy. In his second response to Walkley, he declares that "the truth seems to be . . . that the real offence of '*The Dynasts*' lies, not in its form as such, but in the philosophy which gave rise to the form."[94] He reiterated this position in several letters written at about the same time. To Frederic Harrison, he wrote of the critics, "I wish they would not disguise their objection to the philosophy under the cloak of an objection to the form,"[95] and to Edmund Gosse, he complained that "the British Philistine is already moved by the *odium theologicum* in his regard of it, though the prejudice is carefully disguised."[96] Since he admits that the philosophy "gave rise to the form," we can infer that what his blind spot obscures is the fact that he has mistaken the nature of the philosophy that engenders the form. Hardy's astonishment at his discovery of the form's alienating effects stems from his failure to recognize that the supposed monistic doctrine of the Immanent Will actually represents a de facto plurality.

Auden's stage directions create a much greater unifying effect than do Hardy's, but they fail to overcome the incomprehensibility of the verse spoken by the characters in most of *The Age of Anxiety*. Auden might call each of the reviewers the kind of person for whom, "when he condemns a work or a passage, the possibility never occurs that its author may have foreseen exactly what he is going to say"; but the concurrence of so many critics who condemn the work on the basis of its alienating properties suggests that Auden's precognition of their complaints cannot excuse the inhospitality of the text to the reader. The incomprehensible speech may represent the reality of the isolation endured by individuals in a world that refuses to apprehend the One, but it also defeats communication between author and reader. In his essay "Writing," Auden had, after all, put forth the author/reader relationship as a means of overcoming emotional isolation: "People write in order to be read. They would like to be read by everybody and for ever. They feel alone, cut off from each other in an indifferent world where they do not live for very long. How can they get in touch again; how can they prolong their lives?" (*DH*, 21). In the same essay, he reiterates that "the underlying reason for writing is to bridge the gulf between one person and another," and for that reason decries the modern tendency in which "writing gets shut up in a circle of clever people writing about themselves for themselves" (24). *The Age of Anxiety*, despite its condemnation of solipsism and its optimistic notion that self-recognition and integration can lead to the recognition of the individual's relationship to a transcendent One, demonstrates precisely such a failure to bridge the gulfs between people. The comprehensible speech of the stage directions and the later speeches of Rosetta and Malin prove to be too little and too late.

In the end, the lesson seems to be that for dramatic poetry to provide a unified reading experience, none of the three inherent distances—between poet and text, between speakers, and especially between reader and text—should imitate too effectively a pluralistic belief in the existence of gaps between people. Dramatic verse lacks the unity of speakers engaged in debate that underlies the dialogue of self and soul as well as eclogue forms, and it frequently lacks the unity of action common to the ballad, so that the dramatic form is particularly ripe for a failure of communication to the reader. The reader must be able to form some sort of connection to both poet and speakers; he must be able to appreciate some sort of whole in order for the reading experience to be of value. Extensive prose didascalia may, in certain cases, provide enough of a unifying element to overcome any deficiencies; but, in order for such a strategy to be successful, both prose and verse must create a whole.

3

Two Modern Poets, Body and Soul

WHILE W. H. AUDEN CLAIMS THOMAS HARDY AS HIS FIRST MAJOR influence, Louis MacNeice claims for the entire "Auden school," of which he himself was a prominent member, a heritage derived primarily from T. S. Eliot and W. B. Yeats. "Eliot has much in common with Yeats," MacNeice claims in his study of the latter; although they differ in some respects, he acknowledges, they are both conservative, and "both dislike intensely the flux of the modern world" (*PWBY*, 158). MacNeice asserts that Eliot's reaction to that flux is a "passive impressionism" as opposed to an active attempt by Yeats to impose order, and he differentiates between Eliot and Yeats by associating Eliot with John Donne and Yeats with William Blake; "our aim," MacNeice claims, "was to use our brains, as Donne and Eliot had done, but to follow Blake in not abjuring life or the world of 'created things'" (191). Attributing to the mystics Yeats and Blake a dedication to the material world might seem at first an odd move, but the dualism they both espouse emphasizes the importance of body as well as soul. One's perceived relationship of body and soul depends on one's understanding of the problem of the One and the Many, and the difference between Donne and Blake, Eliot and Yeats, comes down to a conflict between a desire to integrate the One and the Many (through paradox or wit) and the desire to balance One and Many by opposing them (through the recognition of antinomies).

In 1915, *Poetry* published Eliot's "The Love Song of J. Alfred Prufrock"; a few months later, Yeats produced "Ego Dominus Tuus." Both poems concern themselves with dichotomies associated with the problem of the One and the Many, most notably the subject/object split, and both are variations on the conventional debate of body and soul. Reporting on a 1917 conversation

between the two poets on the topic of "psychical research," a
topic that encompasses numerous questions of the relationship
between body and soul, Eliot wryly observed of Yeats that the
subject was "the only thing he ever talks about, except Dublin
gossip."[1] It is hard to know when they first began their metaphysical dialogue in person, but it is tempting to read "The Love
Song of J. Alfred Prufrock" and "Ego Dominus Tuus" as a part
of that conversation, especially because Eliot's poem contains a
number of images that echo incidents recounted by Yeats in his
Memoirs, making J. Alfred Prufrock suspiciously Yeatsian. At
the very least, the two poems provide a useful illustration of
how the poets' different understandings of the subject/object
split generate differences in form. Yeats, who insists on the
maintenance of a separation between oppositions, personifies
subject in one speaker and object in the other; both speakers are
clearly identified and separated on the page. Eliot, who insists
that severing the two sides of the opposition is both undesirable
and unwise, merges subject and object in a portrait of a single
man.

In the 1910s, when Yeats and Eliot were writing "Ego Dominus Tuus" and "The Love Song of J. Alfred Prufrock," both were
undergoing spiritual crises that reinforced their desires to reconcile the subjective and the objective, self and soul, within themselves. Ronald Schuchard claims that Eliot's "spiritual impulses
were desecrated by sexual fantasies"[2] at this time and that Eliot's spiritual quest fits into a pattern repeated by numerous late
nineteenth-century writers: "Out of a disgust with materialism
and conventional religious values, their sensibilities fall into a
rebellion that often takes the form of occultism, satanism, and
'romantic blasphemy.' Then out of a desire to extend the boundaries of emotional and religious experience, they begin an aesthetic and spiritual escape into the self. The delight in perverse
and artificial sensations is followed by an introspective religious
quest that leads ultimately to morbid psychological explorations
of the self and soul."[3] Schuchard lists Oscar Wilde, Francis
Thompson, and Ernest Dowson among his examples;[4] Yeats fits
the pattern equally well. Both Eliot and Yeats descend from
Christian clergy for whom the relationship between body and
soul was not in question. Eliot's paternal grandfather, the Rever-
end William Greenleaf Eliot once declared that "[t]he essential

idea of humanity is not derived from weakness and sin, but from that mysterious connection of the soul and the body, —the immortal spirit with the corruptible flesh, —by which the soul is made subject to earthly influence" and affirmed the soul's superiority.[5] Eliot, however, was not ready to dismiss the value of "earthly influence," though he came to different conclusions than did Yeats about how to reconcile body and soul.

Most Neoplatonic systems envision the spiritual world as the realm of the One and the material world as that of the Many, asserting the superiority of unity over multiplicity and certain of the eventual triumph of the former. In these systems, when "the immortal spirit" escapes from entrapment in "corruptible flesh," as the soul escapes from the body at death, the spirit reassumes its place in the One. Occult systems also regard the body as the "occluding agency" that prevents access to the noumenal, preventing the soul from reaching enlightenment.[6] For Yeats, however, the "ultimate reality," beyond human knowing, exists; but it is "neither one nor many, concord nor discord" (*Vision*, 193). In the world of consciousness, "all things fall into a series of antinomies in human experience" (193), and without consciousness, no life is possible. For the soul to survive as a conscious self, it must remain in this world of antinomies. Reincarnation prevents the human soul from achieving an eternal union with the Absolute that would be a true death: "We come at birth into a multitude and after death would perish into the One did not a witch of Endor call us back" (52). Any soul that would remain disembodied would "perish"; only a continuing opposition of matter to spirit, of flux to stasis, of the temporal to the atemporal allows for the maintenance of selfhood. "All propositions" locating truth on one side of any dichotomy "can only enter rich minds to dislocate and strain, if they can enter at all, and sooner or later the mind expels them by instinct," he writes.[7] In Yeats's deterministic system, he perceives "subjectivity and objectivity as intersecting states struggling one against the other" (*Vision*, 71), and "Ego Dominus Tuus" dramatizes that struggle within the artistic type.

Unlike Yeats, who values the struggle between opposing qualities, Eliot desires to transcend them. MacNeice's comparison of Eliot to Donne is apt according to the terms of James Smith's definition of metaphysical poetry. Smith, in his 1933 essay "On

Metaphysical Poetry," defines metaphysical poetry as that which concerns problems associated with the paradox of the One and the Many, explaining that such problems comprise pairs of oppositions in which "[i]t seems impossible that the nature of things should possess either the one or the other of a pair of qualities; it seems impossible that it should possess both together; it seems impossible that it should not possess both."[8] These circumstances produce a "note of tension, or strain," which he proposes to call the "metaphysical note";[9] such a "metaphysical note," in which aspects of the One coexist with, and yet stand in opposition to aspects of the Many, pervades the entire oeuvre of T. S. Eliot. John Paul Riquelme, in his book, *Harmony of Dissonances*—the title is taken from Eliot's own assessment of Donne's metaphysicality—designates the "note of strain or tension" in Eliot's work as a *coincidentia oppositorum*, "an unstable ambivalence marking the complete passage between opposites"[10] and identifies it as the key to Eliot's modernity.[11] M. A. R. Habib traces the source of this predisposition, which he identifies as Eliot's "integrative impulse," to the philosophies of Bergson and Bradley, whose strategies Habib calls "a philosophy of integration, where distinctions between real and ideal, sense and intellect, past and present, are abrogated."[12] Habib traces Eliot's attempt to "*control* the gulf between unity and diversity" through an "assertion that opposites somehow share a deeper ground of identity."[13] Eliot himself cited Heraclitus for demonstrating that "opposites do not neutralize each other, but may sometimes be the same thing."[14] For Eliot, oppositions exist only as perceptions that depend on one's point of view; from this "deeper ground of identity," a transcendent position, an observer may choose to interpret the world as either One or Many, although no such distinction actually exists.

In his 1936 essay "Modern Poetry," Yeats describes Eliot's vision of reality as "that unknowable something the supports the center of the see-saw" (*E&I*, 503). This "see-saw" metaphor for reality is for Yeats both symptomatic of the modern world and absolutely abhorrent. Yeats blames the "see-saw" mentality for downfall of Florence Farr, who left the Order of the Golden Dawn after a scandal in 1902: "Wit and paradox alike sought to pull down whatever had tradition or passion and she was soon to spend her days in the British Museum reading-room and become erudite in many heterogeneous studies moved by an insatiable, destroying curiosity."[15] Wit and paradox, for Yeats, lead to heterogeneity, to multiplicity, not to unity as they do for Eliot, who might be "the most revolutionary man in poetry," according to Yeats, but whose "revolution was stylistic alone" (*E&I*, 499). Modern philosophy, thinking as Eliot does, "that an object can at the same moment have contradictory qualities"—for instance, "deciding that a penny is bright and dark, oblong and round, hot and cold, dumb and ringing in its own right"—is indicative, Yeats claims, "of a consciousness that has shrunk back, grown intermittent and accidental, into the looking-glass" (406). Yeats explains his aversion to this type of philosophy by alluding to Coleridge's attribution of "mental disease" to "delving in the unwholesome quicksilver mines of metaphysic depths" (407).[16] He considers this paradoxical understanding of oppositions solipsistic, and to consider that the One and the Many are the same thing is, for Yeats, a path to madness.

The dialogue between the occultist Yeats and the philosophy student Eliot on this topic reflects an underlying connection between the two fields; if they discussed the occult during their 1913 meeting, the two poets more than likely discussed the problem of the One and the Many. The esoteric nature of the occult makes it difficult to trace the actual genesis of his system, but Yeats dedicated the 1925 edition of *A Vision*, in which he delineates his system of interpenetrating gyres of "Concord" and "Discord," to Moina Mathers, a member of the Order of the Golden Dawn, which had introduced him to the understanding of the simultaneity of unity and multiplicity as expressed in the concept of emanations descending from a single godhead. The evolution of Eliot's understanding of the One/Many problem is, on the other hand, very well documented. His investment in the quest to hold in tension two opposing qualities dates at least to his days at Harvard, where in the first few decades of the twentieth century, the problem of the One and the Many dominated the thoughts of faculty and students alike. Eliot studied with Babbitt, Santayana, James, and Royce, all of whom lectured and wrote on the subject, and his notes on Greek philosophy demonstrate that he was preoccupied with the problem himself.[17]

Donald Childs suggests that Eliot "found the epistemological practices of many occultists to be similar to his own,"[18] and in the early twentieth century, the occult and philosophy were, in fact, blood kin. It was in Babbitt's class that Eliot was first exposed to theories of Moina Mathers's brother, Henri Bergson. Although he was interested in many of the same metaphysical problems as was his sister, Bergson took a scientific approach and at one time served as the president of the Society for Psychical Research.[19] Much of Bergson's work arises out of the problem of the One and the Many, and in a 1945 letter to Eudo Mason, Eliot affirms that he was under Bergson's influence of at the time that he was writing "The Love Song of J. Alfred Prufrock."[20] In the fall of 1910, Eliot attended Bergson's lectures in Paris, and also, he says, "gave close study to the books [Bergson] had then written."[21] Under Bergson's influence, Eliot was exposed to recurrent musings on the problem of the One and the Many as related to the body/soul duality. In *Matter and Memory*, for example, Bergson suggests that the question of unity versus multiplicity, spirit versus matter, memory versus perception all comes down to the issue: "This problem is no less than that of the union of soul and body."[22] According to Eliot's unpublished notes on Bergson's lectures, Bergson concentrated on the One/Many problem both as a general question and as relating to the status of the self, teaching that the self exists simultaneously as one and as multiple selves.[23] Bergson asks in *Creative Evolution*, "Is my own person, at a given moment, one or manifold?" answering that he is "a unity that is multiple and a multiplicity that is one; but unity and multiplicity are only views of my personality taken by an understanding that directs its categories at me; I enter neither into one nor into the other nor into both at once, although both, united, may give a fair imitation of the mutual interpenetration and continuity that I find at the base of my own self."[24] The idea of a union between body and soul that may exist as equally valid oppositions in "mutual interpenetration" is a radical departure from the conventional Christian notion of the superiority of the soul and much more palatable to Eliot than his grandfather's.

By the time Eliot wrote his paper on Bergson, probably in 1912–13, he had recanted his "temporary conversion," expressing disappointment in his recognition that Bergson's "attempt to occupy a middle ground between idealism and realism" is unsuccessful.[25] His disappointment must have been severe—in his

ssay on ethics, he recounts the story of the ancient Chinese phi-
osopher Ye Bo, who warns his disciples that they would meet
1any wise men who would propose many different solutions to
1e problem of the One and the Many, achieving nothing but
onfusion and sadness for his students.[26] After failing to find a
atisfactory answer to the One/Many problem and the question
f the union of body and soul in Bergsonism, Eliot turned to
radley. According to Bradley, the self always transcends multi-
licity: "At every moment my state, whatever else it is, is a
hole of which I am immediately aware. It is an experienced
on-relational unity of many in one."[27] In the condition of "im-
1ediate experience," subject and object form a continuous
hole, so that they may not be distinguished from one another.
Although Yeats dismisses philosophers as disconnected from
ith, unity, and the eternal, complaining that "[t]hey fill their
1inds with deductions just as they fill their empty houses,
here there is nothing of the past, with machine-made furni-
1re" (Memoirs, 209), Eliot's dissertation concerns itself with
1e spiritual implications of immediate experience. He identi-
es this unity as the function that binds together spirit and mat-
r: "Immediate experience, we have seen, is a timeless unity
hich is not as such present either anywhere or to anyone. It is
1ly in the world of objects that we have time and space and
:lves. By the failure of any experience to be merely immediate,
y its lack of harmony and cohesion, we find ourselves con-
:ious souls in a world of objects" (KE, 31).[28] Eliot also imagines
1e One and the Many as an undifferentiated whole whose per-
:ption depends on one's point of view:

The world, we may insist, is neither one nor many except as that
one or many has meaning in experience, and it is either one or many
according as we contemplate it altogether as an object, talking still,
if you will, of minds, but meaning rather the phenomena which
mind presents to an observer: or as we treat the world as finite centres and their experiences. From the first point of view the world is
a priori one; from the second point of view the world is a priori
many; and I am convinced that this is the only form in which monism or pluralism can appear. And the two views are so far from an-
tagonistic as to be complementary. (KE, 145–46)

:cause the observer can only hold one point of view at a time,
1e mutually dependent relationship between self and world,

therefore, must be viewed alternately as one or as many, th "see-saw" version of reality derided by Yeats.[29]

For Yeats who, according to Harold Bloom, was particularl inclined to accept "any doctrine that sanctified division in th self,"[30] the divisions between One and Many, body and soul, ar externally imposed and cannot be transcended. Unity and mult plicity are completely independent of the observer; he must b aware of both at the same time, and to Yeats, "the two perspec tives were equally real and equally partial."[31] In his system, e pounded in *A Vision*, the fixed relationship between body an soul exists in one of twenty-eight predetermined ratios that d termine personality and are symbolized by the phases of th moon. A basic explanation of this system appears in "Th Phases of the Moon," published along with "Ego Dominu Tuus" in *The Wild Swans at Coole*. In the poem, as the moo waxes, the subjective self becomes more self-oriented until, "A thought becomes an image and the soul / Becomes a body: th body and that soul / Too perfect at the full to lie in a cradle" (l 58–60), and "Body and soul cast out and cast away / Beyond th visible world." As the moon wanes, the self becomes more ol jective; "it takes / Upon the body and upon the soul / The coars ness of the drudge" (ll. 92–94). The subjective self informs th body, and the body grows more beautiful as subjectivity ir creases. As the self loses focus on itself, the body loses the for lent by the soul. Because the objective selves have no will, the have no form and "change their bodies at a word" (l. 113 Human life cannot exist "at the full or the dark" (l. 35), onl when the soul balances between the subjective and the objectiv in opposition to one another can life occur. Uniting subjectiv and objective results not in transcendence, but in death.[32]

The debate of body and soul, a poetic form that dates back t medieval times, provides Eliot and Yeats an opportunity to e plore their respective metaphysical understandings, and bot men wrote poems explicitly labeled as dialogues of body an soul or of self and soul. Eliot's two debates, "First Debate b tween the Body and Soul" (1910) and "Bacchus and Ariadne: 2n Debate between the Body and Soul" (1911) were written at abou the same time as "The Love Song of J. Alfred Prufrock." Yeats

"A Dialogue of Self and Soul" was written long after "Ego Dominus Tuus," but "Ego Dominus Tuus" has more in common with the medieval and Renaissance versions of the debate than does the later poem. Rosalie Osmond, in *Mutual Accusations,* her history of the debate of body and soul, considers Yeats a practitioner of a variation of the type of seventeenth-century body and soul dialogue she calls "philosophical," a category that includes Andrew Marvell's "A Dialogue between the Soul and the Body."[33] This form of the debate arose during the seventeenth century in response to an increasing interest in Neoplatonism at the time,[34] an interest shared by Yeats in the twentieth century. According to Yeats's biographer Norman Jeffares, Yeats objected to the claims of free verse advocates that "the form was accommodated to the matter without restriction" because "the essence of poetry was for him putting the personal into a static form, which he compared to the metaphysical antinomy of the individual and the infinite, the many and the one."[35] In "Ego Dominus Tuus," Yeats inserted his personal struggle into the static form of the debate of body and soul. As Jeffares puts it: "This poem is a dialogue between *Hic* and *Ille* and, as *Hic* defends the objective, *Ille* the subjective, there is some sense in a contemporary Dublin comment that *Hic* and *Willie* would be more correct."[36] Normally, the body would take the objective role and the soul the subjective; but for Yeats, the split—and, therefore, the debate—is between aspects of the self, not between body and soul. For Yeats, the "descent into time" of the "primary reality," or spirit, explains MacNeice, "means a splitting of this primary reality into those secondary half-realities opposed to each other" (*PWBY*, 107); the fall into the material world produces a subject/object split within the spirit itself.

The conventional debate between body and soul recognizes the irreconcilable enmity of the two opponents, elements of the whole self that are at once "essential to one another and yet incompatible."[37] The form serves as a perfect medium for a poet for whom, according to MacNeice, the "secondary half-realities" are pitted against one another in a manner in which their "mutual antagonism implies their mutual dependence" (*PWBY*, 107). For Yeats, according to George Bornstein, "the ideal and subtle were locked in a ritual combat with the actual and common from which neither side expected to emerge victorious" and that are "united into a whole maintained by the internecine warfare of its parts."[38] "Ego Dominus Tuus" has also been referred to as a "duel,"[39] an appropriate word given that "to debate" to medieval authors primarily meant to engage in a fight; the *OED* cites both Chaucer and Spenser using "debate" regarding knights in single combat. In "Ego Dominus Tuus" ("I am Your Master," or perhaps, "I am the Master of You," the subjective is master of the objective), *Ille*'s main point, in fact, is the need to maintain the struggle to approach one's opposite in order to potentiate the creation of art.

If the debate is between the "secondary half-realities," the opposition that *Ille* advocates is essentially that of body and soul. *Ille* seeks wisdom by searching out his "anti-self," an image out of the *anima mundi* that is both his double and "the most unlike." For the poet, who, like Shelley, occupies phase XVII, a phase approaching pure soul, the antiself is the image of the man of phase XIII, a phase approaching pure body. Only struggle by the soul to overcome the necessities of the body results in great art; the modern artist, according to *Ille*, has become overly subjective and, as a result, fails artistically:

> We have lit upon the gentle, sensitive mind
> And lost the old nonchalance of the hand;
> Whether we have chosen chisel, pen or brush,
> We are but critics, or but half create.
>
> (ll. 12–15)

When *Hic* suggests Dante and Keats as examples of poets who created without struggle, *Ille* emphasizes the austerity of the material world as sources of their art. Dante, he suggests, found the image of his antiself by "a Bedouin's horse-hair roof" (l. 29), or "half upturned / Among the coarse grass and the camel-dung" (ll. 30–31) before he could find "The most exalted lady loved by a man" (l. 37). Keats, claims *Ille*, "being poor, ailing and ignorant, / Shut out from all the luxury of the world" (ll. 59–60), produced "luxuriant song" (l. 62). The poet's quarrel is with an antiself dominated by the body.

Recognizing that the dialogue form of the poem reflects its content does not require any great analysis: the voices are distinct from one another, yet they are also clearly in dialogue. *Hic* asks questions or suggests a counterargument, and *Ille* responds directly. *Ille*, as is appropriate, dominates the argument and gets the last word. That the dialogic form expresses Yeats's dialogic philosophy has been widely recognized since the poem's publication. More notable, when applied to this poem, is MacNeice's observation about form and metaphysics: "Those mystics proper who have written poetry, have had in so doing, when trying to express the ineffable, to descend from the mystical plane; they start from a sense of mystical union, a fusion of subject and object, and have to translate this into the language of a world where subject and object are separate and clearly defined" (*PWBY*, 25).[40] Yeats, the mystic, depicts in "Ego Dominus Tuus" a world in which subject and object are separate and clearly defined, providing an interesting contrast with that of "The Love Song of J. Alfred Prufrock," where readers find differentiating subject and object extremely difficult. The "normal poet," according to MacNeice, "starts in this world of distinctions and approaches the mystical plane from below"; because language imposes distinctions, though, although the poet may transcend the world of separation, "he can only do this by a kind of bluff" (25). If Eliot's poem never produces a complete fusion of subject and object, however, the resulting portrait of Prufrock is no failure of language; rather, the poem succeeds in creating a debate of body and soul that takes place in a condition of immediate experience.

"The Love Song of J. Alfred Prufrock" represents such an integrative state; the poem presents a kind of gestalt image in which the unity or multiplicity of its voice depends on the reader's point of view.[41] In this poem, Eliot devised a form whose ambiguities mimic the metaphysical note of its exploration of the tensions between body and soul, subject and object, unity and multiplicity. Because Eliot's interest in the reconciliation of opposites dates to at least as early as 1910, when he attended Bergson's Paris lectures, we should find expect to find the "integrative impulse" permeating Eliot's poetry of the time, including "The Love Song of J. Alfred Prufrock;" yet most critics read this poem as a model of *dis*-integration, as a dramatic monologue whose speaker has splintered into multiple selves.[42] In light of Eliot's demonstrated interest in overcoming dualities, it is at least as useful to read "The Love Song of J. Alfred Prufrock" as a debate of body and soul in which the distinctions have been, to use Habib's word, "abrogated," as it is to read the poem as a fractured dramatic monologue, and it is even more useful to recognize that the poem transcends the two forms so that whether it appears as a dialogue or monologue depends on the reader's point of view. The *OED* defines "gestalt" as "[a] 'shape,' 'configuration,' or 'structure' which as an object of perception forms a specific whole or unity incapable of expression simply in terms of its parts," and "The Love Song of J. Alfred Prufrock" is a structure that cannot be disassembled into the component forms. Because the debate of body and soul offers an objective depiction of a personality while a dramatic monologue provides a subjective portrait, a poem which transcends both forms represents a transcendence of the subject/object duality.[43]

Although the integration of opposing voices within the poem does not proceed through the use of transcendental dialectic as in the type of philosophical dialogue identified by Michael Prince as "comedic," it possesses some features of the comic integrative impulse. Prince designates dialogues that tend to unity as comedic because of the convention that comedies usually conclude with a marriage between lovers who have overcome barriers to their union,[44] and the reconciliation of the division between body and soul in the poem might be read as such a marriage. The poem is, after all, advertised as a love song. And Prufrock's predicament is comical enough as his body and soul war with one another before finally wedding their "you" and "I" into "we" in the final stanza. Although particular lines cannot be ascribed easily to one side or another, enough of the general drift of the dialogue between body and soul comes through in "The Love Song of J. Alfred Prufrock" that some critics have sensed the underlying debate form, and it is possible to pick out some specific lines that focus on one side or another.[45] In the first stanza, which begins "And indeed there will be time," the soul anticipates a future time for the concerns of the Many—for superficial relations with others, for manual labor—but does not act; inaction, according to Bergson, is the hallmark of the man too much devoted to the life of the mind.[46] In the second of these stanzas, Prufrock frets about his body, about his bald spot, his thin arms and legs, his clothing; his decisions and revisions occur on impulse, in a minute, turning back to descend the stair.

Impulse, according to Bergson, living life only in the present "is the mark of the lower animals,"[47] of matter without consciousness.[48] The soul observes without action; the body acts without reflection.

At the end of the poem, however, body and soul speak together as "we," indicating a momentary unity, the immediate experience in which subject and object are one. Bergson imagines just such a state of unity, one that transcends the intellect, as an "ocean of life." The sudden change of scene to the seashore in the last few stanzas signals a unification of body and soul in which Prufrock turns from "the works and days of hands," the labors of the body of the farmer as described in Hesiod's *Works and Days*, to this sea of unity. Bergson describes the process in *Creative Evolution*:

> Harnessed, like yoked oxen, to a heavy task, we feel the play of our muscles and joints, the weight of the plow and the resistance of the soil. To act and to know that we are acting, to come into touch with reality and even to live it, but only in the measure in which it concerns the work that is being accomplished and the furrow that is being plowed, such is the function of human intelligence. Yet a beneficent fluid bathes us, whence we draw the very force to labor and to live. From this ocean of life, in which we are immersed, we are continually drawing something, and we feel that our being, or at least the intellect that guides it, has been formed therein by a kind of local concentration. Philosophy can only be an effort to dissolve again into the Whole.[49]

The effort to "dissolve again into the Whole," however, is thwarted by reason: "It is of the essence of reasoning to shut us up in the circle of the given. But action breaks the circle. . . . Reasoning, in fact, always nails us down to the solid ground. But if, quite simply, I throw myself into the water without fear, I may keep myself up well enough at first by merely struggling, and gradually adapt myself to the new environment: I shall thus have learnt to swim."[50] Prufrock's sojourn in the unity of immediate experience ends when human voices, the voices of the material world and of reason, intrude into his reverie, and he "drowns." The condition of immediate experience is, unfortunately, immediate and cannot be maintained. After drowning, or failing to sustain the unity, Prufrock will once again split into subject and object, but it is a "we" that drown(s) at the end of the poem, and Eliot's use of the present tense insures that Prufrock will remain forever in this state. The reader will leave Prufrock always in the process of division, but never completely divided.

Yeats also identifies water as "experience, immediate sensation" (E&I, 284), but Ille has no wish to drown, preferring works and days to eternal death. Yeats suggests that "[t]he occupations and the places known to Homer or to Hesiod, those pure first artists, might, as it were, if but the fashioners' hands had loosened, have changed before the poem's end to symbols and vanished, caught up as in a golden cloud into the unchanging worlds where religion alone can discover life as well as peace" (295–96). Vanishing, however, puts an end to art; in order to create, the poet must stand, as Ille does, between the "old-wind beaten tower" (l. 2), the symbol of the intellect, and the water, not in it.[51] Ille stands "On the grey sand beside the shallow stream" (l. 1) where, at the end of the poem, he searches for his antiself "the mysterious one who yet / Shall walk the wet sands by the edge of the stream" (ll. 70–71) and stand next to the symbols that "mediate between the one mind and the individual consciousness and link the two together."[52] This meeting with his double, as described by Ille, will occur in the future, a consummation not devoutly desired. The voice of the antiself who will reveal the meaning of the runes Ille has scratched in the sand remains unspoken, and even when he does speak, he will:

> whisper it as though
> he were afraid the birds, who cry aloud
> their momentary cries before it is dawn,
> would carry it away to blasphemous men.
>
> (ll. 76–79)

Not mermaids, who dwell in the ocean where One and Many are united, but birds who soar free of the material world, pure spirits like Keats's nightingale. Were their cries revealing the reality of the One carried to the material world, all life would cease.

Bergson's image of the Ocean of Life differs from the Neoplatonic vision of transcendent oneness in that, although he claims that in order to learn how to swim in this Ocean of Life, "you must thrust intelligence outside itself by an act of will,"[53] he does not suggest that such an act requires the separation of body and soul. The soul does not need to free itself from corruptible matter to ascend to a higher plane; the immanence of the *élan vital* suffuses the complete being. Eliot himself strongly objects to the notion that the soul must separate from the body in order to return to its place in the transcendent One. He notes approvingly that in Dante's poetry, "There is no imagined struggle of soul and body, only the one struggle toward perfection" (*VMP*, 114). Eliot's disapproval of the quest for *ecstasis* is a major component of his dialogue with Yeats and Yeats's companions in the esoteric orders. Ecstatic practices are believed by mystics to be necessary for the attainment of gnosis,[54] and that acquisition of mystical knowledge results from the soul's participation in the One. Evelyn Underhill's *Mysticism: A Study in the Nature and Development of Man's Spiritual Consciousness* appeared in 1911, and Eliot copied out her definition of mysticism as "the expression of the innate tendency of the human spirit towards complete harmony with the transcendental order."[55] Immediate experience, however, unlike mystical practice, requires that body and soul, the objective and subjective halves of a personality, must remain linked.

Throughout "The Love Song of J. Alfred Prufrock," the soul mistakenly, and therefore unsuccessfully, attempts to unyoke itself from the body in order to achieve a mystical union. To convey a sense of such a struggle within Prufrock, Eliot makes use of some standard images of the debate of body and soul. One of the conventional forms of the debate poem, the seventeenth-century "philosophical" dialogues, which include Marvell's "A Dialogue between the Soul and the Body," concerns itself particularly with the incompatibility of the body and soul, where the soul complains of being trapped in the body, and the body complains of having been saddled with the soul.[56] A number of the most famous images in "The Love Song of J. Alfred Prufrock" originate out of this tradition. The body's side of the debate is represented by Prufrock's famous declaration: "I should have been a pair of ragged claws / Scuttling across the floors of silent seas." It seems that the formulation, "I should have been a . . . [fill in your favorite lower form of life]" is a standard complaint of the body that resents the burden of a soul. In the Old English

"Address," the soul declares that the body would have been better off not being a man who must answer for his sins, but should have been a bird or a fish, or even a worm.[57] In the "Irish Homily," the body wishes that it had been a tree so that it would not have suffered from having a soul.[58] And in the medieval poem, "Als I Lay on a Winteris Nyt," the body rues its creation as a human being:

> I scholde have ben dumb as a schep, or as a nouwe, or as a suyn,
> That et and drank and lay and slep, slayn and passid al his pin;
> Nevere of catel he ne kep, ne wyste wat was water ne wyn;
> No leyn in helle that is so dep; never ne wist I of al that was tin.[59]

If Prufrock had been born a crab following its instincts at the bottom of the ocean, he would not suffer the torments of his soul or of his conscience or of society. He could eat and drink and lie and sleep; he would never know of hell, either religious or societal, would never know the snickers of the eternal footman.

On the other side of the debate, one of the common images of the soul's entrapment, that of the chrysalis, underlies Prufrock's self-depiction as an insect wriggling on a pin. The emblem of the chrysalis is not the only means by which English writers have depicted the soul's struggle to distance itself from the body, but it seems to have been particularly compelling to Eliot, who employs the same image in "Bacchus and Ariadne: 2nd Debate between the Body and Soul":

> Yet to burst out at last, ingenuous and pure
> Surprised, but knowing—it is triumph not endurable to miss!
> Not to set free the purity that clings
> To the cautious midnight of its chrysalis
> Lies in its cell and meditates its wings
> Nourished in earth and stimulated by manure.
>
> (ll. 14–19)

This is the classic complaint of the soul unable to break free of the body, and a recognition that death will bring the desired release.[60]

Bergson also employs the image of the chrysalis to underscore the paradoxical nature of consciousness embodied in matter. Regarding the evolution of life, it seems "as if a broad current of consciousness had penetrated matter," a consciousness that brings with it infinite potential; however, "[o]n the one hand," Bergson suggests, "consciousness has had to fall asleep, like the chrysalis in the envelope in which it is preparing for itself wings," and on the other hand, its influence, "its manifold tendencies" appears in the movements of the organism.[61] Life, therefore, which he defines as "consciousness launched into matter" turns either toward intuition [One] or toward intellect [Many].[62] Since "the vital impetus is neither pure unity nor pure multiplicity," when matter "compels it to choose one of the two, its choice will never be definitive: it will leap from one to the other indefinitely."[63] A consciousness pinned cannot make that leap; it remains trapped in multiplicity, soul trapped in body, and Prufrock's soul is unable to "force the moment to its crisis," to make this leap. Bergson also employs the chrysalis image in conjunction with the idea of a transforming moment in life: "[C]rises like puberty or the menopause, in which the individual is completely transformed, are quite comparable to changes in the course of larval or embryonic life—yet they are part and parcel of the process of our aging. . . . In short, what is properly vital in growing old is the insensible, infinitely graduated, continuance of the change of form."[64] "It is often impossible for us to say," according to Bergson, "whether we are dealing with an organism growing old or with an embryo continuing to evolve; such is the case for example, with the larvae of insects and crustacea,"[65] and whether changes result from aging or from evolution depends on one's point of view. What the soul perceives as a transcendent leap forward, the body perceives only as a degradation of form and eventual death: "I grow old . . . I grow old" (l. 120), it complains.

The trapped insect for Yeats is no beautiful butterfly or moth, but a "fly in marmalade" (l. 45). The struggle of the fly, according to *Ille*, represents the production of art by "those that love the world," those who "Grow rich, popular, and full of influence" (ll. 42–43). Instead of being pinned by an unsympathetic, rational, scientific objectivity, these "artists" are victims of their own greedy desires, having entrapped themselves while attempting to feed off sticky sweet goo. "The rhetorician would deceive his neighbours," claims *Ille*, "The sentimentalist himself" (ll. 46–47). As Harold Bloom points out, Yeats, like Blake, flouts convention in "the dialectical audacity of transvaluing the ancient quarrel between the objective and the subjective man,"[66] associating the objective with the sentimental. *Ille*, who champions the subjective, sees the souls of the worldly artists as pests. For those that love the material world, who, per *Hic*, "have made their art / Out of no tragic war, lovers of life, / Impulsive men that look for happiness" (ll. 38–40) their souls could never take flight in beautiful flashes of color even were they to escape the enveloping matter.

The uncoupling of the soul from the body in order for the soul to access a higher consciousness may be accomplished by means other than literal death, and "The Love Song of J. Alfred Prufrock" includes references to other methods, including mystical practices, drugs, and sex. One of the most common motifs for initiation into groups such as the Order of the Golden Dawn and the Theosophists is that of the symbolic death and rebirth.[67] The descent topos enacts the process in which "gnosis was operated by means of an essential transformation or transmutation leading to a transfiguration. There was first of all a 'passing out through oneself,' a mystical death," followed by a rebirth into the knowledge of the "Divine Monad."[68] Dante's *Inferno*, naturally, attracted the attention of occultists who interpreted it as a description of this type of ritual.[69] The epigraph from Dante supplied by Eliot at the beginning of "The Love Song of J. Alfred Prufrock," in which Guido claims that he would not tell his story if he thought that his listener would return to the world of the living, suggests the esoteric nature of the message. "Ego Dominus Tuus" also alludes to Dante as a searcher after mystical knowledge, with a "hunger for the apple on the bough / Most out of reach" (ll. 24–25) the apple of the tree of esoteric knowledge that tantalizes him. In "Ego Dominus Tuus," Yeats, like Eliot, regards *ecstasis* as a failure, not because it is an improper method of achieving unity with the Absolute, but because such unity would result in death. For Yeats at this point in time, esoteric knowledge resides in the antiself, as *Ille* explains, and it is Dante's continual reaching toward that apple, not eating of it, that creates his art.

The apple that Prufrock would eat of is not Tantalus's, but Eve's. "Would it have been worth while," he asks, to have eaten of the tree of knowledge, "to have bitten off the *matter*" (ll. 90–

91), to find gnosis through the body's sexual experience? Many mystics suggest that the experience of orgasm, the *petit mort* or "little death," represents a momentary perception of a separation of body and soul, temporarily allowing the soul to transcend the material world, and occult rituals that reenact the *hieros gamos* (divine marriage) through ritual intercourse are equivalent to those that involve ritual descent, since both acts represent a palingenesis or "backward birth."[70] The Order of the Golden Dawn claims not to know whether sex magic ever formed part of its rituals, but acknowledges that Aleister Crowley was expelled for "sex intemperance" and that Paul Case wrote extensively on the topic.[71] Moina Mathers contends that she had "seen the results of this superficial sex teaching in several Occult Societies as well as in individual cases" and "never met with one happy result."[72] Yeats apparently agreed. Norman Jeffares reports that Yeats believed that "the finest description of sexual intercourse ever written was in Dryden's translation of Lucretius, and it was justified; it was introduced to illustrate the difficulty of two becoming a unity"; the problem for Yeats, as Jeffares describes it, is that "[s]exual intercourse is an attempt to solve the eternal antinomy, doomed to failure because it takes place only on one side of the gulf. The gulf is that which separates the one and the many, or if you like, God and man."[73] Yeats interprets sex as a misguided attempt at unity, one that, even if it might manage to produce an ecstatic experience, still fails to unite the individual with the One.

For Eliot, sex results not in a release of the soul in order to unite with God, but in the Fall, where the acquisition of carnal knowledge isolates the individual from the unity of God and body from soul. The suggestion that Prufrock might "have squeezed the universe into a ball" (l. 92), where the ball continues the forbidden apple imagery, also contains puns on the sexual associations of "ball" and possibly makes reference to the vision of Dame Julian, in which she sees the universe in the form of a nut. In either case, Prufrock does not accomplish the act; he fears that an apprehension of mystical unity will never compensate for a failure to achieve a union with a woman. Even worse, he also recognizes that eating of the fruit of the tree of knowledge is just as likely to lead to a greater division between the One and the Many. When he laments that he has "measured

out his life with coffee spoons" (l. 51), he mourns that he has
been subject to the world of multiplicity in which time, according to Bergson, is perceived as a series of discrete moments. He
claims to have heard other "voices dying with a dying fall" (l.
52), in other words, reenacting the Fall in which Man became
isolated from the One.

"The Love Song of J. Alfred Prufrock" alludes to another
method of disconnecting the soul from the body in order to transcend the material: the use of mind-altering drugs. The famous
opening image of the night spread out like a patient etherized on
a table suggests such a strategy for achieving *ecstasis* and has its
roots in the conventional debate of body and soul. The medieval
debate typically opens with a vision of the body just dead, whose
soul has returned to confront it, and the position of the image of
the etherized patient in the opening stanza of "The Love Song
of J. Alfred Prufrock" corresponds to the position of the body in
William Crashaw's "The Complaint or *Dialgve*, Betwixt the
Soule and the *Bodie* of *a damned man*" and in other medieval
versions of the debate. In the opening stanza of Crashaw's poem,
the voice of the narrator announces:

> In silence of / a Winters night,
> A sleeping, yet / a waking spirit:
> A liueless body / to my sight
> Methought appeared / thus addight.[74]

Traditionally, the visions in debates of body and soul, and in related vision poetry, occur only at night;[75] the appearance of the
vision in the evening or twilight suggests the delicate balance
between body and soul, as the evening is poised between day and
night. Both conditions suggest the union of opposites in which
the states of the patient and the day depend on one's point of
view—alive or dead, day or night. "Ego Dominus Tuus," in contrast, takes place at night, "in the moon," as is appropriate when
the soul dominates. The dreaded disclosure of the secrets of the
Absolute to "blasphemous men" would occur in "the momentary cries" of the birds "before it is dawn," in the fleeting moment where night and day meet. For Yeats, that moment of
unification at dawn or at twilight is to be feared.

This vision of the night spread out as if in a drugged state contrasts with that of a dead body in its implied relationship of body and soul. An etherized patient, in a sense, both sleeps and wakes, existing in a twilight ("evening") sleep while appearing lifeless;[76] in effect, body and consciousness are partially disconnected from one another, but not entirely separate as they would be if the patient were dead. As a student, Eliot took notes on James's theories on drunkenness and on experiments with nitrous oxide, copying out James's conclusion that "our normal waking consciousness, rational consciousness as we call it, is but one special type of consciousness, whilst all about it, parted from it by the filmiest of screens, there lie potential forms of consciousness entirely different."[77] He was also fascinated by James's accounts in *The Varieties of Religious Experience* of altered states of consciousness induced by anesthesia, states in which James believes men may attain a mystical union with a larger consciousness.[78] Yeats's report of one of his experiences with hash, which he took with a friend, illustrates this sense of union in terms that sound remarkably like "The Love Song of J. Alfred Prufrock": "I felt suddenly that a cloud I was looking at floated in an immense space, and for an instant my being rushed out, as it seemed, into that space with ecstasy. I was myself again immediately, but the poet was wholly above himself, and presently he pointed to one of the street-lamps now brightening in the fading twilight, and cried at the top of his voice, 'Why do you look at me with your great eye?'" (E&I, 281). After consuming several cups of coffee, he continues, he "grew very anxious to dance," but was unable to remember how (281). Footmen undoubtedly snickered.

Prufrock's declaration that he has "wept and fasted, wept and prayed" also suggests an abortive attempt to weaken the bonds between body and spirit in search of a mystical experience. At Harvard, Eliot took numerous notes on Murisier's *Les Maladies du sentiments religieux* (1901), focusing on Murisier's description of the attainment of mystic insights as a result of physical deprivations such as loss of blood, lack of sleep, or fasting where the resulting physical debility results in a weakness of the bond between body and mind.[79] Yeats recalls a Theosophist acquaintance who was "accustomed to interrupt long periods of asceticism, in which he would eat vegetables and drink water, with brief outbreaks of what he considered the devil. After an outbreak he would for a few hours dazzle the imagination of the members of the local theosophical society with poetical rhapsodies about harlots and street lamps, and then sink into weeks of melancholy."[80] Madame Blavatsky, according to Yeats, was convinced that the young man's "settled gloom came from his chastity."[81] If Prufrock resorts to self-mortification in order to escape his material being and to join with the One, he fails miserably. The presentation of his head to him on a platter mocks his aspirations by forcing him to recognize his bodily nature, whose temporality is emphasized by his baldness. If he must acknowledge his failure as a prophet, however, he refuses to accord supremacy to the body. The aside "and here's no great matter" (l. 83) refers not to the soul's acceptance of its own lack of mystical adeptness, but instead is a snide comment on the state of the material self which prevents its ascension to the One.

Simply keeping body and soul, subject and object, united is not enough for Eliot. Unlike Yeats, for whom the soul predominates in the artist, as evidenced by *Ille*'s dominance over *Hic*, Eliot disapproves of any imbalance in the body/soul relationship. Prufrock's mortification by society reflects Bergson's theory that the body's oppression of the soul provides the genesis for comedy. In his essay, "Laughter," Bergson explains that "soul imparts a portion of its winged lightness to the body it animates: the immateriality which thus passes into matter is what is called gracefulness. Matter, however, is obstinate and resists. . . . Where matter thus succeeds in dulling the outward life of the soul, in petrifying its movements and thwarting its gracefulness, it achieves, at the expense of a body, an effect that is comic."[82] This laughter, according to Bergson, is designed to bolster the societal spirit: "By the fear which it inspires, it restrains eccentricity, keeps constantly awake and in mutual contact certain activities of a secondary order which might retire into their shell and go to sleep, and in short, softens down whatever the surface of the social body may retain of mechanical inelasticity."[83] The eternal footman's snickers are designed, then, to reduce the individual to an attendant lord, one of the crowd that will swell a progress. Such a movement toward social unity, however, sacrifices the potential contributions of the outstanding individual, and Eliot recognizes this leveling tendency of society as a false and detrimental harmony, writing, "for as genius tends towards unity, so mediocrity tends toward uniformity" (*VMP*, 52). Medi-

crity leads to uniformity and vice versa, and the members of
uch a society become "Politic, cautious, and meticulous; / Full
f high sentence, but a bit obtuse; / At times, indeed, almost ri-
iculous" (ll. 116–18).

Prufrock's appearance as an attendant lord illustrates Berg-
on's theory of social laughter, which addresses the problem of
ie body's dominance over the soul, but his invocation of Ham-
t addresses the opposite problem—the dominance of the soul
ver the body. Where spirit, or subject, fails to unite with matter,
r object, no action may be taken and no progress may occur.
liot's problem with Hamlet is that the prince "is dominated by
a emotion which is inexpressible, because it is in *excess* of the
icts as they appear" (*SE*, 125). "Hamlet's bafflement at the ab-
:nce of an objective equivalent to his feelings" results in paral-
sis; "he cannot objectify" his feeling about his mother, so "it
1erefore remains to poison life and obstruct action" (125). Yeats
:scribes such a moment in his youth when he was unable to
:t in the face of ridicule of by other poets, when, he says,
though getting much angrier, I was silent" (*E&I*, viii). When
1e subjective is unable to form a unity with the objective, the
)irit is unable to actuate its potential, and Prufrock rejects such
state: "No! I am not Prince Hamlet" (l. 111). Such an imbal-
1ce, though unintentional, represents for Eliot yet another un-
1ccessful unyoking of the soul from the body.

Social interaction—the individual's dialogue with others—
:quires recognition of the relationship between self and world,
ne and Many. "It is only in social behaviour," says Eliot in his
.ssertation, "the conflict and readjustment of finite centres,
1at feelings and things are torn apart. And after this separation
1ey leave dim and drifting edges, and tend to coalesce" (*KE*, 24–
5). Prior to social interaction with others, subject and object,
)dy and soul, may remain unified: "There is no reason, so long
; the one feeling lasts and pervades consciousness, why I should
1t off part of the total content and call it the object, reserving
1e rest to myself under the name of feeling"(24). So, as social
.teraction continuously imposes a dualistic point of view, the
.onistic point of view simultaneously tries to reassert itself.
nd so, the human voices that wake Prufrock's body and soul

tear the two aspects apart, so that his voice of the poem appear
split between two halves of a single personality, as a dramati
monologue divided; yet, at the same time, the separate voices i
dialogue construct a single personality.[84]

Eliot represents the "dim and drifting edges" of the incom
pletely separated body and soul through the use of allo-repetitior
defined by linguists as the exact or nearly exact repetition c
words or phrases from one speaker by the next speaker. Thes
repetitions allow speakers to close the gaps between them b
sharing words and sentence structures, and these are the precis
types of repetitions found in "The Love Song of J. Alfred Pru
frock": we read of "The yellow fog that rubs its back upon th
window-panes, / The yellow smoke that rubs its muzzle on th
window-panes" (ll. 15–16) followed, in the next stanza by th
variant, "For the yellow smoke that slides along the street / Rul
bing its back upon the window-panes" (ll. 24–25). Nothing pre
vents us from hearing one voice ask, "And would it have bee.
worth it, after all, / After the cups, the marmalade, the tea,
Among the porcelain, among some talk of you and me, / Woul
it have been worth while, . . ." (ll. 87–90) and hearing anothe
voice rearranging and restating the question: "And would it hav
been worth it, after all, / Would it have been worth while, / Afte
the sunsets and the dooryards and the sprinkled streets, / Afte
the novels, after the teacups, after the skirts that trail along th
floor—" (ll. 99–102). Each line may indicate a change of speake
as each voice affirms its personhood, reiterating that "I" is nov
speaking. In the sequence which contains the lines, "For I hav
known them all already, known them all:—"; "And I hav
known the eyes already, known them all—"; and "And I hav
known the arms already, known them all—" (ll. 49, 55, 62); es
sentially, the conjunction in the second two stanzas may indi
cate that, instead of saying, "I *also* have known the eyes . . ." i
addition to "them all," as many critics have assumed, and whic.
is unnecessary, the speakers are saying, "I, *too*, have know.
them"; you are not the only one. This allo-repetition depict
Prufrock as one self and, at the same time, as its objective an
subjective components, as separated and reuniting coinciden
tally, creating an effect which can, as Riquelme recognizes
"straddle the boundary between monologue and dialogue."[85]

Because the voices in "The Love Song of J. Alfred Prufrock

are indistinct, it is difficult for the reader to determine which belongs to the subjective and which to the objective; the reader cannot even be certain of the number of voices. [86] In *Matter and Memory*, Bergson describes the interaction between the faculties that perceive multiplicity and unity, "the one by which it discerns individuals, the other by which it constructs genera,"[87] as a an oscillation between the body (perpetually in the present) and the memory, which consists of a "thousand individual images into which its fragile unity would break up."[88] Between the body, located at one point in time, and the memory, spread out over time, so that the points of contact between them may be imagined in the shape of a cone, he claims, "there is room . . . for a thousand repetitions of our psychical life."[89] Within this cone of time and memory, there will be room "for a hundred indecisions, / And for a hundred visions and revisions" (ll. 32–33). This is the theory that allows Eliot in "Tradition and the Individual Talent" to question "the substantial unity of the soul" (*SE*, 9). Distinguishing between "the man who suffers"— the body—and "the mind which creates" (8), he associates "soul" with "mind" by attributing the unifying function to both terms. The mind, he claims, "is in fact a receptacle for seizing and storing up numberless feelings, phrases, images, which remain there until all the particles which can unite to form a new compound are present together" (8), and he explains his attack on the unity of the soul by explaining that the poet has "only a medium and not a personality, in which impressions and experiences combine in peculiar and unexpected ways" (9). The voice of the soul, then, is constructed out of fragments, and the voice of the body varies as it emerges from the successive states of personality, so Prufrock's voice is simultaneously one, two, and many.

The manner in which Yeats makes use of allo-repetition, along with his labeling of the two voices of "Ego Dominus Tuus" and their physical separation on the page, serves to reinforce the perception of two halves of the self, subjective and objective, linked together to produce one work of art, but necessarily remaining isolated from one another. In "Ego Dominus Tuus," *Hic* and *Ille* engage in allo-repetition, but the words and phrases that they share are fewer and less distinctive than those shared by the facets of Prufrock's self, so that the connection between the objective and subjective voices is weaker in "Ego Dominus Tuus." The allo-repetition also takes place in the context of rebuttal; the speakers use the same phrases to intensify their opposition to what the other has said. When *Ille* says, "By the help of an image / I call to my own opposite" (ll. 7–8), *Hic* responds, "And I would find myself and not an image" (l. 10). When *Hic* makes a claim that Dante had "utterly found himself," *Ille* replies: "And did he find himself / Or . . .?" (ll. 19, 22–23). When *Hic* suggests that poets exist who "look for happiness / And sing when they have found it," *Ille* shoots back: "No, not sing, / For those that love the world would serve it in action" (ll. 40–42). In the penultimate exchange, *Ille* distinguishes between the poet and his art when he responds to *Hic*'s assertion that Keats exhibited a "deliberate happiness." *Ille* retorts, "His art is happy, but who knows his mind?" (ll. 53–54). By changing the noun form to the adjective, *Ille* emphasizes the difference between materiality and subjective emotion.

Neither "Ego Dominus Tuus" nor "The Love Song of J. Alfred Prufrock" allows for direct communication between poet and reader. Art, for *Ille* in "Ego Dominus Tuus," "[i]s but a vision of reality" (l. 48), and knowledge of that reality for Yeats is transmitted not didactically, but by inspiration through contact with one's antiself. Just as *Ille* rejects the book in the tower of the intellect and the "sedentary toil" needed to master it, Yeats rejects didacticism as a means of passing on that knowledge. In his journal, he indicates his agreement with the observation that "we cannot teach another religious truth, we can only point out to him a way by which he may find it for himself" (*Memoirs*, 170). Besides, it is impossible to communicate a mystical experience of unity in a medium composed of discrete words. When J. Alfred Prufrock exclaims, "It is impossible to say just what I mean!" (l. 104), he echoes Yeats's complaints of his own inability to convey his experiences to the women in his life. Yeats recalls in his journal a time when he attempted to tell Lady Gregory of one of his visions, but "felt a difficulty in articulation and became confused" (*Memoirs*, 128). "I had wanted to tell her of some beautiful sight," he continues, "and could see no reason for this. I remembered then what I had read of mystics not being always [able] to speak, and remembered some tale of a lecturer on mysticism having to stop in the middle of a sentence." On another occasion, he reports that he had thought that Maud Gonne "never really understands my plans, or nature, or ideas" (141). But then, he asks, "what matter? How much of the best I have done and still do is but the attempt to explain myself to her?" (141–42). If it were not for his inability to communicate his experiences to her, Yeats realizes, he would have no reason to go on writing. Just as the life of the self depends on striving toward but remaining apart from one's antiself and Dante's art depends on the apple being always out of reach, Yeats's art depends on never being able to communicate perfectly.

Dialogue poetry allows Yeats a means of presenting a debate without engaging in one with the reader. While Yeats still favors the "literature of suggestion" over the "literature of logic" in 1909 (*Memoirs*, 209), he remarks on both his desire to convince others and his inability to do so. "Nothing is so hard to conquer," he asserts, than the "desire to convince where conviction is unnecessary"; furthermore, a failed attempt to convince "creates in our subordinates a habit of argument and therefore of resistance" (*Memoirs*, 167). He never succeeds, he laments, at one-on-one negotiation and asks himself why: "I know that my error comes in some way from the absence of the feeling for form . . . , but why have I this lack?" (216). The "form" to which he refers is that of etiquette, not logic or poetic form, but his discomfort with attempts to convince directly may have led him a few years later to turn to the dialogue form in which his speakers conduct the argument between themselves, avoiding a debate between himself and the reader. Given the dominance of *Ille* over *Hic*, Yeats's message is clear (hence the *Hic* and *Willie* witticism), but he gives the reader at least a semblance of autonomy instead of inciting resistance to subordination.

The relationship between poet and reader in "The Love Song of J. Alfred Prufrock" is more distant. For Eliot, the purpose of all poetry is metaphysical; through poetry, both poet and reader seek to achieve an immediate experience in which feeling and thought are united.[90] Because immediate experience is a transcendent, not an immanent unity, the poet and reader must access that plane individually; the poem provides a point of contact between the two, but is not meant to transmit experience from one to the other. The transcendent nature of the unity achieved in immediate experience renders direct communication between the poet and reader neither possible nor desirable in Eliot's view. Through the medium of the poem, poet and reader may each connect individually with the unity experienced in the coincidence of thought and feeling, and the fact that they each access the One establishes an indirect connection between them, but the poet and reader can establish no direct relationship with one another:

> [I]n writing poetry, we begin from our own immediate experience. That experience, in itself, has no relation to the experience of society as a whole. All that we are aware of doing, is expressing our own feelings about experience equally private; it simply happens, or it does not happen, that the private experience corresponds to a general state so that it both evokes the private experience, and expresses a public experience of the reader. Significant poetry occurs when there is a triple relation: that of the private experience of the poet to the general conditions, and that of the private experience of the poet *and* the general conditions to the private experience of the reader. (*VMP*, 290)

Mystical experience cannot be transmitted from one person to another, and it is not the role of the poet to attempt to do so. The poets that he admires for their ability to unite thought and feeling, including Donne and Laforgue, Eliot declares, "were no prophets"; nor should they be (224). The business of the poet, according to Eliot, is not to "provide a gospel for the multitude struggling toward the light," rather it is "no more than transposing into poetry the thought of the time" (223–24). The resulting poem should provide a point at which the many private experiences of poet and reader meet with the one public experience.

"The Love Song of J. Alfred Prufrock" represents such a point. The hybrid monologue/dialogue form transcends not only body and soul, but also poet and reader, leaving the reader to unify the disparate voices in order to experience a unity of thought and feeling approximately the same as that experienced by Eliot in the creation of the poem. What Eliot says of Donne applies equally to Eliot's own poem: "In order to get the full flavour . . . , you must construe analytically and enjoy synthetically; you must hold the elements in suspension and contiguity in your mind, as he did himself" (*VMP*, 124). By doing so, we achieve a provisional unity of the multiple images and voices of the poem and momentarily balance body and soul, thought and feeling, One and Many. Had Eliot compressed the voices of the debate into one, as a coherent dramatic monologue, he would have instituted direct communication, albeit through a mask, between himself and the reader. Had he separated body and soul into discrete voices in dialogue, the reader would recognize Eliot's voice as that of a transcendent third which authorizes and directs the debate, thereby communicating a unified message. Since the reader cannot identify Eliot's voice as either that of a single speaker beneath a persona or as a single speaker transcending a dialogue, the poem itself becomes transcendent.[91]

Leon Surrette points out that Eliot and Yeats were speaking to very different audiences, a fact that accounts for the inequality of the criticism leveled at their respective religious and political beliefs.[92] The poets themselves, however, managed to transcend their differences and find the "deeper ground of identity" between them. On several occasions, Eliot asserted that as a young man he found Yeats's early poetry uninspiring, and he dates his first "enthusiasm" for Yeats's work to 1919.[93] That, of course, is the year that "Ego Dominus Tuus" appeared in *The Wild Swans at Coole*, the year that Yeats became a "modern" poet. Eliot later wrote to Ottoline Morrell about a lunch with Yeats that he claimed was "the first time that I have ever talked to him for any length of time alone."[94] He found Yeats at that time to be "altogether stimulating" and "really one of a very small number of people with whom one can talk profitably about poetry."[95] Eliot's approbation of Yeats, he suggests at the end of the first annual Yeats Lecture at the Abbey Theater in 1940, rests on Yeats's balancing of the aestheticism of the late Victorians and the didactic and political needs for art in the modern world; according to Eliot, Yeats "held firmly to the right view which is between these, though not in any way a compromise between them."[96] Yeats might have held to a view in which the spiritual and material were always in danger of fusing, while Eliot held to a view in which the two sides of the dichotomy were always in danger of falling apart; but no matter, they were both there in the middle, close enough for dialogue.

4

"Across the Soul-from-Soul Abyss": Robert Frost's Dialogues of Many and One

Robert Frost's late poem "a never naught song" offers the following description of the creation of the universe:

> It was in a state
> Of atomic One.
> Matter was begun—
> And in fact complete,
> One and yet discrete
> To conflict and pair.

(ll. 6–11)

Although almost all of Frost's work addresses the paradox of the One and the Many, early in his career he was never as explicit about it in his poetry as in "A Never Naught Song," and he almost never engaged in public dialogue on the topic. Late in his career however, while giving a public talk in New York City in 1951, he explained to his audience his understanding of "ultimate things": "Out of one thing—you see we're always talking about the one, and the many—out of the one, the many. If you want to get rid of the many, want to shut your eyes to the many, get to the one—you're only shutting your eyes, because the many must be in the one."[1] Overcoming the conflict for Frost, as for Eliot, means transcending the paradox; but for Frost, that transcendence requires an act of volition rather than a passive state of immediate experience. In one of his notebooks, he defines "life" as "that which can mix oil and water (Emulsion)," going on to clarify this definition by associating the oil and water metaphor with the paradox of the One and the Many. Life, he says, "can hold in unity the ultimate irreconcilables spirit

108

and matter good and evil, monism (cohesion) and dualism (reaction), peace and strife. It o'er rules the harsh divorce that parts things natural and divine. Life is a bursting unity of opposites barely held."[2] All action attempts to emulsify these irreconcilables, especially the creation of poetry. In his essay, "Education by Poetry," Frost declares that the "philosophical attempt to say matter in terms of spirit, or spirit in terms of matter, to make final unity" represents "the greatest attempt that ever failed," but a failure which is "the height of all poetry" (SP, 41).

In many ways, Frost's views regarding the problem of the One and the Many evolved along the same path as those of Eliot. Like Eliot, Frost had a mother who wrote religious poetry and who instilled in him a profound sense of faith in the existence of a spiritual reality beyond the material and temporal world in which we live.[3] Frost experienced in his youth a religious epiphany, a "flash of second sight," according to his biographer Lawrance Thompson—a "new glimpse of the metaphysical design" that came to him in a time of doubt and that confirmed his belief in that spiritual realm.[4] Although he did so a decade earlier than Eliot, Frost also attended Harvard, and they studied with some of the same professors, Santayana and Royce among them. And like Eliot, Frost found himself enamored of the teachings of Henri Bergson, a lasting interest that began with his reading of Creative Evolution in December of 1911, shortly after the translation became available in the United States.[5] It was Bergson's mediation between idealism and naturalism, according to Thompson, that attracted Frost, and it was the same impulse toward the reconciliation of opposites that had attracted him first, and even more strongly, to William James.[6] According to Jay Parini, "Frost found in James a sympathetic spirit: a man racked by self-doubts and religious skepticism who nevertheless understood that one must have a degree of faith—in oneself and in the nature of the universe—to proceed at all."[7] So great was Frost's admiration for James that he enrolled at Harvard after reading The Will to Believe in hopes of studying with its author.[8] As a teacher, Frost brought James's theories into his own classroom, assigning both Psychology: A Briefer Course and Pragmatism to his students at Plymouth Normal School where he taught in 1911. Among the critics who have commented on James's influence is Frank Lentricchia, who credits James as the instigator of Frost's "controlling urge," an urge "to resolve tensions between self and the exterior, and to resolve tensions that reside wholly within the self."[9]

James himself consistently views the interaction between self and world as the controlling relationship. In *Psychology: A Briefer Course*, James begins by criticizing psychological theorists who "set up the soul as an absolute spiritual being," and who study that being "almost without reference to the peculiarities of the world" in which it acts.[10] "Mind and world," he continues, "in short have been evolved together, and in consequence are something of a mutual fit."[11] James envisions the soul (or ego) as a "combining medium" that serves to unite the many selves of the individual and to integrate the individual into the outside world.[12] Interpersonal relationships, according to James, although necessarily imperfect, allow us to maintain integrity within our own selves, because, in order to fulfill the "desire to be 'recognized' by others," each individual must select "his truest, strongest, deepest self" to present to the world and suppress all others.[13] The relationship of self and others, then, not the relationship of the soul to a transcendent One, and not the immediate experience of subject and object within a single personality, is crucial to one's psychological health and well-being. It is man's "sense of activity," James suggests, that may be seen as the "very core and nucleus of our self" and "the very sanctuary of our life."[14] Frost echoes this reliance on interaction with the world as a means of resolving tensions internal to one's self, observing in one of his notebooks, "Soul and body are a mechanical mixture that is only kept together[,] and the body kept from settling to the bottom of [,] by the paddle of action."[15] One's own balance of body and soul is therefore maintained only by interacting with other bodies and souls.

In a "common sense world," James asserts, "we find things partly joined and partly disjoined."[16] The world is partly disjoined in that each mind, as James tells us in *Psychology*, "keeps its own thoughts to itself. There is no giving or bartering between them. No thought even comes into direct *sight* of a thought in another personal consciousness than its own. Absolute insulation, irreducible pluralism, is the law."[17] Or, as Frost puts it in "A Missive Missile": "Far as we aim our signs to reach / Far as we often make them reach, / Across the soul-from-soul abyss, / . . . Two souls may be too widely met" (ll. 47–49, 52) According to James, relationships between individuals generate a world partly joined out of a still-distinct plurality of selves; he takes a melioristic view of the evolution of humanity: as society grows more complex, the Many grow increasingly harmonized. In his chapter on the One and the Many in *Pragmatism*, James concludes that the pragmatist "must equally abjure absolute monism and absolute pluralism. The world is one just so far as its parts hang together by any definite connexion. It is many just so far as any definite connexion fails to obtain. And finally it is growing more and more unified by those systems of connexion at least which human energy keeps framing as time goes on."[18] "Human efforts," according to James, "are daily unifying the world more and more in definite systematic ways. We found colonial, postal, consular, commercial systems, all the parts of which obey definite influences that propagate themselves within the system but not to facts outside of it," and these systems, he concludes, result in "innumerable little hangings-together of the world's parts within the larger hangings-together, little worlds, not only of discourse but of operation, within the wider universe."[19] Each of these systems grows out of tentative communion between one self and another.

Poetry, for Frost, creates such "little hangings-together." He expresses the belief in "The Figure a Poem Makes" that poetry represents "a clarification of life—not necessarily a great clarification, such as sects and cults are founded on, but in a momentary stay against confusion" (*SP*, 18). For Frost, the temporary nature of any such stays against confusion does not detract from their desirability. Poetry links poet and reader, if momentarily, providing at least an impression of unity. In his introduction to E. A. Robinson's *King Jasper*, Frost meditates on the connections between people engendered by art: "It has been said that recognition in art is all. Better say correspondence is all. Mind must convince mind that it can uncurl and wave the same filaments of subtlety, soul convince soul that it can give off the same shimmers of eternity. At no point would anyone but a brute fool want to break off this correspondence. It is all there is to satisfaction; and it is salutary to live in the fear of its being broken off" (*SP*, 61). For Frost, the correspondence between souls is crucial in the absence of true recognition; when we understand that we can never really know another person, we make do by knowing that they share some elements of humanity with ourselves, that their imperfect understanding corresponds to our imperfect understanding, that their emotional experiences correlate with our emotional experiences. He recognizes the responsibility of the poet in establishing a relationship between himself and the reader. After all, he declares, "No tears in the writer, no tears in the reader" (19).

The reader has his own responsibility for establishing a correspondence, although the effectiveness of his approach cannot be known: "The closeness—everything depends on the closeness with which you come, and you ought to be marked for the closeness, for nothing else. And that will have to be estimated by chance remarks, not by question and answer. It is only by accident that you know some day how near a person has come" (*SP*, 44).[20] In "The Constant Symbol," Frost addresses the question of the reader's relationship to the poet, asking, "How can the world know anything so intimate as what we were intending to do? The answer is the world presumes to know." Further on in the essay, he compares the correspondence between poet and reader to a premonition: "When familiar friends approach each other in the street both are apt to have this experience in feeling before knowing the pleasantry they will inflict on each other in passing" (*SP*, 26–27). Such an experience implies the existence of an underlying, though unfathomable, unity between isolated individuals, as do the connections made in poetry by the use of metaphor. So poetry, for Frost, represents the nearest possible access to the One: the reader who "gets close enough to poetry, he is going to know more about the word *belief* than anybody else knows, even in religion nowadays" (44). Even though the reader cannot *know* what the poet intends, so that a barrier will remain always between them, he can *believe* in the message and values communicated to him in the poem and, therefore, he can construct a virtual bond.

Despite his emphasis on correspondence, Frost does not value the One over the Many. "The separateness of the parts," he announced during one of his talks at Bread Loaf, "is equally as important as the connection of the parts."[21] In addition, as a participant in a panel of the topic of "The Future of Man" during the Darwin centennial, Frost declared that "the balance is between our being members of each other and being individuals" and defined a "civilized society" as "a society that tolerates all sorts of divergences, to the point of eccentricity."[22] A failure to maintain separateness, he fears, leads to totalitarianism: "Utopia can let no man be his own worst enemy, take the risk of going uninsured, gamble on the horses or on his own future, go to hell in his own way. It has to concern itself more with the connection of the parts than with the separateness of the parts. It has to know where everyone is; it has to bunch us up to keep track of us."[23] Frost relates the desirability of maintaining the tension between One and Many to the workings of nature, pointing out in a *New York Times* interview that "[w]e live by the breaking down of cells and the building up of new cells. Change is constant and unavoidable. That is the way it is with human beings and with nations, so why deplore it?"[24] and comparing relationships to the workings of gravity: "We have all sorts of ways to hold people; Hold them and hold them off. Do you know what the sun does with the planets? It holds them and holds them off. The planets don't fall away from the sun, and they don't fall into it. That's one of the marvels: attraction and repulsion. You have that with poetry, and you have that with friendships."[25]

"The breathless swing," claims Frost, "is between subject matter and form,"[26] and dialogue forms play a large role in his consistent attempts to balance the two. In order to represent a world that is partly joined and partly disjoined in dialogue poems, the relationships both between the speakers and between poet and reader, must bridge the soul-from-soul abyss to some extent without fully overcoming the gap. Frost's early dialogue poems, especially those in *North of Boston*, exhibit such a pragmatic approach to overcoming the soul-from-soul abyss. Though none of us can know what is in another's thoughts, we manage to find some means of connection through interpersonal interaction, and it is primarily through language, says Frost, that we endeavor to do so: "I've been saying the three greats in our life—the three greats—are religion and science and gossip. And the greatest of these is gossip because it is both a wild and a mild surmise. It's our guessing at each other all day long and all our lives; guessing at each other. . . . And it rises from the ordinary daily gossip into the columns of the newspapers and then into literature, drama; and all the time you get nearer what I mean by the mild surmise. . . . It gets larger and larger, but it's still gossip, still surmise, guessing at each other."[27] In a 1957 interview, Frost associates these same terms explicitly with his early dialogue poems. When Cecil Day Lewis suggests "in the country, where small things that happen—things that are gossiped about—are extremely important. I should think that is a good foundation, isn't it, for telling the sort of stories that you tell?," Frost replies, "And they're all dialogue, aren't they, nearly? . . . they're gossip. And one of the three great things in the world is gossip, you know. First there's religion; and then there's science; and there's—and then there's friendly gossip . . . the biggest of all, is gossip—our interest in each other."[28] In the *North of Boston* dialogues, in which the speakers approach each other through the use of question and response and through definition and redefinition, Frost presents this gossip, or guessing at each other, as a means of establishing correspondence between oppositions associated with the One/Many paradox, holding the two sides in tension.

"Death of the Hired Man" addresses through its speakers Mary and Warren the paradoxical relationship between the tendency to unity, to "marry," and the tendency toward disunity, to "warring." Warren exemplifies the side of the Many, of insularity, hard logic, and individual responsibility, while Mary represents the One through inclusiveness, intuition, and social responsibility. The duality represented by the couple is balanced by another pair representing the same opposition: the hired man Silas whose "one accomplishment" consists of the fact that "He bundles every forkful [of hay] in its place, / And tags and numbers it for future reference" (ll. 92–93) and Harold, the college boy "associated in his mind with Latin" (l. 81), which we can associate with the unities of classicism. Silas has no vision of the whole; Harold none for the parts. Much of Mary's sympathy for Silas is precipitated by his inability to communicate with others. She reminds Warren that Silas "don't know why he isn't quite as good / As anybody" (ll. 150–51). On the old man's return to the farm, she tells Warren, she "tried to make him talk about his travels. / Nothing would do: he just kept nodding off" (ll. 43–44). When he did talk, she says, "He jumbled everything. I stopped to look / Two or three times—he made me feel so queer— / To see if he was talking in his sleep" (ll. 58–60). Mary relates that Silas, who felt inferior in the face of the younger man's education, is now obsessed with finding Harold and debating with him and with passing on some of his knowledge, and she sympathizes with his concern:

> After so many years he still keeps finding
> Good arguments he sees he might have used.
> I sympathize. I know just how it feels
> To think of the right thing to say too late.
>
> (ll. 77–80)

She recognizes that this inability to communicate prevents him from participating in familial or societal relations.

Mary defines kindness as empathetic and charitable, based on Silas's humanity, while Warren seeks to redefine the terms of kindness as justice and fair play, his payment of Silas for specific services received. Their discussion is not a debate, however, and does not consist of competing declarations of thesis and antithesis; instead the couple employs a series of interrogatives and tentative definitions to negotiate an understanding. In Warren's first six lines, he asks four questions. When Mary first tells her husband that Silas has returned and that Warren should "Be kind" (l. 7), he replies, "When was I ever anything but kind to him? / But I'll not have the fellow back" (ll. 11–12). Even in stating his rejection of Silas, he softens it by appending a question: "I told him so last haying, didn't I?" (l. 13). Warren continues to ask questions based on Silas's individual worth: "What good is he? Who else will harbor him / At his age for the little he can do?" (ll. 15–16). When Mary counters that Silas has returned a changed man, no longer recognizable as the individual he once was, Warren presses her for precise facts:

> "Where did you say he'd been?"
> "He didn't say. . . ."
>
> . . . .
> "What did he say? Did he say anything?"
> "But little."
>
> "Anything? Mary, confess
> He said he'd come to ditch the meadow for me."

"Warren!"

                    "But did he? I just want to know"
Of course he did. What would you have him say?
Surely you wouldn't grudge the poor old man
Some humble way to save his self-respect.[29]

Mary admits that Warren is factually correct, but suggests that
he misunderstands Silas's language by taking his words literally
as a unique utterance, failing to appreciate their context. Late
in the poem, she counters Warren's famous definition of "home"
as "the place where, when you have to go there, / They have to
take you in" (ll. 122–23) with a conception of "home" as "Some
thing you somehow haven't to deserve" (l. 125). Mary's defini
tion depicts "home" as an encompassing and universal ideal, to
which one may belong, while Warren's definition describes
"home" as a place rooted in a singular location, as a collection
of individuals. He continues to base his consideration of the
problem on specific facts relating to Silas, asking why Silas has
not sought shelter with his own brother, why he has never spo
ken of his brother, what the brother is like, and what is the na
ture of the quarrel between them, if any. Mary asks to have pity
on the old man, to value him not for his individual worth—
indeed, she describes him as "worthless" (l. 152)—but out of
general principles. By asking questions and answering them
they engage with each other in a way that bridges some of the
distance between their positions. At the end of the poem, the
speakers are neither closer together nor further apart than they
began; the couple sits hand in hand on the porch, the discussion
unresolved after being rendered moot by Silas's death, while
their words are held separate on the page in equally divided
hemistichs.

In "The Mountain," Frost explores the opposition of faith and
reason. The poem consists of a dialogue between a traveler and
a native of a valley town called Lunenburg in the shadow of a
looming mountain that shelters the town. The traveler/narrator
questions the ox-cart driver about the mountain, and the driver
who has lived in its shadow his entire life, supplies him with
answers, though under further questioning it seems that the
man really has no firsthand knowledge. The traveler's quest

ymbolizes that of a man who searches for a One in the form of ruth or God or the source of life, but who requires tangible evilence of the existence of a such essentially unknowable unity. n response to the traveler's questions, the villager obliges with nswers based entirely on faith. When the traveler asks, "Is that he way to the top from here?" (l. 37), the carter recommends ine path over another, though it turns out that he has climbed ieither. When asked the name of the mountain, he replies, "We all it Hor: I don't know if that's right" (l. 97). The name "Hor" inderscores the religious symbolism of the mountain; as Robert 'aggen points out, Mount Hor is where Aaron the high priest lies according to Torah;[30] but "Hor" (spelled "har" in modern Iebrew) also means "mount" and might equally evoke "Hor iinai." The majority of the poem is devoted to talk of a spring ituated on top of the mountain, which the ox-cart driver says ie has heard is unique in that it is cold in the summertime and varm in the winter. Just as have numerous believers described he glories of heaven in minute detail without having proof of ts existence, he vividly describes the winter aspect of the spring ind the joy of seeing "It steam in winter like an ox's breath, / Jntil the bushes all along its banks / Are inch-deep with the rosty spines and bristles—" (ll. 54–56). In the face of this imaginative certainty, the traveler inquires about the view from the irea of the spring, only to be reminded that his informant has iever seen the top of the mountain and, in fact, cannot swear to ts existence:

> "As to that I can't say. But there's the spring,
> Right on the summit, almost like a fountain.
> That ought to be worth seeing."
>   "If it's there.
> You never saw it?'

>   "I guess there's no doubt
> About its being there. I never saw it.
> It may not be right on the very top:
> . . . .
> One time I asked a fellow climbing it
> To look and tell me later how it was."

> "What did he say?"

"He said there was a lake
Somewhere in Ireland on a mountain top."

"But a lake's different. What about the spring?"

"He never got up high enough to see."

(ll. 66–84

The traveler persists, asking again about the apparent paradox o
the spring's temperature in relationship to the season, only to
have the man remind him that he should know that such a thing
is not really possible, that the water remains the same, it only
seems different relative to the air. Despite Frost's approval of the
imaginative perception of the mountain (the ox-cart driver calls
it "fun"), he indicates no disdain for the traveler's rationality
the poem in no way ridicules him nor does it question the sin
cerity of his quest.

In another of the *North of Boston* dialogues that deals with
aspects of the problem of the One and the Many, "The Genera
tions of Men," the speakers balance their identities as part of an
ancestral clan and as individuals capable of romantic love. A
the outset of the poem, a young man and a young woman, pre
viously unknown to each other, meet at an old cellar hole, the
site of their family reunion, only to find that all of the others
have been dissuaded by the weather. The old cellar hole, all that
remains of the familial homestead, represents the One source
out of which the Many generations have emerged.[31] Drawn to
gether by their common history, the young couple is isolated
from family and all others while they talk. They know that they
are tied to each other through a genealogy that reaches back nine
generations, yet they are so distantly related that they have dif
ficulty puzzling out their relationship. Each has a card on which
is traced the branch of the family to which each belongs, but
as the young man points out, the genealogy is so convoluted, so
intermarried, so *unified* in a way, that they cannot be certain o
the nature of their kinship. Through their conversation, they ex
plore each other as individuals and as a possible new union as a
couple, with the man courting the young woman aggressively.

In their exchange of "visions" and "voices," they trade imagi
native proposals as to the significance of their ancestry, and in

doing so they represent two contrasting modes of imagination, the visual, which Frost associates with the Many, and the aural, which he associates with the One. The young woman suggests that both the visual and auditory imaginations originate in the individual: "It's as you throw a picture on a screen: / The meaning of it all is out of you; / The voices give you what you wish to hear" (ll. 141–43). He contradicts her, rejoining, "Strangely, it's anything they wish to give" (l. 144). Frost's identification of voices such as those heard by the boy as proof of the existence of a world beyond stems is well documented and may account for his identification of the aural and "the sound of sense" with the One.[32] Numerous sources report that he began to hear voices in his childhood, voices "outside of himself, so clear it frightened him."[33] According to one of his friends, "To the end of his life, Robert believed he could hear voices, real voices. . . . He liked to be alone just to listen, to communicate with the spirit-world."[34] Frost, in a 1914 letter, implies that the "sentence sound" that underlies the grammatical sentence exists outside the material world, that all sounds pre-exist: "We come into the world with them and create none of them. . . . We summon them from Heaven knows where under excitement with the audial imagination" (SL, 140). As Robert Hass points out, Frost's conception of the "vital sentence" corresponds to Bergson's durée;[35] the sound of sense corresponds as well to James's stream of consciousness, and the young man in "The Generations of Men" listens for his voices in "a brook hidden in trees": "I've never listened in among the sounds / That a brook makes in such a wild descent. / It ought to give a purer oracle" (ll. 138–40). The young man's "voices," which he claims are those of their ancestors, invoke the continuity and authority of history to suggest that the two create a future together. The "voices" also emphasize the atemporal and the universal by invoking mythology: "The voices seem to say: / Call her Nausicaä, the unafraid / Of an acquaintance made adventurously" (ll. 160–61). Through his "voices," the young man proposes that they build a "new cottage on the ancient spot" (l. 173), starting a life of their own on the ground of history. The tension between unity and individuality remains in effect at the end of the poem as the girl insists on leaving alone, but promises to meet the boy again the next day.

Some of the dialogues in *North of Boston*, "Home Burial" being the best known, illustrate the destructive possibilities of a failure to understand social interactions as the proper source of unity; a character who looks only to the spiritual world for oneness achieves only isolation in this world. In these poems, the exchange between the two speakers ceases as one refuses to participate in any meaningful conversation, while the other continues to seek understanding. The grieving mother of "Home Burial" berates her husband for his connection to the material world, for his connection to the earth:

> If you had any feelings, you that dug
> With your own hand—how could you?—his little grave;
> I saw you from that very window there,
> Making the gravel leap and leap in air,
> Leap up, like that, and land so lightly
> And roll back down the mound beside the hole.
> I thought, Who is that man? I don't know you.
>
> . . . .
>
> You could sit there with the stains on your shoes
> Of the fresh earth from your own baby's grave
> And talk about your everyday concerns.
>   (ll. 76–82, 88–90)

She accuses him of an inability to feel emotion for having said "Three foggy mornings and one rainy day / Will rot the best birch fence a man can build" (ll. 96–97) failing to understand "What had how long it takes a birch to rot / To do with what was in the darkened parlor" (ll. 99–100). She rejects any equivalence between the material and the spiritual, body and soul, seeing this world as fallen:

> You *couldn't* care! The nearest friends can go
> With anyone to death, comes so far short
> They might as well not try to go at all.
> No, from the time when one is sick to death,
> One is alone, and he dies more alone.
> Friends make pretense of following to the grave,
> But before one is in it, their minds are turned
> And making the best of their way back to life

> And living people, and things they understand.
> But the world's evil. . . .

(ll. 101–10)

She establishes a perverse bond between herself and the dead child by refusing to turn her mind back to things understood by the living, and by isolating herself, she achieves a kind of stasis or death.

The woman expects an ideal Platonic union, one of minds and feelings, not bodies; the kind of union that James tells us is impossible because each mind "keeps its own thoughts to itself." Frost mocks the Platonic attitude toward the world of matter and flux in his letter to *The Amherst Student*: "The background is hugeness and confusion shading away from where we stand into black and utter chaos; and against the background any small man-made figure of order and concentration. What pleasanter than that this should be so? Unless we are novelists or economists we don't worry about this confusion. . . . If I were a Platonist I should have to consider it, I suppose, for how much less it is than everything" (*SP*, 107). The woman's rejection of her husband implies a rejection of the sexual relationship necessary to create and sustain life in the material world. When he attempts to see things literally from her point of view, by looking out the window she haunts and asking, "What is it you see / From up there always—for I want to know" (ll. 6–7), she interprets attempt to comprehend and share her spiritual state as a kind of rape. Frost describes the man's approach in menacing sexual terms—"Mounting until she cowered under him" (l. 11)—and her reaction as a terrified frigidity: "She in her place, refused him any help / With the least stiffening of her neck and silence" (ll. 13–14). When he proves that he recognizes the child's grave as the object of her attention, she screams, " 'Don't, don't, don't, don't . . . .' " (l. 32). She rejects her husband's pragmatic approach to the marriage in favor of the unattainable ideal and at the end of the poem, as she is on the verge of leaving the house after rejecting all of his attempts to communicate, he finally resorts to a threat to use force to maintain the marriage, another improper means of attempting to maintain a union and one that would certainly result in further disunity.

That the wife values vision over voice indicates her misapprehension of the One and that Frost associates her with the material, not her husband. She meets the husband's attempts to communicate with her, to reestablish their identity as a couple through language, with resistance. He offers to make any changes in his behavior that she wishes if she will only communicate with him: "Tell me about it if it's something human. / Let me into your grief" (ll. 61–62). When he admits, "My words are nearly always an offense. / I don't know how to speak of anything / So as to please you. . . ." (ll. 48–50), and suggests that she teach him what to say, she rejects his overture. When he repeats, "A man can't speak of his own child that's dead," she responds, "You can't because you don't know how to speak. / If you had any feelings . . ." (ll. 74, 75–76). "You—," she says, "oh, you think talk is all . . ." (l. 116). The woman cannot interpret the sound of sense; after she watches the man bury the child and return to the house, she hears the tones of his voice, but does not trust her ears: "Then you came in. I heard your rumbling voice / Out in the kitchen, and I don't know why, / But I went near to see with my own eyes" (ll. 85–87). In her mistrust of this world, she fails to hear the deeper meaning that exists here on Earth. Despite the breakdown of the marriage in "Home Burial," the dialogue itself still maintains a balance between the speakers; the reader may sympathize with both wife and husband and, despite the husband's attempts to communicate, he really does lack sensitivity (he asks, "What was it brought you up to think it the thing / To take your mother-loss of a first child / So inconsolably—in the face of love," ll. 66–68) and shares some of the blame for his failure. The poem ends with the wife poised on the doorsill—in the process of leaving, but still there.

If "Home Burial" demonstrates how the poet can maintain balance between dualities even when the two speakers fail to do so, "Build Soil," a parody of Virgil's first eclogue, demonstrates how he can favor one side of the dialogue over the other while still keeping the two sides in tension. "Build Soil" deals with a world in which Frost finds that the balance between One and Many has swung too far toward unity and, as a corrective, he advocates increasing plurality. The poem complains that "we are too unseparate" (p. 297) and that we have such a need to retreat from this excess of togetherness that not only should colors on a palette be kept apart, they should be kept on different plates scattered around the room (p. 293). Throughout the eclogue, Frost as Tityrus derides attempts at unity among men. In speculating on the nature of pure socialism, were it possible, he says he does not know what it would be like, but: "I have no doubt like all the loves when / Philosophized together into one— / One sickness of the body and the soul" (p. 291). "Thank God," he says, "our practice holds the loves apart / Beyond embarrassing self-consciousness . . . ." (p. 291). Tityrus's advocacy of the need for isolation perversely turns pragmatism against James's optimistic vision of social interaction:

> We're always too much out or too much in.
> At present from a cosmical dilation
> We're so much out that the odds are against
> Our ever getting inside again.
> But inside is where we've got to get.
> My friends all know I'm interpersonal
> Away 'way down inside I'm personal.
> Just so before we're international
> We're national and act as nationals.
>
> . . . .
> It's hard to tell which is the worse abhorrence
> Whether it's persons pied or nations pied.
> Don't let me seem to say the exchange, the encounter,
> May not be the important thing at last.
> It well may be. We meet—I don't say when—
> But must bring to the meeting the maturest,
> The longest-saved-up, raciest, localest
> We have the strength of reserve in us to bring.
>
> (p. 293)

He suggests cynically that the pragmatic balance of the One and the Many need not result from good intentions only: "We congregate embracing from distrust / As much as love. . . ." (p. 296). The only practical thing to do, Frost/Tityrus claims, is to retreat to our own homes and to our own thoughts.

The distance between the speakers derives from differences of both philosophy and of status; Meliboeus takes on the subordinate role of inquiring student and Tityrus lectures him. In a letter to Frost responding to "Build Soil," an idealistic young man named Ferner Nuhn sympathizes, "Poor Meloebeus (if I have his name right), I do feel he got rather talked down, and went away not so much convinced as subdued, and when *he* got by himself again, much *he* had to say came back to him, and he grumbled at not being as articulate as he might have been."[36] Frost replied to Nuhn that "[b]oth of those people in the dialogue are me. I enjoyed having one part of me impose on the other."[37] Thompson recommends taking this declaration with a grain of salt, writing that while "[i]t was true that Frost had been fashioning poems, for years, out of the dramatic conflicts between the opposed sides of his own nature," at the time he wrote "Build Soil," he had no sympathy for Meliboeus's position whatsoever.[38] That lack of sympathy is evident as Meliboeus cedes to Tityrus at the end of the poem; when asked if he will agree to the conditions of retirement set by Tityrus, he replies, "Probably, but you're far too fast and strong / For my mind to keep working in your presence" (p. 296). Nevertheless, he assents, "We're too unseparate. And going home / From company means coming to our senses" (p. 297). The "singing contest" between the shepherds turns into a rout, and Tityrus's thesis wins the debate without ever really facing an antithesis.

Although Frost frequently encouraged, or at least failed to discourage, classifying the *North of Boston* poems as eclogues,[39] fitting them into that genre can be difficult due to their lack of a *locus amoenus* or shepherds in what is clearly not a golden age. Faggen makes a valiant attempt in his essay "Frost and the Questions of Pastoral" despite admitting that "[i]f we adhere to strict definitions then Frost definitely appears out of place: his landscapes are often barren, his shepherds seem to be rather tough farmers, and contemplation always appears threatened and mingled with hard labor."[40] In fact, although the *North of Boston* dialogue poems have speakers representing opposite sides of various dualities and rural locations for their settings, they do not otherwise resemble eclogues. These poems bear a much closer resemblance to another typically rural form, the ballad. The *Princeton Encyclopedia of Poetry and Poetics* lists three characteristics of the ballad: 1) "Ballads focus on a single crucial episode," 2) "Ballads are dramatic. . . . Protagonists are allowed to speak for themselves, which means that dialogue bulks large," 3) "Ballads are impersonal. The narrator seldom allows his or her own attitude toward the events to intrude."[41]

Each of the *North of Boston* dialogues focuses on a single dramatic episode, and they all include narration, not a conventional feature of the eclogue and not present in "Build Soil." The difference is important because ballads inherently create more of a balance between unity and plurality than do eclogues. Frost himself recognizes that the ballad tends toward unity; in his introduction to *The Hearsay Ballad*, he writes, "It may seem to be going to pieces, breaking up, but it is only the voice breaks with emotion."[42] Ballads, Frost suggests, "lead their life in the mouths and ears of men by hear-say"[43] or, in other words, are forms of gossip. One of the primary ways that ballads represent smaller distances between individuals than do eclogues is that the dialogue usually takes the form of question and response rather than debate, and this is how the conversations proceed in Frost's early dialogues. The ballad also allows for a more intimate approach for the reader than does the eclogue, in large part because of the presence of a narrator who speaks directly to the reader, in part because its folk origins and rusticity require little or no educational background to appreciate, and in part because the folk speech of ballads conveys sincerity as opposed to the artifice of the eclogue's elevated diction.

Frost intimates that narration has provided him with a means of bridging dualities associated with the One/Many problem in his poetry:

> Clash is all very well for coming lawyers politicians and theologians. But I should think there must be a whole realm or plane above that— all sight and insight, perception, intuition, rapture. Narrative is a fearfully safe place to spend your time. Having ideas that are neither pro nor con is the happy thing. Get up there high enough and the differences that make controversy become only the two legs of a body the weight of which is on one in one period, on the other in the next. Democracy monarchy; puritanism paganism; form content; conservatism radicalism; systole diastole; rustic urbane; literary colloquial; work play. I should think too much of myself to let any teacher fool me into taking sides on any one of these oppositions. . . . I have wanted to find ways to transcend the strife-method. I have found some. (*SL*, 324–25)

Narration transcends the oppositions represented by the speakers of dialogues and supplies a provisional connection between poet and reader as well. In order to represent a world that is partly joined and partly disjoined in dialogue poems, the relationships both between the speakers and between poet and reader must bridge the soul-from-soul abyss to some extent, but must be limited to surfaces and exteriors without access to interior thoughts or emotions, and the narration in the *North of Boston* dialogues performs precisely this function. The few lines of narrative suggest a personal knowledge of the circumstances of each dialogue on the part of the poet so that each of the voices constitutes a part of his unique experience. But while he uses narrative to impose some unity, Frost avoids tipping the scale too far toward the one, preserving some distance between himself, the characters, and the reader by including only description, not commentary, in the narration, and by reserving autobiographical detail.

Perhaps the most telling effect of the limited narration in establishing a tension between the One and the Many in these dialogues results from the temporality imparted by the use of the past tense. For one thing, the use of the past tense situates the poet and reader in the same time frame, whereas the speakers of the dialogue exist at some prior point in time. The resulting temporal and spatial distance provides perspective so that the conversations themselves appear as a single incident in which the idea shifts back and forth within a predetermined outcome. Without this distance and without the unifying force of the narrator's memory, the reader would shift back and forth synchronously with the speakers. Additionally, the use of the past tense by the narrator positions him and the reader as participants in the One of a continuous history, while the speakers of the dialogues exist only in isolation of the present tense, in a singular moment in time. Through the conjunction of the two time frames, Frost allows the reader to experience the atemporality of monism and the temporality of pluralism at the same time.

The presence of the narrator also helps to overcome one of the sources of distance inherent in dialogue forms, an "eavesdropping" effect that results when the speakers direct their lines to each other instead of the reader. The lack of an invitation to join or to listen in on the conversation may evoke or intensify a feeling of unease, alienation, or even guilt in the reader, which increases the sense of distance. Ferner Nuhn's apparent discomfort in reading the trouncing of Meliboeus by Tityrus is a case in point. In the earlier dialogues the limited use of narration helps to overcome this effect to some extent, although reading highly charged scenes such as the dialogue between the grieving parents of "Home Burial" may still feel voyeuristic and intrusive. The narration creates the illusion of a direct address from the poet; at the same time, we know that the narrator is a persona; we are aware that the poet both is and is not establishing a connection with us; whereas, "Build Soil" not only lacks a narrator to create this relationship, but we get a triple distancing effect: Frost masking as Virgil masking as Tityrus, who completely ignores the reader.

The narrator sets the scene and the mood, giving the reader some context, some sense of the characters' emotions without giving access to either his own or the characters' interior thoughts. In fact, Frost refrains from any presentation of his speakers' internal states, and his narrators make no judgments on any of their actions, even in poems like "The Mountain" and "The Housekeeper," with first-person narrators. Instead, the limitations of the narrator emphasize the impenetrability of the consciousnesses of individuals and that our attempts to commune consist only of guesses and surmises; we are partly joined together, *and* the world remains irreducibly plural. The narrator provides information on the settings and backgrounds of the scenes, as in the first lines of "The Death of the Hired Man":

> Mary sat musing on the lamp-flame at the table
> Waiting for Warren. When she heard his step,
> She ran on tip-toe down the darkened passage
> To meet him in the doorway with the news
> And put him on his guard. . . .
>
> (ll. 1–5)

These lines set the mood, giving the reader some sense of the characters' emotions without giving access to the characters' interior thoughts. With a few minor exceptions, Frost refrains from any presentation of his speakers' internal states, and his narrators make no judgments on any of their actions. Victor Vogt, writing about "The Death of the Hired Man," regards this as Frost's "strategic withdrawal"; in the short narrative passages, he writes, "we again see Frost's calculated refusal: he deliberately avoids a crucial resource open to tellers of tales in order to exploit the measured subtleties of implied commentary stemming from juxtaposition and ironic understatement."[44] The fact that the commentary remains implied reinforces the notion that our attempts to commune with each other consist only of guesses and surmises. Frost once reported to Louis Untermeyer that Ezra Pound had told him that what he was attempting to do in these dialogues was to write short stories.[45] Certainly the dramatic situations of the poems could warrant such treatment, but the creation of prose stories, or even of narrative poems, would upset the balance of the one voice of the poet and the many of the characters by shifting the emphasis to the one voice of the narrator, and Frost avoids doing so.

Although most of Frost's early dialogues feature a narrator who transcends the dualities of the speakers, "West-Running Brook," which appeared in 1928, is a fascinating exception to the rule. Thompson comments that Frost's lifelong desire to hold in tension "naturalism and idealism, physics and metaphysics, skepticism and mysticism" was generally successful, but his occasional swings from one extreme to another puzzled not only his readers, but also his family and Frost himself.[46] These swings become less puzzling when we recognize that the relationships between dualities associated with the problem of the One and the Many vary depending on the nature of the unity theorized. For example, while James sees a plurality where tenuous interpersonal connections form a whole, Bergson sees a whole divided into individual lives in which a "current, running through human generations, subdividing itself into individuals," the *élan vital*, provides unity.[47] Widely acknowledged as Frost's most Bergsonian work, "West-Running Brook," a poem that Thompson calls "a study in Bergsonian contraries,"[48] features a narrative voice that appears within parentheses, rising from within the dialogue instead of transcending it, a position particularly appropriate to a Bergsonian stance. In "West-Running Brook," a couple stands beside a stream which, contrary to expectations, runs west rather than east toward the ocean. Thompson identifies Frost's source for this poem as this passage from *Creative Evolution*: "Life as a whole, from the initial impulse that thrust it into the world, will appear as a wave which rises, and which is opposed by the descending movement of matter. . . . On the other hand, this rising wave is consciousness, and, like all consciousness, it includes potentialities without number which interpenetrate and to which consequently neither the category of unity nor that of multiplicity is appropriate, made as they both are for inert matter."[49] In the poem, the husband, Fred, emphasizes the immanence of the life force inherent in and symbolized by the brook:

> It is from that in water we were from
> Long, long before we were from any creature.
> Here we, in our impatience of the steps,
> Get back to the beginning of beginnings,
> The stream of everything that runs away.
> Some say existence like a Pirouot
> And Pirouette, forever in one place,
> Stands still and dances, but it runs away,
> It seriously, sadly, runs away
> To fill the abyss' void with emptiness.
> It flows beside us in this water brook,
> But it flows over us. It flows between us
> To separate us for a panic moment.
> It flows between us, over us, and *with* us.
>
> (ll. 40–53)

The couple in this poem tries out different methods of speaking about the brook, with her fanciful personification emphasizing unity and his wistful realism emphasizing disunity; but, unlike the dialogues in *North of Boston* this poem ends in synthesis with the words (presumably hers), "Today will be the day of what we both said" (l. 75). The internal coherence of the speakers leads Jay Parini to note that "[t]he husband-wife dialogue has none of the edginess of the dramatic lyrics (as in "Home Burial," where the dramatic tension is brought to a fierce climax)," and he refers to "West-Running Brook" as "a kind of meditative lyric couched in the spoken voice."[50]

Unlike the *North of Boston* dialogues, "West-Running Brook" does not begin with a short narrative introduction. Instead, the dialogue begins with four hemistichs set on opposite sides of the page followed by a narrative intrusion which unifies the lines:

"Fred, where is north?"

                                "North, North is there, my love.
        The brook runs west."

                                "West-running Brook then call it."
        (West-running Brook men call it to this day.)

                                                        (ll. 1–3)

The parenthetical comment provides a temporal link between the poet and reader; it is unnecessary here for the narrator to unify opposing sides of a debate because Fred's response to his wife's question begins in the second half of the first line, continues to the first half of the second line, and is flanked by the woman's two half-lines so that the hemistichs represent not debate but two speakers mingled together. A few lines later, the poem contains, as Tyler Hoffman has pointed out,[51] an unusual tripartite line that symbolizes the trinity of man, wife, and the spirit represented by the brook:

        "What are we?"

                    "Young or new?'

                                "We must be something.
        We've said we two. Let's change that to we three.
        As you and I are married to each other,
        We'll both be married to the brook. We'll build
        Our bridge across it, and the bridge shall be
        Our arm thrown over it asleep beside it."

                                                    (ll. 10–15)

The "bridge" created by the middle third of the line appears not only "over it" and "beside it," as she says, but also within. The wife speaks of the wave in the middle of the brook in terms of creation, as marriage and annunciation, and the husband describes the flow of life in the brook as "The universal cataract of death / That spends to nothingness" (ll. 56–57). In the middle, another parenthetical intrusion emphasizes the infinite struggle in the wave between Bergson's rising life and descending matter ("And the white water rode the black forever, / Not gaining but not losing" ll. 21–22), so that the narrator internally balances the opposing points of view asserted by the couple.

"West-Running Brook" shares with the *North of Boston* ballads the New England setting that gives those poems their universal appeal. Frost himself asserted that his use of regional settings and diction takes advantage of the relationship between the regional and the universal. In a 1917 interview, he acknowledges that "[w]e think the word 'provincial' is a shameful word here in America," but points out that "[y]ou can't be universal without being provincial, can you?"[52] On the flyleaf of a copy of *North of Boston*, he makes a similar point: "I suffer from the way people abuse the word colloquial. All writing, I don't care how exalted, how lyrical, or how seemingly far removed from the dramatic, must be as colloquial as this passage from 'Monadnoc' comes to. I am as sure that the colloquial is the root of every good poem as I am that the national is the root of all thought and art. . . . One half of individuality is locality: and I was about venturing to say the other half was colloquiality." (*SL*, 228). At the beginning of "The Hear-Say Ballad," Frost quotes Joseph Addison approvingly: "An ordinary song or ballad that is the delight of the common people cannot fail to please all such readers as are not unqualified for the entertainment by their affectation or their ignorance."[53] The use of regional locations, situations, and characters in the early dialogues promotes the paradox, and the continuing popularity of dialogues like "Death of the Hired Man" and "Home Burial" attests to their universal appeal, to their ability to establish correspondences with readers. Conversely, abstractions distance readers. In 1931, Frost gave an interview to *Rural America* in which he claims that "poetry is very, very rural—rustic" and that "it might be taken as a symbol of a man, taking its rise from individuality and seclusion." In the same interview, however, he explains his current philosophy in the same terms he uses in "Build Soil": "We are now at a moment when we are getting too far out into the social-industrial and are at the point of drawing back—drawing in to renew ourselves."[54] At this time, he says, it is time "to take corrective measures" and concludes that "[t]he individual and the social—I know those two things are always getting something out of each other. But I am mostly interested in solitude and in the preservation of the individual. I want to see people sufficiently drawn

into themselves."[55] This corrective turn away from unity to plu
rality paradoxically produces a poem that contains nothing truly
rustic or regional and that parodies a poem that has been handed
down from generation to generation throughout the history of
Western civilization.

In his notebooks, Frost mocks Yeats's contention that the art
ist must adopt one of seven universal poses. "Don't believe i
children," he writes, "There is such a thing as sincerity."[56] In
large part, the intimacy and sincerity projected by Frost's poems
derives from their folk speech, with its colloquial diction, un
adorned, hesitant, and sometimes semiarticulate. Frost valued
sincerity as a means of achieving closeness between himself and
the reader, and he praised the speech of his New England coun
trymen—their ' gossip," their guessing at each other—as partic
ularly conducive to overcoming the distances between people
In a letter to William Stanley Braithwaite, he relates:

> There came a day about ten years ago when I made the discovery
> that though sequestered I wasnt [sic] living without reference to
> other people. Right on top of that I made the discovery in doing The
> Death of the Hired Man that I was interested in neighbors for more
> than merely their tones of speech—and always had been. I remember
> about when I began to suspect myself of liking their gossip for its
> own sake. . . .
> I like the actuality of gossip, the intimacy of it. Say what you will
> effects of actuality and intimacy are the greatest aim an artist can
> have. The sense of intimacy gives the thrill of sincerity. (SL, 159)

In a 1915 interview, Frost also specifically associates folk speech
with the sound of sense. "All folk speech is musical," he claims
"In primitive conditions man has not at his aid reactions by
which he can quickly and easily convey his ideas and emotions
Consequently, he has to think more deeply to call up the image
for the communication of his meaning."[57] This idea follows
fairly closely his assertion that "[i]f we go back far enough we
will discover that the sound of sense existed before words, that
something in the voice or vocal gesture made primitive man
convey a meaning to his fellow before the race developed a more
elaborate and concrete symbol of communication in language."[58] Since words represent the discrete and the rational part

f language, and the sound of sense correlates to the continuous
nd irrational, he indicates that folk speech balances the two
ides of the dichotomy, so that it is appropriate for dialogues that
ry to balance unity and multiplicity. The meter and semiaca-
demic diction of "Build Soil," on the other hand, are sorely lack-
ng in musicality. For example, this stirring passage: "I keep my
ye on Congress, Meliboeus. / They're in the best position of us
ll / To know if anything is very wrong." Or: "There's only dem-
cratic socialism, / Monarchic socialism—oligarchic, / The last
eing what they seem to have in Russia." If anything, the effect
s staccato, emphasizing discontinuity.

In later dialogue poems, such as "The Literate Farmer and the
Planet Venus" and the two masques, although Frost continues
o express a pragmatic understanding of a world partly joined
nd partly disjoined, the poems exhibit a profoundly cynical
iew of human relationships inconsistent with James's opti-
mism regarding the unifying power of social systems. The mock-
ng diction and tone of these poems represent increased distance
etween the speakers and impose a certain amount of distance
etween poet and reader as well. In a letter to Untermeyer, Frost
ecognizes the distancing effects of humor: "At bottom the
vorld isn't a joke. We only joke about it to avoid an issue with
omeone to let someone know that we know he's there with his
uestions: to disarm him by seeming to have heard and done jus-
ice to his side of the standing argument. Humor is the most en-
aging cowardice. With it myself I have been able to hold some
f my enemy in play far out of gunshot."[59] Significantly, he rec-
gnizes that humor holds people on and holds them off simulta-
eously, attracts and repels, engages and ducks, holds in play but
ut of the range of fire. Although the tension between One and
Many remains in these poems, Frost's understanding of the One
s changing. Satire implies absolute values that transcend this
vorld; to mock someone's views as wrong requires the satirist
o believe that he knows what is right.

"The Literate Farmer" begins when a traveler knocks at the
oor of a farmer and inquires into the nature of a bright light in
he sky. The farmer asserts that the "star" (Venus) is really an
xperiment of Edison's, an electric light that is intended to cure
atred by pushing Man to evolve so as not to need sleep and
herefore never to get up on the wrong side of the bed:

> That is the source perhaps of human hate,
> And well may be where wars originate.
> Get rid of that and there'd be left no great
> Of either murder or war in any land.
> You know how cunningly mankind is planned:
> We have one loving and one hating hand.
> The loving's made to hold each other like,
> While with the hating other hand we strike.
> The blow can be no stronger than the clutch,
> Or soon we'd bat each other out of touch,
> And the fray wouldn't last a single round.
> And still it's bad enough to badly wound,
> And if our getting up to start the day
> On the right side of bed would end the fray,
> We'd hail the remedy. But it's been tried
> And found, he says, a bed has no right side.
>
> (ll. 108–23)

Robert Faggen asks, "Is the farmer a buffoon who has absorbed popular accounts of Darwinism, or does he spout this ideology to the vagrant to let him know that he's none too charitable toward his fellow man?"[60] This is a difficult question to answer, and Faggen never really does so; but while he ridicules the farmer's solution to the problems of "human hate," Frost sounds serious about the diagnosis of the problem. Venus traditionally represents love, beauty, and order and, as Faggen points out, is often opposed to Mars, the god of war. Although Frost does not quite at this time turn to religious faith, his transcendent image of unity here is quite literally over men's heads. The traveler who counts himself a liberal "willing to give place / To any demonstrably better race" (ll. 49–50), bases his assumptions about the star on religion, beauty, and intuition:

> Here come more stars to character the skies,
> And they in the estimation of the wise
> Are more divine than any bulb or arc,
> Because their purpose is to flash and spark,
> But not to take away the precious dark.
> We need the interruption of the night
> To ease attention off when overtight,
> To break our logic in too long a flight,
> And ask us if our premises are right.
>
> (ll. 75–83)

The farmer responds disparagingly, "Sick talk, sick talk, sick sentimental talk!" (l. 84) and Frost takes the traveler's politically correct talk of racial equality, of unity among men, hardly more seriously than he does the farmer's evolutionary meliorism. The poem's humor derives not only from the absurdity of the farmer's claims and from puns like, "There's a star that's Serious by name" (l. 29), but also from the verse itself. In addition to the rhyming couplets and the tumbling rhythm that give the entire poem a comic tone, the farmer's lines incorporate a number of multisyllabic, feminine rhymes worthy of Lear or Nash. Per the farmer: "The slave will never thank his manumitter; / Which often makes the manumitter bitter" (ll. 90–91). He also rhymes "inherited" with "merited," "meet with them" with "Bethlehem," and "rubbing sticks" with "pterodix" (ll. 55–56, 33–34, 138–39). While early in his career Frost valued the folk speech of ballads for its sincerity and musicality, for its immanent unity, he turns to this highly artificial dialogue when the One appears unavailable within this world.

Artificiality in a more typically modern mode suffuses the two masques, *A Masque of Reason* and *A Masque of Mercy*, that Frost produced in the mid-1940s. In the masques, Frost addresses a transcendent unity, that of the Judeo-Christian God. Anthony Hecht describes *A Masque of Reason* as an "impudent work, markedly devoid of the usual forms of reverence, not only for God but for Yeats"; Frost's allusions to golden birds and "Greek artificers," Hecht suggests, and particularly "the Byzantine contraption of a throne that cannot stand on its own," symbolize the "jerrybuilt contrivance of Yeats's entire theory of historical necessity."[61] The lack of "the usual forms of reverence" does not imply a lack of reverence, and Hecht suggests that in taking this shot at Yeats, Frost is attacking the atheism he perceives in Yeats's system.[62] Although Frost protested during a 1960 interview, "Don't make me out to be a religious man," he did not mean to deny faith in God, only that he was not "a man who has all the answers. I don't go around preaching God. I'm not a minister"; in fact, he believed strongly, explaining, "It's like climbing up a ladder, and the ladder rests on nothing; and you climb higher and higher, and you feel there must be God at the top. It can't be unsupported up there."[63] The "up there" that

transcends this earth had by the 1940s replaced James's social
unity for Frost as the only One.

Frost's upbringing might have dissuaded him from religious
belief early on—he sometimes referred to his mother's religious
convictions as "incipient insanity," although he also recalled: "I
looked on at my mother's devoutness and thought it was beautiful"[64]—but by the time he was ready to write the masques, pragmatism had long since given way to faith. A 1942 letter to
Untermeyer suggests that he approached religion uncertainly
and resignedly:

> To prayer I think I go,
> I go to prayer—
> Along a darkened corridor of woe
> And down a stair
> In every step of which I am abased.
> I wear a halter-rope about the waist.
> I bear a candle end put out with haste.
> For such as I there is reserved a crypt
> That from its stony arches having dripped
> Has stony pavement in a slime of mould.
> There I will throw me down an unconsoled
> And utter loss,
> And spread out in the figure of a cross.—
> Oh, if religion's not to be my fate
> I must be spoken to and told
> Before too late![65]

Critics, particularly Thompson, who, in light of Frost's earlier
attitudes toward religion, interpreted A Masque of Reason as an
attack on Christianity, angered Frost; "They're very doctrinal,
very orthodox, both of them," he insisted.[66] Parini finds A
Masque of Mercy "less interesting as poetry than as evidence of
a shift in Frost's thinking," a shift which moved from justice to
mercy,[67] or, in other words, from a focus on rationality and fair-
ness to the Many to faith in the grace of the One God.

Frost's choice of the masque form reflects a preference for
faith over reason, or at least a recognition that reason fails us
when it comes to questions of God's nature. In a 1960 talk, he
acknowledges the near futility of any attempt to understand ra-
tionally the questions addressed in the masques: "There's a cer-

tain debate in your life that you don't ever feel you've got the best of, that there's still something unsettled. If He's a God of mercy, is He also a God of justice? Naturally, there's a constant, natural conflict between justice and mercy. The big joke is that somebody on earth ought to balance them up. Probably God does. It could be assumed. That is the most Godlike thing to balance them—mercy for justice or a just mercy. But there's something there that's almost too hard for a mortal man to get."[68] God's justice and mercy must be taken as a matter of faith, and neither rhetoric nor dialectic can successfully contend for belief or intuition; their very natures would contradict the argument. In *A Masque of Reason*, Job demands once again to know why God mistreated him so cruelly. In response, God thanks him for helping to "Establish once for all the principle / There's no connection man can reason out / Between his just deserts and what he gets" (p. 374). Frost addresses the relationship between unreason and the morality play explicitly when God insists that the reason for the episode with Job had to occur because "Society can never think things out: / It has to see them acted out by actors" (p. 380). If one believes that a poem can operate by reason, then the burden of communication rests on the poet, and he must establish a clear understanding between himself and the reader. However, if the poet believes that only unreason will communicate his meaning, then the entire burden falls to the reader, and it is incumbent on the poet only to lay out the materials and stand back so that the willing (and worthy) reader may interpret them. Other than a few terse stage directions, neither masque contains any direct address from Frost to the reader, and in neither poem can any of the characters be associated directly with the poet. The shift in the masques to a transcendent unity accessible only through faith puts Frost more in line with Eliot or Pound than he was early in his career, and the masques employ typically modernist techniques appropriate to such a belief. Instead of intensely regional and individual situations as in the earlier dialogues, the later poems incorporate themes and references from throughout the history of Western civilization. The conflation of biblical stories with examples of Greek philosophy and with modern references such as the Kodak camera emphasizes the universality and timelessness of Frost's subject. Allusions to Blake, Browning, Yeats, Shakespeare, Milton, Robinson,

O'Neill, and others situate these poems as part of tradition, while, at the same time, restricting understanding of the works to readers worthy of receiving the knowledge they contain, those who, as Eliot writes in "Tradition and the Individual Talent," have worked "to obtain it by great labour."

Parini credits Frost's venture into verse drama to the influence of *The Dynasts*, which, according to Parini, "made a strong impression on Frost."[69] Reginald Cook also notes similarities between Frost's worldview and that of Hardy: "Frost contemplates without commitment the validation of an all-powerful universal force which does govern in things both large and small, then and now, waywardly, and with purpose, if any, beyond our ken, like Hardy's 'knitter drowsed' whose 'fingers play in skilled unmindfulness.'"[70] The stance of the poet in the masques, distancing himself from poem and readers, brings to mind *The Dynasts* as well. Frost once expressed a desire to take up a position akin to that of the spirits in *The Dynasts*: "I sometimes have the whimsical desire to see all civilization obliterated in order to stand, timeless at some cosmic vantage point and watch the slow, painful process of rebuilding."[71] Cook attributes the comedy of the masques to such a stance, suggesting that the drama, "like the peripatetic on his porch or the sophist on the street corner, has its *point d'appui* in philosophic detachment. When we stand off just far enough from human or divine institutions, no matter how big, heroic, grand, imposing, and serious they are supposed to be, they *can* look funny. Obviously, this is the way the institution of religion looked to the poet."[72] The comedy of the masques, however, derives not from a burlesque of institutional religion, but from the idea that individuals could ever comprehend God's will and, as a result of that understanding, assert their own. In the early part of the twentieth century, Frost had seized on James's optimistic view that acts of human volition would serve to unify the world. In the early 1940's Frost had, within the past decade, lost two of his remaining children and his wife, and he had watched the promised world order disintegrate into World War II. Although he had come to believe that the One exists in a world that transcends our own, like Hardy he recognized that any desire for communion with that One is fruitless, and like Hardy, he ends up writing about a de facto pluralism.

5

"Let Everything be Vanity or One": Louis MacNeice's Eclogues

IN HIS "PERSONAL ESSAY," *MODERN POETRY*, LOUIS MACNEICE COM plains that critics tend to pick out one characteristic of a poet's work on which to focus as if that single feature constitutes the entirety of his poetics; "It would be a more valid method," Mac-Neice argues, "for the critic to try to work out in each poet a kind of Hegelian dialectic of opposites, remembering again to stress the fusion of these opposites rather than their opposition" (*MP*, 78). In MacNeice's case, ironically, his dialecticism *is* the single issue seized upon by critics. Although each critic uses different terms to specify the opposition, each recognizes Mac-Neice's struggle to find a balance between the One and the Many. Peter McDonald names this process a dialectic of "historical situation and personal artistic history."[1] For Edna Longley, MacNeice's poetry exhibits an "unusually acute version" of the "drive to reconcile the demands of form and content."[2] Terence Brown specifically employs the language of the One/Many paradox to describe the tensions inherent in the poetry: "Together the flux of life and the awful permanence of death create the tension which men need, to stimulate mind, heart and senses to full vigour. The two inseparable opposites of the infinite unchanging One into which all being goes, and the multiple flux of all that now is, seem to MacNeice to give each other value, to co-exist in a metaphysical relation which the poet can accept with bittersweet emotions, and can trust as real. This is a sceptical faith, which believes that no transcendent reality, but rather non-being, gives being value."[3] Like Eliot, Yeats, Frost, Hardy, and Auden, MacNeice seeks to balance unity and plurality in his dialogue poetry. Unlike these other poets, however, he eventually rejects monism completely, and his dialogues reflect an increasing bias towards plurality.

Early in his career, MacNeice found himself unable to discover any balance between the One and the Many. He recalls that when he went up to Oxford he "had no system which could at the same time unify the world and differentiate its parts significantly" (MP, 62). Reiterating this point in his essay "When I Was Twenty-One: 1928," he reminisces that during his college years, "having reacted violently against the Christian ethic," he felt himself "morally naked and spiritually hungry," which led him to search both plurality and monism for some sort of answer: "Let everything be vanity or One! It was to take me some time to close for a middle way."[4] Vanity, the concern of the individual, he links with reason—"the Gallic grain of salt"—as opposed to the "hidden magic of the Rheingold" of German Idealism, and both offered potential a potential "cure" for his spiritual crisis.[5] MacNeice's poetry of this period, published in *Blind Fireworks* (1929), consists of modernist, impersonal expressions of what Edna Longley calls a "hothouse solipsism"[6] that reflect his desire for both vanity and One. His 1930 poem "Neurospastoumenos" includes lines that indicate a certain sense of loss in his recognition of the absence of that middle way: "Regards not us the One but plays at being Many, / Regards not us the Point but dreams of three dimensions, / Regards not us the Absolute."[7] Whereas in immediate experience, as propounded by Bradley and Eliot, the human mind is the observer that determines whether the world is One or Many, here One and Many interchange identities without regard to any human viewpoint, and MacNeice finds himself unable to exert any control over his experience.

By the late 1930s, however, MacNeice discovered his middle way, a means of imposing order on the flux of life without reliance on a transcendent unity. In *Autumn Journal* (1938), a poem he describes as "half-way between the lyric and the didactic poem,"[8] and a poem which Peter McDonald calls MacNeice's most successful "amalgam" of self and world,[9] he created a work that occupies a space poised between the personal and the universal. Just before *Autumn Journal*, as he was searching for a middle way between the One and the Many, MacNeice found in the eclogue an apt form in which to conduct the exploration. Be-

tween 1933 and 1937, he produced four of these poems: "An Eclogue for Christmas," "Eclogue by a Five-Barred Gate," "Eclogue
from Iceland," and "Eclogue Between the Motherless." Each of
the eclogues addresses in some way the question of how to de-
velop a relationship between self and world, a relationship that
none of the speakers in any of these poems has yet established.
As is consistent with speakers searching for unity but still isolated, each of the poems employs dialogue with no apparent unifying voice. And as is consistent with works that assume a unity
that as yet remains undiscovered, although the poet's One voice
is not apparent on the surface of the poems, such a unity is available to anyone willing to search for it.

As MacNeice himself asserts, "Literary criticism should always be partly biographical," and "a certain knowledge of the
poet's personal background will help us to understand" him (*MP*,
75, 89), and such an approach to the eclogues reveals that all of
the speakers in the poems represent past and present aspects of
the poet himself. Debates between two aspects of a writer's self
have a long tradition in Western literature, including dialogues
by Augustine, Abelard, and Petrarch.[10] MacNeice's use of two
selves separated by time is consistent with an observation in his
study of Yeats, when in a discussion of Yeats's contention in his
essay "Anima Hominus" that "[w]e make out of the quarrel
with others, rhetoric, but of the quarrel with ourselves, poetry,"
MacNeice suggests that such internal poetic debates occur between present and past selves: "The poet is always quarreling
with himself, perhaps because he half remembers himself in a
past life as having been some one different" (*PWBY*, 116). Auden,
one of MacNeice's close friends, validates the concept of a debate between past and present aspects, declaring that, "The only
duality is that between the whole self at different stages of development—e.g. a man before and after a religious conversion. The
old life must die in giving birth to the new."[11] In the eclogues,
then, MacNeice stages dialogues between speakers who have at
once different identities and the same, Many and One in the
same person. At the same time, the concealment of his personal
associations with the speakers allows him to maintain a certain
amount of distance from the reader as he comes to the conclusion that he must interact with the world, but has not yet begun

to do so, has not yet readied himself for the revelations of the first-person diary form of *Autumn Journal*.

As a group, the four eclogues record a transition in MacNeice's understanding of the One from that of a transcendental monism to a belief in a tentative social unity that has similarities to the ideas of William James, who claimed that business, diplomatic, and even postal systems constitute "innumerable little hangings-together of the world's parts."[12] At the end of this period, MacNeice's newfound interest in such "little hangings-together" resulting from interpersonal relationships allowed him to conceive of a tension between society and the individual, between unity and plurality, which had eluded him previously. Although he had rejected the Christian ethic of his father, a clergyman, MacNeice at the beginning of his career still sought for a means of defending a belief in a religious or Idealistic unity in the face of a materialistic world: "I wanted the world to be One, to be permanent, the incarnation of an absolute Idea" (*SF*, 124). One of his early poems, "The Creditor," which affirms a religious unity, opens the *Collected Poems*:

> The peacefulness of the fire-blaze
> Will not erase
> My debts to God for His mind strays
> Over and under and all ways
> All days and always.

(ll. 10–14)

He longed for the comfort of such a belief, recognizing later that "[t]he Form of the Good, the One, may be food or it may be dope but it stops the hunger of the waifs of Here and Now" (*SF*, 125). After rejecting his father's religion, the young MacNeice looked to philosophy to satisfy his spiritual hunger for a transcendent One. In Canto XIII of *Autumn Journal* (1938), he recalls the attraction of the Idealism he was taught at Oxford and the security of such a belief:

> And it made one confident to think that nothing
>   Really was what it seemed under the sun,
> That the actual was not real and the real was not with us
>   And all the mattered was the One.

And they said "The man in the street is so naïve, he never
    Can see the wood for the trees;
He thinks he knows he sees a thing but cannot
    Tell you how he knows the thing he thinks he sees."
And oh how much I liked the Concrete Universal,
    I never thought that I should
Be telling them vice-versa
    That they can't see the trees for the wood.

(p. 126)

After finding his middle way, when MacNeice rejected the notion of a transcendent One in favor of social unity and began to focus on the trees as well as the wood; he did so emphatically, concluding his commentary in Canto XIII with a farewell to Plato and Hegel: "The shop is closing down; / They don't want any philosopher-kings in England, / There ain't no universals in this man's town" (p. 127). By 1940, he was even more outspoken on the subject, vehemently rejecting monism in a poem explicitly titled "Plurality":

The smug philosophers lie who say the world is one;
World is other and other, world is here and there,
Parmenides would smother life for lack of air
Precluding birth and death; his crystal never breaks—
No movement and no breath, no progress nor mistakes,
Nothing begins or ends, no one loves or fights.

(ll. 2–7)

Like Parmenides, "The modern monist too castrates, negates our lives" (l. 11). MacNeice rejects transcendent monism on the grounds that it is the flux of life and the differences between individuals that constitute life and art. Using the same metaphor as does Frost in "Build Soil"—the mixing of colors—MacNeice declares in "Poetry To-day" (1935), "We must maintain differences. Or else we must be honest monist-nihilists and not meddle with the arts. It is honest to say of a picture 'It doesn't matter which colour goes there, it's all canvas underneath,' but it is not honest, if one holds this point of view, to become a painter" (SLC, 18). His rejection of Idealism also led to his sympathy for the contemporary leftist aesthetic, as he declared in 1938 that art "has often been regarded recently as an escape from the actual to some transcendent reality on the pattern of Plato's Forms, whereas Marxist materialism ignores *transcendent* realities and is therefore a good creed for the artist who must move in a concrete world" (*MP*, 25). It is not the belief in reality that he rejects, only the belief in an abstraction which transcends and controls this world, leaving no room at all for individuality.

MacNeice's rejection of monism, then, does not preclude for him a belief in the possibility of an ephemeral social unity comprised of active individuals; he envisions a paradoxical oneness in which, as in an agglomerate, the character of the whole depends on the discreteness of its parts. This is an *e pluribus unum* philosophy in which, as Peter McDonald suggests, "the political good resides in individuals rather than in *the* individual" and, "the blueprint for a just society is . . . a socialized dialogue of self and soul in which one individual is incomplete without others."[13] MacNeice insists that the resulting society "is more than men in the mass, just as a man is something more than a conglomeration of cells. The fact that soul is inseparable from body does not disprove soul" (*SLC*, 113). In such a unity, society acquires a value beyond the sum of its parts, and MacNeice comes to view the creation of poetry as dependent on the same process of immanent unification. In *Modern Poetry*, he writes approvingly of the *New Signatures* conception of the poem as a union of individual experiences which synthesizes the One and Many of human experience: "On the one side is concrete living—not just a conglomeration of animals or machines, mere flux, a dissolving hail of data, but a system of individuals determined by their circumstances, a concrete, therefore, of sensuous fact and what we may call 'universals'; on the other side is a concrete poet—not just an eye or a heart or a brain or a solar plexus, but the whole man reacting with both intelligence and emotion . . . to experiences, and on this basis presenting something which is (a) communication, a record, but is also (b) a creation—having a new unity of its own, something in its shape which makes it poetry" (*MP*, 29–30). This type of unity, he says, relies on the free expression of individual will, and at the end of "Plurality," he expresses approval for the Sisyphean efforts of man to "transcend and flout the human span: / A species become rich by seeing things as wrong / And patching them" (ll. 64–66). The rewards of such transcendence result not from a static truth situated beyond our world, but in the process of imposing order on the chaos of the universe, for "Raising a frail scaffold in a never-ending flux" (l. 69), man may become "conscious also of love and the joy of things and the power / Of going beyond and above the limits of the lagging hour" (ll. 77–78). He continues to emphasize that it is the unending process of the creation of order that is important, not the transient structure created. "Human efforts are daily unifying the world more and more in definite systematic ways" writes James in *Pragmatism*; "[w]e found colonial, postal, consular, commercial systems. . . . The result is innumerable little hangings-together of the world's parts within the larger hangings-together, little worlds."[14] MacNeice, in the Europe of 1938, recognizes the impermanence of colonial, diplomatic, and financial systems, but he maintains the value of the effort:

> Who am I—or I—to demand oblivion?
> I must go out to-morrow as the others do
>   And build the falling castle;
> Which has never fallen, thanks
>   Not to any formula, red tape or institution,
> Not to any creeds or banks,
>   But to the human animal's endless courage.[15]

When systems fail to hang together, when things fall apart, we must look, he says, not to some transcendent authority, but to ourselves, and the faith he expresses is a faith in humanity's ability to create more than one unity out of the flux.

The eclogues reflect MacNeice's movement toward this philosophy. In the first poem in the series, "An Eclogue for Christmas" (1933), he begins a quest for the middle way. This eclogue focuses on his disenchantment with the oppositions of One and Many; by taking up a position outside of the apparent duality, he ends up rejecting both sides. In the next poem, "Eclogue by a Five-Barred Gate" (1934), he rejects the ideas of unity he perceives as available to him, denouncing two different types of transcendence: Idealism and Death, both of which he views as escapist. At the end of "Eclogue from Iceland" (1936), the speakers take the final step toward his eventual conception of a just society as they reject Romantic notions of the isolated hero in favor of the active, engaged individual. The last of the "eclogues," "Eclogue Between the Motherless" (1937), pushes the boundaries of the poet's movement toward pluralism, emphasizing the limitations of interpersonal relationships. Subtle differences in MacNeice's relationship to the reader in these dialogues correspond to the focus of each poem, with "Eclogue from Iceland" demonstrating the closest approach and "Eclogue Between the Motherless" the most distant. Together, the four poems provide a record of the internal debates that led to MacNeice's adoption of the middle way of *Autumn Journal*.

In the first of the series, "An Eclogue for Christmas," two speakers labeled "A" and "B" meet on Christmas Day, the anniversary of the Incarnation. Despite the split into two separate voices, they represent a single personality (MacNeice himself) who stands outside of the duality of country and city, in which the apparent One of history and the promised One of communism both give way to mechanistic materialism. Both speakers decry the decline of their respective civilizations. In the tradition of the Virgilian eclogue, the poem consists of an encounter between the urban and the rural, but A's pilgrimage to the countryside occurs in no golden age—he says they meet "in an evil time" (p. 33)—nor is B's countryside any *locus amoenus*. "B" recognizes "A" as an "analogue of me," and advises him that "One place is as bad as another" (p. 33). "A," a denizen of London, criticizes the city's obsession with temporal pleasures, and "B," the country man, opposes the oblivion of history, the "bland ancestral ease" of his neighbors. Together, A and B comprise a sort of Janus-faced speaker who looks in one direction toward a decadent society concerned only with the present and in the other direction toward a decaying society embedded in its past. A's city and B's countryside represent the two radically opposed environments between which MacNeice found himself torn as a youth: as the son of an Irish clergyman, his home life centered on religion and morality, while at school, his classmates embraced a fashionable aestheticism, a duality that Brown cites as the genesis of MacNeice's skepticism.[16]

B represents the grown-up MacNeice who rejects the ideals of a youth spent in the Irish countryside. As a young child, he came under the influence of his sister Elizabeth, his elder by several years, who "took refuge in a cult of the Old," an escape abetted by their surroundings, which included an atmospheric Norman church and castle (*SF*, 50). This resort to the unity of history probably provided a sense of stability for two motherless children, but in B's countryside, stability has hardened into stasis. B imagines that the rural gentry, petrified in their cult of the Old, will fall to obsolescence and subsequent extinction while the moon "Jeers at the end of us, our bland ancestral ease" (p. 34). Because they cannot adapt B predicts, "They will die in their shoes" (p. 35). The inhabitants of the countryside cannot accept the flux of life, so their only future lies in extinction.

B's "analogue," A, takes the role of a MacNeice disenchanted with his schoolboy aestheticism. He recalls in his memoir that his expectation when he arrived at Oxford was of life as "a Pateresque affair of hard gemlike flames, a sequence of purely aesthetic sensations, except of course for the erotic ones" (*SF*, 231). Under the influence of prep school classmate Anthony Blunt, he became enamored of "pure form," but this quest for the One led only to fragmentation. Like a Picasso portrait, he says, he has been "sifted and splintered in broken facets," a man who has "not been allowed to be / Myself in flesh or face, but abstracting and dissecting me / They have made of me pure form, a symbol or a pastiche" (p. 33); as a result, he has become nothing more than an unthinking "automaton." His schoolboy aesthetics remained on the side of the Many through his time at Oxford as he recalls: "Style remained more important than subject. The magic words—Relativity and the Unconscious—were always on our lips and we were pathetically eager to be realist (which meant the mimesis of flux)" (*SF*, 118). MacNeice links this worship of the flux to the urban settings in which he lived as a young adult; A's city, with its streets dug up for the installation of "Ever-changing conveniences," where "nothing comfortable remains / Unimproved" (p. 34), is inhabited by soulless materialists desperately undertaking continual Protean shifts in an effort to escape the past, trying always to experience some new sensation, and continuously on the move to the sounds of jazz music.

Through A and B, MacNeice rejects two illusory unities—the theoretical unity of communism, to which British poets of the 1930s were flocking, and the stagnating traditionalism of the bourgeoisie. Both city and country in "An Eclogue for Christmas" flaunt their materialism, inviting communist revolution. While the city dwellers are "choked with furs" (p. 34) and stockinged in silk, the country gentry, according to B, have become nothing more than their possessions, the "flotsam of private property, pekinese and polyanthus" and will die in "a paltry fizzle" (p. 35) when the state appropriates their ancestral homes and hunting grounds. A and B see a country ripe for overthrow and ask what will happen when private property is abolished. The answer, according to B, is that communism will only institute new insults against humanity: "the whore and the buffoon / Will come off best; no dreamers, they cannot lose their dream / And are at least likely to be reinstated in the new régime" (p. 36). According to MacNeice's account in *The Strings Are False*, his distrust of communism in conjunction with his disgust at British society's materialism led directly to the composition of this poem. "I had a certain hankering to sink my ego," he recalls, "but was repelled by the priggishness of the Comrades and suspected that their positive programme was vitiated by wishful thinking and over-simplification. I joined them however in their hatred of the *status quo*, I wanted to smash the aquarium" (*SF*, 146). He wrote the eclogue "with a kind of cold-blooded passion and when it was done it surprised me. Was I really as concerned as all that with the Decline of the West? Did I really feel so desperate? Apparently I did" (146).

Further on in *The Strings are False*, MacNeice explains why he views both the bourgeoisie and the Communist Party as adherents of the Many: "While there were many motives driving the intelligentsia towards the C.P., there was one great paradox nearly always present; intellectuals turned to communism as an escape from materialism. Materialism, that is, in the popular sense—that materialism which in more easy and archaic pockets of the country bolsters up the physical comfort of individuals and which, in places where people think, had for so long acknowledged the principle of enlightened self-interest, of mere utilitarianism, as man's only ideal in a mechanistic universe" (*SF*, 169). In a 1935 essay, MacNeice derides both the bourgeoisie and the communists as proponents of the Many: "The individualist is an atom thinking about himself (Thank God I am not as other men); the communist, too often, is an atom having ecstaies of self-denial (Thank God I am one in a crowd)" (*SLC*, 6). He rejects both the "enlightened self-interest" of the gentry and the "hankering" to extinguish his personality in a collective, and he takes up a position outside the conflict. His desire for unity therefore paradoxically leads him to retreat to a unique vantage point. Establishing a position outside a duality was nothing new for MacNeice; circumstances had relegated him to the role of outsider since childhood, a role he later relished. In *The Strings Are False*, MacNeice recounts a number of incidents in which he discovered that the world was divided into two groups and that he belonged to neither. He recalls the first time (at age nine) that he came to this realization after seeing a farmwoman mistreating a dog, an incident he says taught him that the "Lower Classes were dour and hostile" (*SF*, 58). "Not that the Gentry were much better," he continues; he sensed that they barely tolerated him, the son of a clergyman. Later, at Oxford, the young MacNeice discovered that at that university, "homosexuality and 'intelligence,' heterosexuality and brawn, were almost inexorably paired," and this dichotomized social structure, he writes, "left me out in the cold and I took to drink" (103). At Oxford, MacNeice's friend John Hilton found him to be self-absorbed in a manner that would guarantee his alienation from any number of social groups or institutions. According to Hilton, MacNeice was uninterested in others; "he was concerned largely with his own forces—and the aspects of the outer world that got reflected in or swept along with and transmogrified by their currents" (240). And as the native son of a country split between Catholics and Protestants, MacNeice removed himself from that debate by marrying a Jew and declaring himself agnostic.[17]

By taking up a stance outside the duality, MacNeice achieves a viewpoint similar to that of the observer from the Overworld in *The Dynasts*, the position accorded to the artist by Schopenhauer. Michael O'Neill and Gareth Reeves find that MacNeice assumes this outsider position throughout his work and attribute it to "the attempt to find poetic life in the demotic," an attempt that "demands a scrutinizing frame of mind."[18] But MacNeice himself, in "An Eclogue for Christmas," suggests that his outsider role indeed originates in Schopenhauer. Both A and B subscribe to the Schopenhauerean concept of an underlying Will that controls the behavior of an unknowing populace, but

which superior individuals like themselves are able to discern
As in Hardy's *The Dynasts*, people think that they are individu
als, but only because they are "blind / To the fact that they are
merely the counters of an unknown Mind" (p. 34), that they are
merely wind-up toys set in motion by "A Mind that does no
think, if such a thing can be, / Mechanical Reason, capricious
Identity" (p. 34). MacNeice, who according to classmate John
Hilton, "preferred to study mankind indirectly," regarding them
"as specimens, bearers of the potentialities of the race, concrete
universals perhaps" (*SF*, 241), explains his behavior (and that of
A and B) by citing Schopenhauer's idea of the Will, which should
provide great freedom for the individual, but "one lets it rip
then cannot put the drag on, the Will runs away with the lot of
us, we have no more choice in the matter than a falling stone"
(32). As a result of this runaway individuality, he continues, "I
like many others, though wrongly, have lived a life of episodes
isolating incidents or people or aspects of people in the hope of
finding something self-contained, having despaired of a self
contained world" (33). A and B, at the end of the poem, set off to
resume this life of episodes, recognizing the futility of the search
for self-contained world—"The old idealist lie" (p. 36), B calls it
Yet they have no choice but to "lie once more"; since they have
no way to connect to any underlying unity, they each agree to
continue as individuals in their own societies.

At the end of the poem, MacNeice introduces the prospect of
attaining some sort of order in the flux of life, as B entreats, "Let
all these so ephemeral things / Be somehow permanent like the
swallow's tangent wings." He then reminds A that this is the
day of the Incarnation: "this morn / They say, interpret it you
own way, Christ is born" (p. 36). On Christmas day, not only i
the body united with the spirit, but the fleeting span of human
life is united with the eternal presence. On Christmas day, Mac
Neice suggests, Christ *is* born, not Christ *was* born—the cycl
repeats perpetually because neither is God perpetually incarnate
nor is God pure spirit. B's plea for unity is no more than a wistfu
prayer, and he has no idea how such ephemeral things might be
come permanent, but he suggests that a unity composed of the
ephemeral, the material, is the only proper One. In *The Poetr
of W. B. Yeats*, MacNeice declares that, in discussions of abstrac
tions, "we tend to suppose a gulf between this abstracted valu

and the thing which is valuable. This seems to me wrong. . . . Idealist philosophers in talking about their Absolutes and Universals have made them vulnerable by hypostatizing them, whereas the only invulnerable Universal is one that is incarnate" (*PWBY*, 15). He returns in "Plurality" to the image of the swallow's wings to illustrate his mature conception of this potential unity:

> And, if we use the word Eternal, stake a claim
> Only to what a bird can find within the frame
> Of momentary flight (the value will persist
> But as event the night sweeps it away in mist).
>
> (ll. 55–58)

As they part, A and B each agree to return to their respective lives and, as Robyn Marsack suggests, "accept their doom with a kind of morbid relish;"[19] MacNeice has not yet fully developed his solution to the problem of the One and the Many in "An Eclogue for Christmas," the ephemeral things do not attain permanence, and the flight of a swallow does not help them relate to society.

In "Eclogue by a Five-Barred Gate" (1934), MacNeice creates another dialogue between representatives of his former selves, in the form of two shepherds "of the Theocritean breed" who practice an escapist (Georgian) poetics, and "Death," the embodiment of a universal (modernist) aesthetic, which MacNeice views as another type of escape. The two sides of the discussion in effect represent two different conceptions of unity: Idealism on the part of the shepherds and the nullification represented by eternity on the part of Death. Neither of these conceptions of the One represents a proper engagement with life. Instead of standing outside of the duality in "Eclogue by a Five-Barred Gate," MacNeice's shepherds ("1" and "2") veer from one side to the other. Between the oblivion of Idealism and the oblivion of Death, they momentarily find themselves as individuals, but cannot sustain those identities.

MacNeice uses the convention of the singing contest associated with the eclogue form to illustrate an improper unity, a recourse to a history from which modern man gains no insights and to which he has no emotional connection. One of his problems with Georgian poetry is the poem's disconnection from the subject matter; he suggests in *Modern Poetry* that any subject matter is fit for poetry as long as it is of "intellectual or emotional or moral significance" for the poet, but without that significance, the poem will have "no backbone" (*MP*, 6). The conventional eclogue exemplifies poetry lacking such significance, a form which, from the time of Theocritus, has idealized the pastoral life to such an extent that it bears no relationship to the reality of such a life; the defining features of the eclogue include what W. W. Greg called "those delicate touches of refined sentiment that in Theocritus appear so incongruous with the rough coats and rougher banter of the shepherds."[20] The reason that the eclogue never attained any status as significant poetry, according to Greg, was that despite the popularity of such poems in various societies, up to and including those of Pope and Spenser, "the simple sensuous ideal was too much hampered by the ungenuine paraphernalia which the conventions of these various societies had gathered round it to take rank among the permanent and inevitable forms of literary art."[21]

In the mechanistic twentieth century, the paraphernalia of pastoral poetry seems even more ungenuine than in the rural past, and the shepherds of "Eclogue by a Five-Barred Gate," in their foolishly consistent mimicry of eclogue conventions, produce verse that has no significance for them; they have no knowledge of the meaning behind the words they write, as they reveal when confronted by Death at the entrance to his domain:

> D. This won't do, shepherds, life is not like that,
>   And when it comes to death I may say he is not like that.
>   Have you never thought of death?
> 1.   Only off and on,
>   Thanatos in Greek, the accent proparoxytone—
>
> (p. 37)

MacNeice associates Georgian poetry in particular with this type of escapism; he identifies Theocritus as an escapist poet (*MP*, 7) and associates the Georgians with the stylized shepherds of the conventional eclogue form, contending that they "idyll-

ized the country-side without being rooted . . . in their subject"
and that "[t]hey are mainly townsmen on excursion" (8). In the
world of jazz musicians, smog, and traffic described by A in "An
Eclogue for Christmas," the resort to pastoral poetry has no intellectual or emotional or moral significance.

In his condemnation of the escapism of the two shepherds,
Death at first appears to encourage them as individuals to find
such significance in their own poetry. At the beginning of the
poem, they speak in Georgian tones and are mocked by Death in
return; in response to 2's fanciful, "But certainly poets are
sleepers, / The sleeping beauty behind the many-coloured hedge—"
(p. 37), Death responds, "All you do is burke the other and terri-
ble beauty, all you do is hedge / And shirk the inevitable issue,
all you do / Is shear your sheep to stop your ears" (pp. 37–38).
When 1 evades a question as to whether he ever feels old by saying, "It is a question we all have to answer, / And I may say that
when I smell the beans or hear the thrush / I feel a wave intensely bitter sweet and topped with silver—" (p. 38), Death reminds them of their mortality, of their temporality:

> All time is not your tear-off jotter, you cannot afford to scribble
> So many false answers.
> This escapism of yours is blasphemy,
> An immortal cannot blaspheme for one way or another
> His trivialities will pattern in the end;
> But for you your privilege and panic is to be mortal.
>
> (p. 38)

In mocking the self-conscious artificiality of the shepherd-poets,
Death mocks the poetry of MacNeice's own youth and therefore
appears at this point in the poem to represent the poet's present
self.

MacNeice devotes an entire chapter of *Modern Poetry* to a
self-accusation strikingly similar to Death's condemnation of
the shepherds' escapism. In this chapter, he recalls that as a
youth he perceived his life as "so inadequate to my emotional
demands that I fled towards euphuism on the one hand and a
dream-world on the other" (*MP*, 52–53). Looking back on his
past theories of poetry, in which he advocated all of the traits
ridiculed by Death in "Eclogue by a Five-Barred Gate," he exam-

ines one of his Oxford term papers which claims: "[W]e should exploit our self-consciousness and not fall into trances of automatic writing. To be thoroughly conscious of oneself is very difficult, and this is, I think, the first reason why men write poetry. It is to introduce myself to me." In reading this passage MacNeice admits that at the time, "Metaphysically, I was very near solipsism" (64). He continues: "Then, on the metaphysical ground that all plurality is make-believe anyway, I write: 'If you must write poetry, don't decline the charge of artificiality. It is only a further link in a chain of artifices—Life, men, society, language. The more the sounder. Lie often enough and your lies will be truth." The poetry that he produced during this same period at Oxford appears in his first book, *Blind Fireworks* (1929), in which, according to McDonald, "the self-consciousness of its use of mythological metaphor as deferral of reality entails a general retreat from reality into system which its rather precious ironies are insufficient to reverse."[22] If life, society, and language are only artifices, then the ultimate reality from which the poet retreats would be death.

While Death does represent some aspect of the poet's present self in his rejection of MacNeice's past acceptance of Idealism and artificiality, he also symbolizes a transcendent unity that results in the failure of poetry altogether, so he may be associated with the poet's early desire for such a One. Invoking one of the conventions of the eclogue, the singing contest, Death offers the shepherds a prize for the best description of one of their dreams. When he asks them to search the unconscious world of dreams, he is asking them to search their personal mystical level in order to find a transcendent unity, much as do the characters in *The Age of Anxiety*. The shepherds do as he asks, finding dreams true to their individual selves, but their success results in nullification. Both of the shepherds report a connection in their dreams with a transcendent world. Shepherd 1 dreams that "a face was swung in my eyes like a lantern / Swinging on the neck of a snake / And that face I knew to be God, and I woke" (p. 39), And 2, whose sensual dream includes a sexual encounter—"I found her with my hands lying on the drying hay, / Wet heat in the deeps of the hay as my hand delved, / And I possessed her, gross and good like the hay (p. 39)"—sees a vision of Jacob, angels ascending, and descending ladders to heaven. McDonald interprets both of the dreams as instances of recognition of the other by the previously self-centered shepherds, where the first represents "the awareness of the other discovered inside the self" and the second symbolizes "the point of real communication—sexual and non-verbal—with the other as it exists outside the self,"[23] but both find in the plane below consciousness not only an other, but intimations of a transcendent One. Death accepts both of their dreams and, as their "prize," invites the shepherds to enter his land, but as soon as they walk through his gate, they cease to exist. The gate to Death's land, he says, is nothing more than "the façade of a mirage" (p. 40). In their recognition of and confrontation with Death, the two shepherds learn to face a reality outside of themselves, but by entering into his One, they nullify their individual lives.

Throughout his later works, MacNeice insists on the potential destructiveness of a monistic reality. In "Plurality," he imagines unity itself as a kind of death, and life consists of Man's struggle against "the One," the "Absolute, the row of noughts where time is done, / Where nothing goes or comes and Is is one with Ought / And all the possible sums alike resolve to nought" (ll. 34–36). In *The Poetry of W. B. Yeats*, he explains why Death's way negates the production of poetry specifically, why when the shepherds move from searching their unconsciousnesses to entering into the transcendent unity, the possibility of poetry ceases to exist; poets must remain in the world, neither giving in to the animal urges impelling them from a lower stage, nor ascending permanently to mystical union with the One, because "the poet's job is to be articulate and man cannot be articulate unless he makes distinction; the logical outcome of mysticism is silence" (*PWBY*, 24). Whereas his friend Auden advocates the desirability of the Ones of both the internal and external planes, and particularly the latter, in *The Age of Anxiety*, MacNeice rejects both. Life and poetry might originate out of immanent and transcendent unities, but life does not *happen* in those realms. Both life and poetry rely on flux and therefore cannot occur in the stasis of the One.

The defiance of the Absolute partially defines man according to MacNeice, and Brown finds the apprehension critical to this philosophy: "The sceptical MacNeice believes in no transcendent reality but rather in the possibility of non-existence. The value of life depends on the possibility of death. The land is valuable because of the eroding sea, a garden is valuable in view of the great waste outside. Value is found in the fact, in view of the non-fact. It is to be found in things themselves, not in any transcendent realm of Ideas or religious otherworld. Value depends on a dialectic, between life and death."[24] The possibility of death, not death itself, provides this value. In one of the poems in which MacNeice addresses the value of such a dialectic, "The Stygian Banks," he imagines the river that bounds Death's land as a limit that fosters creation:

> The closed window,
> The river of Styx, the wall of limitation
> Beyond which the word beyond loses its meaning,
> Are the fertilizing paradox. The grill
> That, severing, joins, the end to make us begin.
>
> (p. 267)

The river surrounding Death's land stimulates life by providing a boundary, but once the river is crossed, all limits dissolve within Death's realm. In "Eclogue by a Five-Barred Gate," while mocking the escapism of the shepherds, Death asserts to them that "poetry is not only the bridging of two-banked rivers," and 2 replies, "Who ever heard of a river without a further bank?" (p. 38). McDonald suggests that Death "epitomizes the idea of a 'river without a further bank'" in the poem,[25] and MacNeice himself associates this particular image with Death when he recalls a day when he came upon a river covered by a fog that was "so thick that the river had no further bank. A Lethe where everything ends and nothing begins" (SF, 153). Where water, or life, has no boundaries, all resolves to nought, an idea that MacNeice also highlights later in the poem. In response to the shepherds' anxiety that their dreams will not "wear well," Death employs an image similar to Bergson's vision of life as a rising wave: "Water appears tower only while in well— / All from the same comes" (p. 39). Without the confines of the body, the spirit will return to its source and will return to the One—a positive prospect for Bergson, but disaster in MacNeice's eyes.

By the time he produced "Eclogue from Iceland" in 1936, Mac-Neice had almost fully developed his notion of a unity comprising unique, active individuals, and his poetry was becoming more personal and more autobiographical. He and Auden traveled together to Iceland in the summer of 1936, having been commissioned to write a book about their experiences there (*Letters from Iceland*), and they appear in the poem as "Ryan" and "Craven," respectively. The discussion takes place between the two poets, who embrace the notion of the Romantic hero as the ideal man, and the ghost of Grettir Asmundson, who for them represents such a man. However, Grettir, a timeless figure, desperately desires to rejoin society and is prevented from doing so only by an ancient curse. He advises the poets that they must return to society, that the retreat into isolation is not the answer. Despite the overt identification of Ryan with the poet, the speakers all represent aspects of MacNeice's past and present selves. Together Ryan and Craven represent MacNeice's past tendency to withdraw into idealism and Grettir his present desire to "build the falling castle" or to raise "the frail scaffold" in defiance of unending flux.

As would-be Romantic rebels and poets, Ryan and Craven admire loners like Grettir "who working from / The common premises did not end with many / In the blind alley where the trek began" (p. 46). As such, they represent the school-age Mac-Neice who, by his seventeenth year, considered Shelley as "*the* great poet" and wrote "a number of Shelleyan poems defying or renouncing everyday life and its codes" (*MP*, 50). His adoration of the individual who shuns society continued during his years at Oxford, where he found himself enamored of Nietzsche—"'Up Dionysus!' became my slogan," he recalls (*SF*, 110). Ryan and Craven share the young poet's enthusiasm for "those who go their own way, will not kiss / The arse of law and order nor compound / For physical comfort at the price of pride," those who "prefer to taunt the mask of God, / Bid him unmask and die in the living lightning" ("Iceland," p. 44) and they put forth a series of examples of such men, including Chekhov and Stephen MacKenna.

At the outset of the poem, Grettir, a self-described outlaw, appears to the two poets as an archetype of the Romantic hero, the epitome of the mode in which they imagine themselves. In previous drafts of the poem, MacNeice further emphasized their identification with the saga hero by having Ryan inquire at Grettir's entrance, "Who could it be / Except the echo of you and me"?[26] Grettir quickly dismisses Ryan and Craven's illusions of his desirability as a role model, establishing a certain distance from his two visitors from his first appearance. For one thing, the poets can never achieve his status because he exists only as a ghost, a legendary one at that, and he forthrightly identifies himself as such. Grettir highlights his status as a figment of the imagination by warning Ryan and Craven to beware the dangers presented by illusory companions; he recalls men who died when they embraced "Wives of mist" ("Iceland," p. 41) Not only does Grettir not represent their own kind, but he insults the travelers by inquiring whether they are among the "Greedy young men . . . / . . . / Who leap the toothed and dour crevasse / Of death on a sardonic phrase?" (p. 41). If Ryan and Craven choose to identify with his status as an exile, Grettir cannot stop them; but, in his speeches he emphasizes his differences from these intellectuals fleeing their responsibilities. Grettir lives in exile not as a result of his own volition, but as the result of a curse. He is a "man of will and muscle" who revels in physical challenges, not a poet or thinker and, unlike Ryan and Craven, he has "Always had to move on; craving company" (p. 42).

The two poets have fled their homes because they find no companionship in their fellow men and women who revel in their existence as Many, precluding the appreciation of any sort of unity. Craven describes his peers as possessed of "that compelling stare / Stare which betrays the cosmic purposelessness" and backed by a "nightmare noise" of "Time sharpening his blade" (p. 46). Among these people, the possibility of true communion is unknown. The women who "never loving would be loved by others," according to Craven live alongside men who appear loyal, but "Who yet are ready to plug you as you drink" (p. 47). Ryan describes the women's devotion to the material:

> The permutations of lapels and gussets,
> Of stuffs—georgette or velvet or corduroy—
> Of hats and eye-veils, of shoes, lizard or suede,
> Of bracelets, milk or coral, of zip bags
> Of compacts, lipstick, eyeshade and coiffures.
>
> (pp. 47–48)

MacNeice dismisses all such ornamentation as "surface," and Craven claims this is all that they have found on their travels. Even on their trip to Spain before the civil war,[27] they found in the beggars, the architecture, the bullfights, even in the "scrawled hammer and sickle," nothing but "copy—impenetrable surface." And in Iceland: "More copy, more surface" ("Iceland," p. 42). Like A in "An Eclogue for Christmas," they expected to find a simpler, more complete life in a less developed society, but have found that one place is no better than the other.

If Craven and Ryan seek validation from Grettir, they do not get it; he advises them to return and face the forces of the Many directly. In the face of their objections, Grettir insists, saying, "I tell you still / Go back to where you belong" ("Iceland," p. 47) The poets agree, but assert that they can do little in the cause of the One; as mere mortals, they can do nothing but martyr themselves. Grettir assures them that the effort itself matters: "Minute your gesture but it must be made—" (p. 47). The castle may continue to fall, but they must continue to build it back up through the "assertion of human values." "It is your only duty," he says, "And, it may be added, it is your only chance" (p. 47). Whereas in "An Eclogue for Christmas," MacNeice has A and B agree to return to their respective societies and accept their fates passively, praying to the unknown god to impose some unity, in "Eclogue from Iceland," he insists that the poets must take an active, if futile, role.

Taking an active role requires taking a stand, and MacNeice no longer depicts his past and present selves standing outside of the duality; "Eclogue from Iceland" contains real debate, and he gives Grettir the last word, indicating the dominance of Grettir's position. MacNeice also communicates a clear disapproval of the two exiled poets' Romanticism. Craven acknowledges that his and Ryan's roles as poets have been nothing but pose and pretence and that their understanding of real artists is superficial and secondhand at best. They will return to Europe, he admits, "To preen ourselves on the reinterpretation / Of the words of obsolete interpreters" and to "leaning forward to knock out our pipes / Into the fire protest that art is good" (p. 44). In addition to the two poets' own admissions of shallowness and pretense, MacNeice satirizes their escapism through his choice of names—mocking his own self-importance through the name "Ryan" ("little king" in Gaelic) and insinuating their cowardice with "Craven"—and by having them speak their opening lines in awkward rhyming couplets (R: This is the place, Craven, the end of our way; / Hobble the horses, we have had a long day, p. 40).

MacNeice's identification of his present self with Grettir becomes clear when he allows Grettir to prevail in the argument, and his approval becomes even clearer when "Eclogue from Iceland" is read in conjunction with *Autumn Journal*. Not only does Grettir's stance correspond to the philosophy expressed by MacNeice in *Autumn Journal*, but as a "man of will and muscle" he represents an ideal of the active man, the kind that MacNeice lauds in this poem:

> Aristotle was right to think of man-in-action
>   As the essential and really existent man
> And man means men in action; try and confine your
>   Self to yourself if you can.
>
> (p. 136)

Leading up to this declaration in Canto XVII, MacNeice presents some of his clearest statements of the need for engagement. The escapism of solitude, in which "all our trivial daily acts are altered / Into heroic or romantic make-believe" (p. 134), he suggests, can never provide lasting pleasure; we relish the sybaritic pleasures of a hot bath, but soon "this lagoon grows cold, we have to leave it" and ask ourselves, "Who could expect—or want—to be spiritually self-supporting, / Eternal self-abuse?" (p. 135). "Why not admit," he asks, "that other people are always / Organic to the self, that a monologue is the death of language" (p. 135). Although MacNeice in *Autumn Journal* puts it much more elegantly than does Grettir in the eclogue, they agree in substance on the need to face reality and to interact with others.

The last of the four eclogues, "Eclogue Between the Motherless" (1937) demonstrates the limits of MacNeice's trend toward a pluralistic viewpoint. Most critics treat this poem separately from the other three poems (if at all) because it abandons all pretense of claim to the eclogue tradition, consisting of a dialogue between speakers A and B on the subject of loneliness and marriage. The discussion is dominated by A, who represents the desire for pluralism in his desperation to escape his past by marrying a soulless "perfect stranger." B, in his relatively few lines, expresses a vain desire for unity, for a continuity with the past which he sought in marriage; but he has found such oneness impossible to achieve. The absence of any of the conventions of the eclogue, the lack of a pastoral setting or names or a singing contest, also accords with A's move toward the temporality of the Many, since the poem itself eschews any place in the One of tradition. And, unlike the other eclogues, which are anchored by a situation and a location, "Eclogue Between the Motherless" appears as a single point in time; MacNeice provides the discussion no dramatic frame at all, no setting, and no announcement by the speakers of their identities. The two speakers remain at odds at the end of the poem (B: "You must be out of your mind," p. 51), and the only underlying unity derives from the identification of both speakers with aspects of MacNeice, with A representing his present and B his past.

A, whose mother died in childbirth, is haunted by the past and by family associations and wishes to escape both. At his home, the house and gardens fall to ruins while his father drinks and his sister resents her role as housekeeper; about his visit there, he says, "In a way it went too far, / Back to childhood, back to the backwoods mind; / I could not stand a great deal of it" ("Motherless," p. 48). He dreams of his mother, and each worn item associated with his childhood in the house haunts him: "all kept reminding me, binding / My feet to the floating past" (p. 49). Life cannot proceed without change; frozen in the stasis of history, he cannot move forward. Only by breaking free from the unity of the past will he be able to live, and if he marries a replica of his mother, he will never escape. He seeks to replace his mother with a "stranger" and to detach himself from his family.

Form rather than content is what A seeks. Attempting to overcome a past that has come too close, he pursues distance. The perfect woman will be "Someone immutably alien" (p. 50) who will "Be careless, be callous, be glass frolic of prisms / Be eyes of guns through lashes of barbed wire, / Be the gaoler's smile and all that breaks the past" (p. 57). Assuring himself that he may marry while remaining essentially alone, he has written a proposal to a woman he barely knows. When B demands to know to whom he has proposed, A refuses to divulge her name, revealing only that she is in India and has only a year to live. Marsack points out that A's proposal to a dying woman imposes a limit on the relationship; she suggests that he does this so that the end "is no one's 'fault.' "[28] Placing such a boundary on the relationship, however, also assures that it will represent a discontinuity in time, an anomaly that will not become part of the continuity of history that haunts him. The limitation also ensures that the woman will never unite with him; he will not become half of a couple, and his individuality will be preserved.

B, on the other hand, has sought both human connection and continuity with his past through marriage, yet has found himself alone. Of his marriage, he says, the beginning "Is heaven come back from the nursery—swansdown kisses—/ But after that one misses something" (p. 48). He regrets his attempt to find happiness in marriage, explaining to A that "One marries only / Because one thinks one is lonely—and so one was / But wait till the lonely are two and no better" (p. 48). B's wife represents hollow surface and soulless materialism, symbolized by her empty gloves that keep moving after she has taken them off (p. 49). Reprising the image of the surface represented by the gloves later in the poem, B responds to A's desire for such a woman:

> Odd ideals you have; all I wanted
> Was to get really close but closeness was
> Only a glove on the hand, alien and veinless,
> And yet her empty glove could move.
>
> (p. 57)

As in "An Eclogue for Christmas" and "Eclogue for Iceland," MacNeice communicates the hollowness of the body, her disassociation from the soul, through sumptuous images of material goods. Not only does B associate his wife with the gloves, but also recalls the image of her with their car at a gas station, draped in camelhair, where she appeared "Comfortable, scented and alien" (p. 50). He regrets his lack of connection with her and discourages the search for unity in marriage.

B's failed marriage echoes MacNeice's own marriage to Mary

(or Mariette) Beazley, which began at Oxford and ended in 1935, when Mary ran off with their houseguest. B's description of "heaven come back from the nursery" correlates to MacNeice's description of his marriage to Mary in a letter to Anthony Blunt: "Perhaps being married to M. was a sort of prolonged child-hood—many toys, much comfort, painted furniture, running one's hand over materials, handtomouth [sic] idyll as all idylls are."[29] Both MacNeice and B correlate marriage with childhood in the wake of the loss of a mother. Jon Stallworthy suggests that MacNeice associated Mary's abandonment with that of his mother, who, as the result of depression after a hysterectomy, was sent to a nursing home when Louis was five and never re-turned.[30] MacNeice's father later married Georgina Beatrice Greer, a member of one of the Carrickfergus's wealthiest fami-lies.[31] In "Eclogue Between the Motherless," B describes a simi-lar situation at home, doubting that his father could be happy married to a rich woman who wears jodhpurs and rides out be-fore breakfast.

After the breakup of his marriage, MacNeice himself, like A, discovered the charms of empty surfaces. In *The Strings Are False*, he describes a relationship he experienced in 1937 with an actress: "[A]ll eye-veils, furs and egotism. . . . My relationship with her was make-believe on both sides and it ended with her throwing a teatable at me" (*SF*, 170–71). *Autumn Journal* also provides evidence that A's wish for a surface relationship repre-sents aspects of MacNeice's own desires as concerned women. In Canto XXII, he declares:

> For, where there is the luxury of leisure, there
>   There should also be the luxury of women.
> I do not need you on my daily job
>   Nor yet on any spiritual adventure,
> Not when I earn my keep but when I rob
>   Time of his growth of tinsel:
> No longer thinking you or any other
>   Essential to my life—soul-mate or dual star;
> All I want is an elegant and witty playmate
>   At the perfume counter or the cocktail bar.
> . . . .
>   I need you badly,
>   Whatever your name or age or the colour of your hair;

> I need your surface company (what happens
> Below the surface is my own affair).

(Autumn Journal, pp. 146–47)

A few lines later, he reiterates that he badly needs this "age-old woman apt for all misuse / whose soul is out of the picture" (p. 147). Later in 1937, after his affair with Leonora, MacNeice had carried on an affair with a married woman named Nancy Coldstream, who like A's intended in India was unattainable. Such a woman allows him to fulfill his material needs without interfering with his spiritual life; he rejects any relationship which would hamper his role as the active individual.

While MacNeice implored critics to examine the "fusion" of dichotomies in a poet's work, his own work sometimes lacked the tension between the One and the Many required for such unification, a propensity which he himself notes in his essay "Experiences With Images" (1949): "But I think that, generally speaking, my basic conception of life being dialectical (in the philosophical, not in the political sense), I have tended to swing to and fro between descriptive or physical images . . . and *faute de mieux* metaphysical, mythical or mystical images" (*SLC*, 156). As he moved toward a philosophy that leans toward the Many, his poetry naturally swings in the direction of plurality. O'Neill and Reeves note, "Finding it difficult to free his mind from the attempt to reconcile the 'ephemeral' and the 'permanent,' in poetic terms the concrete and the abstract, . . . he is liable in some of his thirties poems to fall back on propounding a philosophy of the impermanent."[32] This "philosophy of the impermanent," however, is not a fallback position, but MacNeice's conception of the proper method for balancing One and Many. His eclogues of the mid-1930s demonstrate a bias toward plurality. The balance between the one voice of the poet and the many voices of the speakers in pure dialogue forms inherently tips slightly toward the Many unless the poet imposes some means of unifying the speakers and some means to emphasize his own voice, and MacNeice's failure to take advantage of any such techniques suggests that he was already well on his way to a wholehearted embrace of plurality. Nothing in the form of his eclogues places any emphasis on unity; he refrains from using any narrative that would provide him with a direction communication with the reader, and he maintains clear distinctions between his speakers. He also conceals the only consistent source of unity in the poems—the association of all of the speakers with his past and present selves.

Subtle differences in the distance between the speakers, however, can be correlated to the evolution from a mild bias toward unity to a distinct bias toward plurality. In the earliest of the poems, "An Eclogue for Christmas," a poem which expresses a longing for the One, the speakers A and B exhibit the greatest concord of any group of speakers in the eclogues. They agree with each other completely from the beginning—only their circumstances differ—and MacNeice states explicitly their status as "analogues." Because both agree in principle, although they face different challenges, MacNeice's own voice, his condemnation of materialism, is evident. However, the next poem, "Eclogue by a Five-Barred Gate," with its condemnation of different types of unity, lacks communion between the speakers; the exchange is dramatic, not dialectical, and Death directs the two shepherds throughout the piece, instead of engaging them in debate. Because Death dominates the poem, his voice appears consistent with that of MacNeice; MacNeice's disapproval of the limitlessness of Death's unity is not immediately evident, and the poet's voice is therefore partly suppressed.

In all likelihood, it is the inconsistencies in the relationships between the speakers in these two poems that has engendered some debate among critics as to whether or not the dialogues consist of dialectic. Marsack asserts that the eclogues "have a genuinely dialectical structure" and suggests that the eclogue form allows MacNeice to engage in "debate without requiring a resolution," that the "statement and counter-statement helped improve the construction of his poetry," an improvement she deems necessary because he fails elsewhere to "impose a clarifying order on his impressions, could just slide from one to the next."[33] McDonald objects to Marsack's characterization of the eclogues on the grounds that she implies that the poems "are partly exercises in inconclusion, their modish image-displays leading to nowhere but the poet's own 'uncertainty.'"[34] Marsack's remark that MacNeice slides from one position to the

other would seem to imply that she sees his viewpoint in flux
but McDonald interprets her statement as forcing MacNeice
outside of the dialogue:

> It is perhaps necessary to stress that "dialectic," from Plato onwards
> cannot be without direction, a rhetorical trick for getting nowhere
> if there is a sense in which the eclogues embody only a very slight
> progression of ideas, and seem to be without specific conclusions,
> then criticizing them in terms of "dialectic," a word whose Marxist
> associations MacNeice distrusted, may be inappropriate. In any case,
> it is easy to confuse this "dialectic" with drama, and so forget the
> significance of the eclogue form in the first place. A reading of these
> poems as debate that has been stage-managed so as to be without
> resolution sets MacNeice, as stage-manager, on precisely that "terra
> firma" somewhere above "the bewildering flux of modern life" men-
> tioned by Day-Lewis. However, a great many of the poet's contem-
> porary critics saw him as carefully avoiding this position.[35]

McDonald attributes the lack of dialectic to a fidelity on Mac-
Neice's part to the conventional eclogue form, in which the traditional singing contest "is in no sense part of any larger,
dialectically achieved meaning."[36] While he is correct in claiming that neither poem contains dialectic, his explanation fails to
take into account that MacNeice shows no allegiance to the eclogue form and, in fact, satirizes its conventions in "Eclogue by
a Five-Barred Gate," and both he and Marsack fail to recognize
that one poem lacks dialectic because the speakers are too close
and the other because the speakers are too far apart.

At the conclusion of "Eclogue from Iceland," the speakers do
engage in a bit of dialectic, resulting in their agreement that active individuals must work to build some sort of unity in society, and the relationships between the speakers over the course
of the poem echo this philosophy. After the dramatic introduction of the situation, Ryan, Craven, and Grettir move into a type
of singing contest where each speaks in turn, listing examples of
other exiles and loners. At the end of the poem, though, they
come together to engage in a debate that ends with agreement
among the three that Ryan and Craven should return to their
homes. MacNeice makes his own viewpoint clear by having the
two poets accede to Grettir's directive to return to society, a position that he verifies when he recalls that in the late 1930s he

was "reacting over much . . . against the concept of the solitary pure-minded genius saving his soul in a tower without doors" (*SF*, 173). Not only does he make his own voice prominent in this poem, but the use of names, rather than numbers or letters for the speakers, also suggests a greater engagement with the world, and with the reader in particular.

The last dialogue in the series, "Eclogue Between the Motherless," a poem whose theme is the want of closeness in interpersonal relationships, appropriately contains the least opportunity for communion between poet and reader of all the eclogues. Although labeled an eclogue, the poem blatantly disregards any conventions of place, subject matter, and identity of the speakers that readers might recognize from the conventional form. Besides detaching the poem from the unity of tradition, the lack of a physical or temporal setting helps to keep the reader at a remove from the speakers, and MacNeice provides no clues to the identities of the speakers; we do not know anything about them other than that they are both motherless and loverless. Because the reader knows nothing of the setting or the participants in the conversation, "Eclogue Between the Motherless" suffers badly from the eavesdropping effect, in which the reader feels that he is intruding on a private conversation and should leave. That effect is heightened in this poem because the exchange between the characters does not provide enough information for the reader to understand what is happening. The two speakers talk at each other for much of the poem, with A's long lyrical reminiscences dominating the talk. Because the dialogue contains no dialectic and no argument on either side, A's insistence on finding an empty relationship remains unexplained and confusing, and the reader remains unclear as to the point of the discussion.

This failure in "Eclogue Between the Motherless" to provide points of recognition for the reader violates MacNeice's own formulation for communication between poet and reader, suggesting that he means to overemphasize plurality in this poem. Although he does not consider poetry a vehicle for achieving a deep communion between poet and reader, he generally believes that some understanding between them is necessary and that the poet must provide the reader with something recognizable in order for that relationship to exist. In a 1936 essay on "Subject in Modern Poetry," MacNeice emphasizes that poetry should not be expected to create any intimacy between poet and reader: "We must never forget that poetry is made with words, that words are primarily for communication, that verbal communication is, if you like, a surface ritual" (*SLC*, 70). Nevertheless, he writes, "it is a human characteristic that the poet must try to explain and the reader to comprehend why, how and what the poet writes" (10). In "Eclogue Between the Motherless," not only does he make no effort to explain, he ensures that the reader will not comprehend.

If verbal communication is only a "surface ritual," it still has value, and MacNeice considers the means by which this, as Frost would put it, "guessing at each other" occurs in both his poetry and his prose. In "The Stygian Banks," while he objects to absolute Oneness—"We must avoid / That haunting wish to fuse all persons together; / To *be* my neighbour is banned"—he also recognizes an inchoate unity among individuals and between aspects of the self:

> We have no word for the bridges between our present
> Selves and our past selves or between ourselves and others
> Or between one part of ourselves and another part,
> Yet we must take it as spoken, the bridge is there.
>
> (p. 259)

Poetry can provide such an invisible bridge: "There is the thing *A* and his own reaction to it *B*, but as he is a poet (and, as a poet, only properly or fully existent when making a poem) his *poet's* reaction to *A* is not realized till the thing *A* has been transported (a mysterious process) right into his poem, when it is no longer *A* but α, and with this α is fused his own poetic reaction to it—β. Or, more strictly, instead of the still segregated *A* and *B* there is now only the resulting poetic unity $\alpha\beta$." (*MP*, 21). Then, because in poetry which avails itself of "some traditional scheme of values," readers "can tumble to $\alpha\beta$ because they recognize the *A* behind it and have themselves had the experience *B*" (22). The first three dialogues resort to the traditional scheme of values associated with the eclogue, a scheme recognizable to any reader who, like MacNeice, was classically educated. Although he satirizes the conventions of the form, the eclogue tradition nevertheless provides the reader with a starting point, a touchstone that is missing in "Eclogue Between the Motherless."

By the time he wrote *Autumn Journal*, "Plurality," and "The Stygian Banks," MacNeice had found a middle way in both his philosophy of the One and the Many and in poetic form. He had come to accept that the lyric voice presented a valid method of expressing both personal emotion and universal truths, and he moved from dialogue to first-person statements on the subject. *Autumn Journal*, he wrote, presents a "constant interrelation of abstract & concrete" and has a dramatic quality in that "different parts of myself (e.g. the anarchist, the defeatist, the sensual man, the philosopher, the would-be good citizen) can be given their say in turn."[37] In his essay "Experiences with Images" (1949), he insists that the lyric is not "a sort of emotional parthenogenesis which results in a one-track attitude," but instead is inevitably dramatic (*SLC*, 155). "There may be only one actor on the stage," he continues, "but the Opposition are on their toes in the wings," and, furthermore, "all poems . . . contain an internal conflict, cross-talk, backwash, comeback or pay-off." MacNeice's relegation of the "opposition" to waiting in the wings, along with his substitution of consecutive speeches for dialogue, marks the end of his essays into dialogue poetry; he never published any more eclogues.

At midcentury, any hope for a solution to the problem of the One and the Many had evaporated. In his 1948 essay on Yeats, Auden recognizes that times had changed since the beginning of the modernist era, when "the great conflict was between the Religion of Reason and the Religion of Imagination, objective truth and subjective truth, the Universal and the Individual."[38] At the turn of the twentieth century, Yeats was negotiating his way from the side of Imagination toward a balance with Reason at the same time that Hardy, starting from the other side of the conflict, sought the same balance. Frost and Eliot's generation, reacting against that "great conflict" was educated to believe that in finding a middle way between the One and the Many, philosophy "may recover a reality that it has scarcely possessed since the debates of Socrates and the sophists."[39] But after World War II it became clear that any possibility of recovering any such reality was nothing more than wishful thinking, in part because the sciences, as Auden puts it, "no longer claim to explain the meaning of life . . . nor—at least since the Atom Bomb—would any one believe them if they did."[40] Given the failure of both sides of the conflict between objectivity and subjectivity, Auden says, the combatants move either to relativity or to any one of a multiplicity of absolutes, defended as a moral, rather than philosophical choice.[41] In such a climate, he argues, dialogue becomes impossible, and when two people engage in debate, "each tends to spend half of his time and energy not in producing evidence to support his point of view but in looking for the hidden motives which are causing his opponent to hold his. If they lose their tempers, instead of saying, 'You are a fool,' they say, 'You are a wicked man.'"[42] The postmodern era had arrived, the quest for the absolute One had ended, and dialogue had given way to argument. MacNeice's plurality of voices talking in turn in *Autumn Journal* do not expect to find the meaning of life, only to represent its multiplicity.

Notes

Chapter 1. Introduction

1. Irving Babbitt, *The Masters of Modern French Criticism* (Boston: Houghton Mifflin, 1912), xi.

2. Ibid., viii.

3. William James, *Pragmatism: A New Name for Some Old Ways of Thinking* (New York: Longman Green, 1907), 50.

4. Ibid., 60.

5. Bertrand Russell, *The Problems of Philosophy* (1912; repr., London: Oxford University Press, 1977), 100.

6. Babbitt, *Masters*, 371.

7. Josiah Royce, "The One, the Many, and the Infinite," supplementary essay to *The World and the Individual. First Series: The Four Historical Conceptions of Being* (1900; repr., New York: Dover, 1959), 473.

8. Ibid., 500–501.

9. Edward C. Halper, "One-many Problem," in *The Cambridge Dictionary of Philosophy*, ed. Robert Audi (Cambridge: Cambridge University Press, 1995), 546–47.

10. Ibid.

11. For a useful history of various dualities and clarifies their relationships to monism and pluralism, see Rosalie Osmond, *Mutual Accusations: Body and Soul Dialogues in Their Literary and Theological Context* (Toronto: University of Toronto Press, 1990), 3–20.

12. Paul Douglass, *Bergson, Eliot, and American Literature* (Lexington: University Press of Kentucky, 1986), 12.

13. Henri Bergson, *Creative Evolution*, trans. Arthur Mitchell (New York: Henry Holt, 1911), 14.

14. Ibid., 258.

15. Babbitt, *Masters*, viii–ix.

16. Ibid., ix.

17. George Santayana, *Three Philosophical Poets: Lucretius, Dante, and Goethe*, Harvard Studies in Comparative Literature, Volume 1 (1910; repr., New York: Cooper Square, 1970), 23.

18. James Smith, "On Metaphysical Poetry," *Scrutiny* 2 (1933): 228.

19. Ibid., 227.

20. See Patricia Rae, *The Practical Muse: Pragmatist Poetics in Hulme, Pound, and Stevens* (Lewisburg, PA: Bucknell University Press, 1997) and Michael H. Levenson, *A Genealogy of Modernism: A Study of English Literary*

Doctrine, 1908–1922 (Cambridge: Cambridge University Press, 1984) for Hulme's indebtedness to James and Bergson.

21. T. E. Hulme, "A Lecture on Modern Poetry," in *The Collected Writings of T. E. Hulme*, ed. Karen Csengeri (Oxford: Clarendon Press, 1994), 52.

22. Michael Levenson, *The Genealogy of Modernism*, (186).

23. Numerous critics from Richard Poirier to Jay Parini have examined the influence of Bergson and James on Frost's poetry, and both Manju Jain in *T. S. Eliot and American Philosophy: The Harvard Years* (Cambridge: Cambridge University Press, 1992) and M. A. R. Habib in *The Early T. S. Eliot and Western Philosophy* (Cambridge: Cambridge University Press, 1999) assert that Eliot's preoccupation with the One Many problem while he was at Harvard formed the basis for much of his later thought and poetry.

24. Walter F. Wright, *The Shaping of "The Dynasts": A Study in Thomas Hardy* (Lincoln: University of Nebraska Press, 1967), 44.

25. This interest was not restricted to poets; in her recent book *The Phantom Table*, Ann Banfield traces Russell's and G. E. Moore's ideas on unity and plurality as they appear in the aesthetics of Virginia Woolf and Roger Fry. Ann Banfield, *The Phantom Table: Woolf, Fry, Russell and the Epistemology of Modernism* (Cambridge: Cambridge University Press, 2000).

26. Levenson, *Genealogy of Modernism*, 189.

27. The dramatic poem, "Metal Checks," by Louise Driscoll; Cloyd Head's drama, "Grotesques;" Robert Frost's "Snow" and "The Witch of Coös;" "The Old Woman," a drama by Marjorie Seiffert; "The Box of God" by Lew Sarrett; Ford Madox Ford's (then Hueffer's) prosopoetic poem, "A House," in which all the items of the house speak; and "Pianissimo," a dialogue by Alfred Kreymborg.

28. In 1912, *Georgian Poetry* published a dialogue by Lascelles Abercrombie between a sea captain, a doubting Thomas, and a mysterious stranger, called "The Sale of Saint Thomas," along with James Elroy Flecker's "Joseph and Mary" and T. Sturge Moore's long pastoral, *A Sicilian Idyll*. The next edition of *Georgian Poetry* contained dialogue poems by Gordon Bottomly, Wilfrid Gibson, and Harold Monro. The 1916–17 edition contained Siegfried Sassoon's "They" and Robert Graves's "Star-Talk," in which the constellations hold a conversation. Graves also had three dialogue ballads published in the 1918–19 *Georgian Poetry*, along with Abercrombie's "Witchcraft—New Style." Longer works in book form included Edgar Lee Masters' 139-page *Lee: A Dramatic Poem* (MacMillan, 1926), on the subject of Robert E. Lee. Other verse dramas include Djuna Barnes's *The Antiphon* and Archibald MacLeish's *Nobodaddy*.

29. Edward Mendelson, *Early Auden* (1981; repr., New York: Farrar, Straus and Giroux, 2000), xviii.

30. Michael Prince, *Philosophical Dialogue in the British Enlightenment: Theology, Aesthetics, and the Novel* (Cambridge: Cambridge University Press, 1996), 14.

31. Ibid., 4.

32. Ibid., 2.

33. Ibid., 16.

34. Ibid., 15–19.

35. Osmond, *Mutual Accusations*, xi.

36. Ibid., 99.

37. Prince, *Philosophical Dialogue*, 2.

38. Quoted in Jiri Veltruský, *Drama as Literature* (Lisse: Peter de Ridder Press, 1977), 60.

39. Walter W. Greg, *Pastoral Poetry and Pastoral Drama: A Literary Inquiry, with Special Reference to the Pre-Restoration Stage in England* (1906; repr., New York: Russell & Russell, 1959), 13.

40. Robert Wells, introduction to *The Idylls of Theocritus* (New York: Carcanet, 1988), 22. On the other hand, Auden claims that "[i]f a civilization be judged by this double standard, the degree of diversity attained and the degree of unity retained, then it is hardly too much to say that the Athenians of the fifth century B.C. were the most civilized people who have so far existed." *The Complete Works of W. H. Auden*, vol. 2: *Prose: 1939–1948*, ed. Edward Mendelson (Princeton: Princeton University Press, 2002), 359.

41. "Eclogue," in *The New Princeton Encyclopedia of Poetry and Poetics*, ed. Alex Preminger and T. V. F. Brogan. (Princeton: Princeton University Press, 1993),

42. T. V. F. Brogan, "Ballad," in *The New Princeton Encyclopedia of Poetry and Poetics*, 116–18.

43. Ibid.

44. Alan Richardson, *A Mental Theater: Poetic Drama and Consciousness in the Romantic Age* (University Park: Pennsylvania State University Press, 1988), 1.

45. Ibid., 7.

46. Coleridge defines "esemplastic" as "molding into unity."

47. As opposed to verse drama that is meant for the stage. I am restricting the designation of "dramatic verse" to closet dramas, or shorter works, intended for reading rather than performance.

48. Prince, *Philosophical Dialogue*, 2.

49. Ibid., 9.

50. Jay Parini claims in his biography that Frost was so enamored of *The Dynasts* that he decided to try his own hand at dialogue verse. *Robert Frost: A Life* (New York: Henry Holt, 1999), 124. Parini, unfortunately, cannot remember where he read that, though he told me in an e-mail (July 6, 1999) that he is "sure it's true."

CHAPTER 2. "LOOKING AT LIFE . . ."

1. Review of *The Age of Anxiety*, *Times Literary Supplement*, October 23, 1948, 596.

2. Randall Jarrell, "Verse Chronicle," review of *The Age of Anxiety*, by W. H. Auden, *Nation*, October 18, 1947, 424.

3. Considering that Auden wrote the poem while hopped up on benzedrine, that might not be an unreasonable suggestion. See Humphrey Carpenter, *W. H. Auden: A Biography* (Boston: Houghton Mifflin, 1981), 265.

4. H. A. L. Craig, "Poetry," review of *The Age of Anxiety* by W. H. Auden, *Spectator*, December 10, 1948, 774.

5. David Bromwich, "An Oracle Turned Jester," reprinted from *Times Literary Supplement*, September 17, 1976, 91–100, in *Modern Critical Views: W. H. Auden*, ed. Harold Bloom (New York: Chelsea House Publishers, 1986), 98.

6. Richard Hoggart, *Auden: An Introductory Essay* (New Haven: Yale University Press, 1951), 194.

7. Herbert Greenberg, *Quest for the Necessary: W. H. Auden and the Dilemma of Divided Consciousness* (Cambridge, MA: Harvard University Press, 1968), 168.

8. Hardy to Isabelle Oppenheim, February 12, 1904, in *Letters of Thomas Hardy*, vol. 3: 1902–1908, ed. Richard Little Purdy and Michael Millgate (Oxford: Clarendon Press, 1982), 3:106.

9. "Mr. Hardy's Drama," review of *The Dynasts: A Drama*, part 1, by Thomas Hardy, *Times Literary Supplement*, January 15, 1904, 11.

10. A. B. Walkley, "'The Dynasts': A Suggestion," *Times Literary Supplement*, January 29, 1904, 30. In appendix E, *The Complete Poetical Works of Thomas Hardy*. 5 vols., ed. Samuel Hynes, (Oxford: Clarendon Press, 1995), 5:386–88. The attacks on the form of *The Dynasts* at first surprised Hardy, then angered him to the point that he looked for any target on which to focus blame for the bad reviews. One of the great difficulties, he claimed, was that the majority of his reviewers were female; "[s]urely Editors ought to know," he fumed to Henry Newbolt, "that such a subject could hardly be expected to appeal to women" (*Letters*, 3: 112). Hardy's mood could not have been improved by the enthusiastic review of a work by a Mr. A. M. Buckton, entitled "A 'Ballad Epic' of the Boer War," on the very next page after the original *TLS* review, particularly since Hardy himself had originally intended to write *The Dynasts* in the form of a "ballad-sequence" (*Life*, 117).

11. Ibid., 386.

12. Ibid., 387.

13. Anthony Hecht, *The Hidden Law: The Poetry of W. H. Auden* (Cambridge, MA: Harvard University Press, 1993), 294.

14. "A Literary Transference," *Southern Review* 6 (1940–41): 83.

15. Interestingly, Auden defines war and peace in terms of dialectic: "Whenever man attempts to solve any kind of problem dialectically he is in a state of peace; whenever he attempts to solve it eristically he is in a state of war" (*CW*, 289). He also comments on the poetic uses of war: "As poetic experience the incidents of war have nothing special about them; they are on an equality with all the other incidents that form the general flow of history out of which poetry is made, and the poetic use to which they can be put, the translations they undergo in the process of becoming poetry depend always on the poet's individual character and gift. (*CW*, 152).

16. Mendelson, *Early Auden*, xx.

17. Wright, *Shaping*, 53.

18. In a letter he never sent, Hardy states that his primary interest is in "non-rationality," which he defines as "a principle for which there is no exact

name, lying at the indifference-point between rationality and irrationality" (*Life*, 332).

19. Hardy to Roden Noel, April 3, 1892, *Letters*, 1:261.

20. Hardy comments that "[p]eople who to one's-self are transient singularities are to themselves the permanent condition, the inevitable, the normal, the rest of mankind being to them the singularity. Think that those (to us) strange transitory phenomena, their personalities, are with them always, at their going to bed, at their uprising!" and continues, noting that "London appears not to *see itself*. Each individual is conscious of *himself*, but nobody conscious of themselves collectively, except perhaps some poor gaper who stares round with a half-idiotic aspect. There is no consciousness here of where anything comes from or goes to—only that it is present" (*Life*, 215).

21. Monism, which declares that no distinction exists between the material and the spiritual, usually implies an immanent unity; a dualistic worldview corresponds to a concept of transcendent unity, because the soul represents a part of the One which has become entrapped in the lower, or material, world.

22. Hardy to Noel, March 6, 1892, *Letters*, 1:260.

23. Wright, *Shaping*, 53.

24. For a much more comprehensive history of Hardy's monistic influences and beliefs, see C. Glen Wickens, *Thomas Hardy, Monism, and the Carnival Tradition: The One and the Many in "The Dynasts"* (Toronto: University of Toronto Press, 2002).

25. On the occasion of losing a tooth, Hardy asks plaintively, "Why should a man's mind have been thrown into such close, sad, sensational, inexplicable relations with such a precarious object as his own body!" (*Life* 265).

26. Quoted in Edward Mendelson, *Later Auden* (New York: Farrar, Straus and Giroux, 1999), 143, 144.

27. *CW*, 2:100–101. In one of his 1929 notebooks, Auden writes: "Body and mind are distinct, but neither can exist alone, nor is there rightly a rivalry between them. Attempts to turn body into mind (Manichaeism) or mind into body (Arianism) lead to disease, madness, and death." Quoted in Mendelson, *Later Auden*, 76.

28. Auden is well aware that most people will never attain this paradise. Rainer Emig points out the similarity of the images in Simeon's speech to those in Eliot's *Four Quartets*. Emig notes that "rather than following Eliot in leading the manifold to a synthesizing oneness—in which past, present, and future merge—Auden insists on the dialogue of one and many. This excludes simple determinism. It abstains from certainty, too, and these two rejections have direct consequences for language and poetry." Rainer Emig, *W. H. Auden: Towards a Postmodern Poetics* (New York: St. Martin's Press, 2000).

29. Reproduced in Mendelson, *Later Auden*, 240.

30. Ibid. Auden describes the "Hell of the Pure Deed" as "power without purpose" and associates it also with "pure aesthetic immediacy," "pure ethical potentiality," cyclical time, blind superstition, dadaist art, and tyranny. The "Hell of the Pure Word," or "knowledge without power," is associated with "aesthetic nonentity," "pure ethical actuality," eternal time, logical positivism, "state art," and anarchy.

31. Mendelson, *Later Auden*, 174. Synthesis may be attainable temporarily for the individual mystic, but as Auden recognizes, it will never be achievable for society as a whole in this world. The uncertainty inherent in this condition can be read quite rightly as proto-postmodernist.

32. Ibid., 140–41.

33. Ibid., 141.

34. Auden continues: "As long as we continue to do so [ignore relations between individuals], disorder will seem due to the social differentiation itself instead of to our false conception of it."

35. Delmore Schwartz, "Delmore Schwartz on Auden's 'Most Self-Indulgent Book,'" *Partisan Review* 14 (September–October 1947): 528–31, reprinted in *W. H. Auden: The Critical Heritage*, ed. John Haffenden (London: Routledge & Kegan Paul, 1983), 369–70.

36. Prince, *Philosophical Dialogue*, 1–20.

37. Mendelson, *Later Auden*, 424.

38. Schwartz, "Delmore Schwartz," 369.

39. Greenberg, *Quest for the Necessary*, 169.

40. Hardy to Theodore Spencer, quoted in John Fuller, *W. H. Auden: A Commentary* (Princeton, NJ: Princeton University Press, 1998), 370.

41. Mendelson, *Early Auden*, 21.

42. Ibid., 22.

43. Wright, *Shaping*, 44.

44. See Susan Dean, *Hardy's Poetic Vision in "The Dynasts": The Diorama of a Dream* (Princeton: Princeton University Press,1977), a comprehensive study of the poem as diorama.

45. Katherine Kearney Maynard, *Thomas Hardy's Tragic Poetry: The Lyrics and "The Dynasts"* (Iowa City: University of Iowa Press, 1991), 100.

46. For Auden, a dictator's ruthlessness results from an imbalance between his conception of the One and his own place among the Many: "What Hitler, Napoleon and Alexander lacked was a consciousness of their finiteness, a lack that can be disastrous." Howard Griffin, *Conversations with Auden*, ed. Donald Allen (San Francisco: Grey Fox Press, 1981), 8.

47. In the second of his two ripostes to a bad review in the *TLS*, he confirms his pessimism as to the advisability of identifying an underlying unity: "I am convinced that, whether we uphold this or any other conjecture on the cause of things, men's lives and actions will be little affected thereby, these being less dependent on abstract reasonings than on the involuntary intersocial emotions, which would more probably be strengthened than weakened by a sense that humanity and other animal life (roughly, though not accurately definable as puppetry) forms the conscious extremity of a pervading urgence, or will. Hardy, "'The Dynasts': A Postscript," *Times Literary Supplement*, February 19, 1904, 53. In appendix E, *Complete Poetical Works*, 5:396. Although Hardy crisscrosses the usual associations of reason with the Many and irrationality with the One, he leaves little doubt as to his convictions that humanity is better off living in ignorance of the immanent unity that controls their destinies.

48. Quoted in Mendelson, *Later Auden*, 261.

49. Ibid.

50. Ibid., 260.

51. Griffin, *Conversations with Auden*, 11.

52. Hecht, *Hidden Law*, 256.

53. Auden also developed his own schemes, both tetradic and triadic, which have relevance to *The Age of Anxiety*. In the 1950s, after he left the Jungian system behind, he devised, in an essay titled "The Virgin & The Dynamo" (a play on the famous Henry Adams essay), another tetradic scheme in which he claims that "Man exists as a unity-in-tension of four modes of being: soul, body, mind and spirit" (*DH*, 65). He explains further that "[a]s soul and body, he is an individual, as mind and spirit a member of a society. Were he only soul and body, his only relation to others would be numerical and a poem would be comprehensible only to its author; were he only mind and spirit, men would only exist collectively as the system Man, and there would be nothing for a poem to be about" (*DH*, 65).

Under this scheme, we might assign Quant, with his interest in mythology and Emble (ROSETTA: "But you're handsome, aren't you? even now / A kingly corpse"), to the positions of soul and body, respectively. Rosetta, who looks to rejoin the Jewish people, the people of the Law, represents mind; and Malin, who embraces Christian faith, stands for spirit. The division of these faculties into individual and social categories explains why Quant and Emble appear not to have found their places in any transcendent unity at the end of the poem. Only Rosetta and Malin, having undergone the necessary integrative experience, come to find their places in the universe; but, if the other two were never meant to reach beyond the individual, then their failure to do so does not mean that the shared vision had no effect on them. In "The Virgin & The Dynamo," Auden also describes the self as a "unity-in-tension of three modes of awareness" consisting of "a consciousness of the self as self-contained, as embracing all that it is aware of in a unity of experiencing," a second mode that is "a consciousness of beyondness, of an ego standing as a spectator over against both a self and the external world" and an active mode that represents "the ego's consciousness of itself as a striving-towards, as desiring to transform the self, to realize its potentialities" (*DH*, 65–66). This three-part system reflects the transitions of Rosetta and Malin from isolated individuals to a position between the Many (self) and the One (world), then to searchers for their parts in the One.

54. Hecht, *Hidden Law*, 38.

55. Mendelson, *Later Auden*, 251. Auden outlined the symbolic journey as follows: "It begins in the belly, the center of the body, goes on to the general region around the heart, then to the hands (symmetrically, two by two), then to the nose and throat (the capital), then north to the eyes where Rosetta goes in and the others describe it from outside, then to the forehead complex (the museum), the ears (gardens) through which one receives spiritual direction, the hair (woods), and finally they look down the back, the desert—there's nothing farther." Just knowing that the symbolism derives from the *Zohar* does not help Mendelson, who writes, "The details Auden described explain the structure and wit of 'The Seven Stages,' but knowing them does not help make it memorable or convincing. Auden's efforts to write a poetry of the body were

frustrated by his insistence on writing about symbols of the body instead of the body itself." If Auden were attempting to write a "poetry of the body," that might be true, but this section of *The Age of Anxiety* concerns the temporary unification of particulars.

56. Gershom Scholem, *Kabbalah* (1974; repro, New York: Meridian, 1978), 98.

57. Ibid., 103.

58. Ibid., 100.

59. Ibid., 107.

60. Various kabbalistic systems assign various parts of the body to each of the *sefirot*, none of which matches Auden's scheme completely, but the general direction of the journey can be described. The four characters of *The Age of Anxiety* begin in the torso, which represents *Tiferet*, or "beauty" (Scholem, *Kabbalah*, 107), and move to the hands, which represent *Chesed* (love) and *Din* (judgment). According to Scholem, *Tiferet, Chesed, and Din*, the fourth, fifth, and sixth *sefirot*, respectively, comprise the "psychic" stage, which we may associate with the soul (107). *Keter* (crown), *Chokhmah* (wisdom), and *Binah* (intelligence), the first three emanations, symbolize three parts of the brain (106–7), the "intellectual" *sefirot*, and might reasonably encompass Auden's nose/throat (where all of the travelers reunite: "EMBLE: Here we are. MALIN: As we hoped we have come / Together again" [75]), eyes, and forehead. The characters complete their journey through an increasingly uncivilized natural world—gardens, woods, desert—which corresponds roughly to *Hod* (majesty), *Yesod Olam* (the foundation of the world) and *Malkhut* (kingdom). In this last stage, Auden modifies the bodily symbolism of the *Zohar*, since *Hod* and another emanation called *Nezach* (lasting endurance) are represented by the legs, which the characters do not visit, according to his explanation. However, if we take Auden's identification of "the hair," as a euphemism for the sexual organ, then the woods corresponds to *Yesod Olam*, and the desert to *Malkhut*, which represents the entire body. The characters' experiences as they descend through the lower emanations correspond to their increasing return to individuality; in the gardens, they become aware of physical ailments; in the woods, they feel abandoned and unloved, and in the desert ("ROSETTA: Terror scatters us / to the four coigns" [97]), they once more become aware of the world at war, a world in which "The primary colors / Are all mixed up; the whole numbers / Have broken down" (98).

61. Edward Mendelson mistakenly attributes the narrator's withholding of the fact of her Judaism until she reveals it herself to racial sensitivity on Auden's part: "The moral point of not identifying her earlier as a Jew is that the poem does not categorize her by ethnicity or race: her Judaism is a creed, and the poem takes no interest in it until she does." Mendelson, *Later Auden*, 256. Auden, however, certainly knew that Judaism has no such thing as a creed. A few years before the publication of *The Age of Anxiety*, according to Mendelson, he socialized with Jews almost exclusively, told jokes in Yiddish, immersed himself in a study of Judaism and even went so far as to consider conversion (259). Even Mendelson acknowledges that Rosetta's "self-deceptions dissolve when she at last remembers her inescapable obligation to her Juda-

ism" (255). In the aftermath of the Shoah, Rosetta's ethnicity is clearly *the* inescapable point.

62. Ibid., 63.

63. Ibid., 64.

64. Hardy himself referred to the Preface as "being outside the drama" in a letter to Morley Roberts dated April 28, 1906 (*Letters*, 3: 204).

65. Michael Issarachoff, *Discourse as Performance* (Stanford, CA: Stanford University Press, 1989),
18–23.

66. Ibid., 20.

67. Ibid., 4.

68. Ibid., 17.

69. Mary Ann Frese Witt, "Reading Modern Drama: Voice in the Didascaliae," *Studies in the Literary Imagination* 25 (Spring 1992): 104.

70. Hardy, *The Complete Poems of Thomas Hardy*, ed. James Gibson (New York: MacMillan, 1976), 331. J. Hillis Miller discusses Hardy's use of time to establish such a "clear-eyed distance" as characteristic of much of his work: "The horizons of time establish one important kind of distance—distance of one time from another time which makes up the temporal form of all those poems in which someone looks back at an earlier time in his own life; distance in the fiction between the narrator's retrospective view and the time of the characters as they live from moment to moment moving toward the future. The openings within time itself, as Hardy experiences them, are constitutive of these narrative and poetic structures. His writing attempts to close these fissures, to bring the perspective of narrator and character together, to reconcile then and now in the poetic persona's life, or to possess all time in a single moment, as do the choruses of spirits in *The Dynasts*." J. Hillis Miller, *Thomas Hardy: Distance and Desire* (Cambridge, MA: Belknap Press of Harvard University Press, 1970), xii–xiii.

71. Bonamy Dobrée, "The Dynasts," *Southern Review* 6 (1940–41): 115.

72. Dean, *Hardy's Poetic Vision*, 77,78.

73. Auden, "Practiced Topophile," *Town and Country*, July 1947, 101.

74. M. M. Bahktin, *The Dialogic Imagination*, ed. Michael Holquist, trans. Caryl Emerson and Michael Holquist (Austin: University of Texas Press, 1981), 304.

75. Ibid., 316.

76. Ibid.

77. Hardy to Edmund Gosse, January 31, 1904, *Letters*, 3:102.

78. Hardy did not necessarily believe that the characters always should speak in appropriate diction for their stations for the sake of plausibility. In a letter to May Sinclair on July 12, 1909, he describe his reaction to an operatic performance of *Tess of the D'Urbervilles*: "Think of a Wessex dairymaid singing in choice Italian. But when the first sense of incongruity is past it seems natural enough—especially to me who can accept musical convention to any extent" (*Letters*, 4: 32).

79. Kenneth Millard, "Hardy's *The Dynasts*: 'words . . . to hold the imagination,'" reprinted from *Edwardian Poetry* (Oxford: Clarendon Press, 1991), 59–

79, in *Critical Essays on Thomas Hardy's Poetry*, ed. Harold Orel (New York: G. K. Hall, 1995), 179.

80. Ibid.
81. Ibid.
82. Dean, *Hardy's Poetic Vision*, 4.
83. Ibid., 284.
84. Ibid., 289.
85. Hardy, "'The Dynasts': A Postscript," 53.
86. Hardy to Arthur Symons, March 11, 1909, *Letters*, 3:305.
87. Hardy steadfastly denied biographical identification with his novels, even where the parallels are obvious. On the subject of *Jude the Obscure*, he asserted, "Some paragraphists assured the public that the book was an honest autobiography, and Hardy did not take the trouble to deny it till more than twenty years later, when he wrote to an inquirer with whom the superstition still lingered that no book he had ever written contained less of his own life—which of course had been known to his friends from the beginning" (*Life*, 289). He makes the same argument about *A Pair of Blue Eyes*, which "has been considered to show a picture of his own personality as the architect on this visit. But in addition to Hardy's own testimony there is proof that this is not the case, he having ever been shy of putting his personal characteristics into his novels" (76).
88. Jarrell, "Verse Chronicle," 424.
89. *Times Literary Supplement*, October 23, 1948, 596.
90. Mendelson, *Later Auden*, 265.
91. Ibid., 255.
92. Ibid., 254.
93. Hardy to Blanche Crackanthorpe, December 3, 1903, *Letters*, 3:91.
94. "'The Dynasts': A Postscript," 395.
95. Hardy to Frederick Harris, January 24, 1904, *Letters*, 3:99.
96. Hardy to Edmund Gosse, January 17, 1904, *Letters*, 3:98.

CHAPTER 3. TWO MODERN POETS

1. Eliot to Eleanor Hinckley, March 23, 1917, in *The Letters of T. S. Eliot*, vol. 1, ed. Valerie Eliot (San Diego: Harcourt, Brace, Jovanovich, 1988), 169.
2. Eliot's guilty feelings about his sexuality likely also made an equivalence of body and soul attractive. Lyndall Gordon devotes much of *T. S. Eliot: An Imperfect Life* to an assertion that sexual guilt is responsible in some way for a poetic career that demonstrates "a consuming search for salvation" (4). According to Gordon, "Eliot was gradually formulating a choice all through his juvenilia: an Absolute or Pure Idea or Soul set against women, time and society, who were the Absolute's enemies" (34). Given Eliot's penchant for overcoming dichotomies, it seems likely that he would prefer to reconcile his bodily and spiritual needs rather than choosing between them. Lyndall Gordon, *T. S. Eliot: An Imperfect Life* (New York: W. W. Norton, 1999).

3. Ronald Schuchard, *Eliot's Dark Angel: Intersections of Life and Art* New York: Oxford University Press, 1999), 143–44.

4. Ibid., 143.

5. Quoted in Sigg, *The American T. S. Eliot: A Study of the Early Writings* Cambridge: Cambridge University Press, 1989), 1.

6. Leon Surette, *The Birth of Modernism: Ezra Pound, T. S. Eliot, W. B. eats, and the Occult* (Montreal: McGill-Queen's University Press, 1993), 84.

7. W. B. Yeats, *Memoirs*, ed. Denis Donoghue (New York: MacMillan, 972), 151.

8. James Smith, "On Metaphysical Poetry," *Scrutiny* 2 (1933): 227.

9. Ibid.

10. John Paul Riquelme, *Harmony of Dissonances: T. S. Eliot, Romanti- ism, and Imagination* (Baltimore: Johns Hopkins University Press, 1991), 4.

11. Ibid., 2.

12. Habib, *Early T. S. Eliot*, 58.

13. Ibid., 14.

14. Quoted in Benjamin Lockerd, *Aethereal Rumours: T. S. Eliot's Physics nd Poetics* (Lewisburg, PA: Bucknell University Press, 1998), 43.

15. W. B. Yeats, *The Autobiography of W. B. Yeats* (Garden City, NY: Dou- leday Anchor Books, 1958), 81.

16. S. T. Coleridge, *Biographia Literaria. The Collected Works of Samuel aylor Coleridge*, vol. 7, ed. James Engell and W. Jackson Bate (Princeton: rinceton University Press, 1983), 17.

17. Jain, *T. S. Eliot and American Philosophy*, 198.

18. Donald J. Childs, *From Philosophy to Poetry: T. S. Eliot's Study of nowledge and Experience* (New York: Palgrave, 2001), 89.

19. William James also served as president of the society. The Society for sychical Research. http://www.spr.ac.uk. December 14, 2004. James's father, Ienry, was a Swedenborgian. See Linda Simon, *Genuine Reality: A Life of Wil- am James* (New York: Harcourt Brace, 1998), 29–34.

20. Peter Ackroyd, *T. S. Eliot: A Life* (New York: Simon and Schuster, 1984), 1.

21. Quoted in Piers Gray, *T. S. Eliot's Intellectual and Poetic Development, 909–1922* (Sussex: Harvester Press, 1982), 2.

22. Bergson, *Matter and Memory*, 1908, trans. Nancy Margaret Paul and /. Scott Palmer (New York: Zone Books, 1988), 180.

23. Habib, *Early T. S. Eliot*, 87.

24. Bergson, *Matter and Memory*, 257–58.

25. Habib, *Early T. S. Eliot*, 42.

26. Jain, *T. S. Eliot and American Philosophy*, 198.

27. F. H. Bradley, *Essays on Truth and Reality* (Oxford: Clarendon Press, 914), 175.

28. Eliot's explanation of the coincidence of the One and the Many sounds :markably like Gershom Scholem's description of the simultaneous unity nd multiplicity of the godhead and its emanations in kabbalistic mysticism. ccording to Scholem, "The hidden God in the aspect of *Ein-Sof* and the God 1anifested in the emanation of *Sefirot* are one and the same, viewed from two ifferent angles." Scholem, *Kabbalah*, 98.

29. Eliot also addresses in his dissertation the problem of the One and the Many as it concerns the relationship between body and soul. The soul, he says, may contain within it a number of finite centers, a number of different points of view; although, if the soul has a defined (unified) personality, then it may approximate a finite center in its own right (*KE*, 148). As such, "the more of personality it is, the more harmonious and self-contained, the more definitely it is said to possess a 'point of view,' a point of view toward the social world" (148). The soul then as finite center tries to unify its world, "passing, when possible, from two or more discordant viewpoints to a higher which shall somehow include and transmute them" (147–48). In a supplement to the dissertation, Eliot attempts to clarify how the soul and body must exist as both one and many: [I]f there are other souls, we must think of our own soul as more intimately attached to its own body than to the rest of its environment; we detach and idealize some of its states. We thus pass to the point of view from which the soul is the entelechy of its body. It is this transition from one point of view to another which is known to Mr. Bradley's readers as transcendence (205–6). He goes on to refute explicitly Leibniz's conclusion that the soul's status as entelechy of body and soul produces "animated matter," i.e., the subordination of the soul to the body, claiming that it is unnecessary "if one recognizes two points of view, which are irreconcilable and yet melt into each other" (206). In Eliot's view, the soul is just as dependent on the body for its identity as is the body dependent on the soul for its vitality, and it is the recognition that both of these points of view together constitute the reality of the individual which constitutes the transcendent point of view. In the relationship of body and soul, as well as that of self and world, it is the *coincidentia oppositorum* which results in transcendent unity, not the existence of a *tertium quid*.

30. Harold Bloom, *Yeats* (New York: Oxford University Press, 1970), 75.

31. Thomas R. Whitaker, *Swan and Shadow: Yeats's Dialogue with History* (Chapel Hill: University of North Carolina Press, 1964), 9.

32. Harold Bloom suggests that Yeats might have believed that to meet his antiself, "as Shelley himself by tradition did, just before drowning, would be to meet his own death." Bloom, *Yeats*, 205. According to George Bornstein, "The joining of the two selves cannot be permanent, for they are one pair of those antinomies into which life falls in our consciousness; for that reason death is sometimes the symbol of the completed union." George Bornstein, *Yeats and Shelley* (Chicago: University of Chicago Press, 1970), 133.

33. Osmond, *Mutual Accusation*, 101.

34. Ibid.

35. Norman A. Jeffares, *W. B. Yeats: Man and Poet*, 1962 (New York: St. Martin's Press, 1996), 242.

36. Ibid., 172.

37. Osmond, *Mutual Accusation*, xi.

38. Bornstein, *Yeats and Shelley*, 119.

39. Whitaker, *Swan and Shadow*, 67.

40. It should be noted that MacNeice does not consider Yeats a true mystic, that he only "believed in mysticism" (*PWBY*, 25), and he may well be correct.

but as Yeats certainly imitated the behavior of mystics, MacNeice's observation about form should apply.

41. In the early 1930s, W. H. Auden at least once referred to a gestalt version of the "real," specifying that "[t]he sense is the philosophical one as in the *real* wholes in Gestalt psychology." Mendelson, *Early Auden*, 7.

42. Eric Sigg goes so far as to suggest that the split in Prufrock's personality is so radical that the two opposing selves nullify one another. Sigg, *American T. S. Eliot*, 82, 101.

43. Sigg, among others, identifies the struggle within Prufrock as an opposition between matter and spirit, but wrongly suggests that the poem depicts an irreconcilable dualism. Ibid., 76. Mary Ann Gillies, who contends that the poem "is a dramatic monologue," also acknowledges that "the poem exemplifies the subject-object split." She recognizes that the poem "swings back and forth between . . . two approaches, and by so doing it attempts to find a middle ground between subject and object." Mary Ann Gillies, *Henri Bergson and British Modernism* (Montreal: McGill-Queen's University Press, 1996), 86–87. While Gillies attributes Eliot's treatment of the subject-object split in the poem to the influence of Bergson, Donald Childs has recently argued a position close to mine that poem's philosophy is derived from Bradley: "Eliot found in 'The Love Song of J. Alfred Prufrock' while writing his dissertation the very distinction between self as observer and self as observed object that he was analysing in the dissertation. The 'you and I' of the poem are simultaneously continuous and discontinuous—a paradoxical condition of consciousness itself, as Eliot points out in the dissertation." Childs, *From Philosophy to Poetry*, 82.

44. Prince, *Philosophical Dialogue*, 4.

45. Lyndall Gordon actually suggests that "The Love Song of J. Alfred Prufrock" is "a more dramatic and complicated version of Eliot's earlier debates between body and soul," although she offers no explanation of this interpretation. Lyndall Gordon, *Eliot's Early Years* (Oxford: Oxford University Press, 1977), 47. Eric Sigg proposes that "Prufrock's difficulties stem from the familiar Romantic alienation between frustrated subject and unresponsive object and from an even more traditional estrangement between spirit and flesh" Sigg, *American T. S. Eliot*, 76. Jewel Spears Brooker argues that by alternating "gustatory" and "rhetorical" images, Eliot "manipulates a parallel between eating and talking together," and she invokes the ultimate union of body and soul, the Incarnation, in suggesting that "The Love Song of J. Alfred Prufrock" represents a mass in which Prufrock himself is consumed as the host. Jewel Spears Brooker, "Substitutes for Religion in the Early Poetry of T. S. Eliot." *Southern Review* 21, no. 4 (1985), reprinted in *Mastery and Escape: T. S. Eliot and the Dialectic of Modernism*, by Jewel Spears Brooker (Amherst: University of Massachusetts Press, 1994), 132.

46. Bergson, *Matter and Memory*, 153.

47. Ibid.

48. John T. Mayer recognizes this dichotomy, noting that Prufrock "is typically torn between detachment and involvement, between observing and seeking." John T. Mayer, *T. S. Eliot's Silent Voices* (New York: Oxford University Press, 1989), 16.

49. Bergson, *Creative Evolution*, 191.

50. Ibid., 192.

51. See Bornstein, *Yeats and Shelley*, 92.

52. Ibid.

53. Bergson, *Creative Evolution*, 193.

54. Surette, *Birth of Modernism*, 85.

55. Jain, *T. S. Eliot and American Philosophy*, 194.

56. Osmond, *Mutual Accusation*, 97–101.

57. Ibid., 63.

58. Ibid.

59. Quoted in Osmond, *Mutual Accusation*, 66.

60. The same image appears in Tennyson's "The Two Voices," another debate poem which may have influenced Eliot. Eliot included this poem in the syllabus for the extension class in Modern English Literature that he taught in 1916. Schuchard, *Eliot's Dark Angel*, 33.

61. Bergson, *Creative Evolution*, 181.

62. Ibid., 181–82.

63. Ibid., 261.

64. Ibid., 19.

65. Ibid., 18–19.

66. Bloom, *Yeats*, 68.

67. Surette, *Birth of Modernism*, 16.

68. G. R. S. Mead quoted in Surette, *Birth of Modernism*, 17–18.

69. Surette, *Birth of Modernism*, 35.

70. Ibid., 15.

71. www.golden-dawn.org/biocase.html, www.golden-dawn.org/bioffarr.html, September 5, 2004.

72. www.golden-dawn.org/biocase.html, September 5, 2004.

73. Jeffares, *W. B. Yeats*, 243.

74. Osmond, *Mutual Accusation*, 197.

75. Ibid., 81.

76. The *OED* gives a 1912 citation for "twilight sleep" as the condition of a patient under anesthesia.

77. Jain, *T. S. Eliot and American Philosophy*, 174.

78. Ibid.

79. Ibid., 170.

80. Yeats, *Autobiography*, 120.

81. Ibid.

82. Bergson, "Laughter," 1900, trans. unknown, in *Comedy*, edited by Wylie Sypher (New York: Doubleday Anchor Books, 1956), 78–79.

83. Ibid., 73.

84. During the period in which he was an acknowledged Bergsonian, Eliot wrote two poems which he labeled explicitly as debates of body and soul, although neither is in dialogue form. The first, titled "First Debate between the Body and Soul," is dated January 1910. The other, titled "Bacchus and Ariadne: 2nd Debate between the Body and Soul," is dated February 1911. The use of semidistinct voices in "The Love Song of J. Alfred Prufrock" contrasts with

Eliot's techniques in the other debates; while neither of the two debate poems is written in the form of a dialogue between discrete voices, the relationship between body and soul in each of these poems shapes the form of each, so that in the "1st Debate," where the body (matter) prevails, the dualistic viewpoint reigns, and in the "2nd Debate," in which the soul dominates, a single voice appears. In the "1st Debate," matter overwhelms the spirit.

85. Riquelme, *Harmony of Dissonances*, 159.

86. Because the voices in "The Love Song of J. Alfred Prufrock" cannot be clearly distinguished, it is extremely difficult to determine the number of speakers, and some critics perceive many more than two voices. Mayer, for example, proposes that we hear, along with Prufrock, the voices of the mermaids, of John the Baptist, of Polonius, of Hamlet, of the women talking of Michelangelo, etc. He suggests that "[i]t is more helpful to think of "Prufrock" as an interplay of competing, overlapping awarenesses rather than as a debate between "you" and "I," the primary voices." Mayer, *Silent Voices*, 14. Although the interplay of multiple voices and/or aspects of personality might seem incompatible with a debate of body and soul, a Bergsonian would find them not only compatible, but necessarily concomitant. In Bergsonian terms, the debate between body and soul translates roughly to an interchange between an outer, material, temporal self, which may appear in successive guises, and an inner, spiritual, atemporal self, which, in turn, consists of interpenetrating voices. Bergson describes the unity-in-multiplicity of the inner self in *Time and Free Will*: "We should therefore distinguish two forms of multiplicity, two very different ways of regarding duration, two aspects of conscious life. Below homogeneous duration, which is the extensive symbol of true duration, a close psychological analysis distinguishes a duration whose heterogeneous moments permeate one another; below the numerical multiplicity of conscious states, a qualitative multiplicity; below the self with well-defined states, a self in which *succeeding each other* means *melting into one another* and forming an organic whole." Bergson, *Time and Free Will: An Essay on the Immediate Data of Consciousness*, translator F. L. Pogson (London: George Allen and Unwin, 1910), 128.

87. Bergson, *Matter and Memory*, 161.

88. Ibid., 162.

89. Ibid.

90. The role of the metaphysical poet, according to Eliot, is to reassociate thought and feeling, body and soul, in a type of the Incarnation. Eliot claims that feeling, which Bradley defines as "the general state of the total soul not yet at all differentiated into any of the preceding special aspects" (qtd. in *KE*, 20), is completely deficient in the poetry of Milton and Dryden, who "triumph with a dazzling disregard of the soul" (*SE*, 249). Even worse, in Eliot's opinion, is the domination of the unconscious in Romantic poetry at the expense of thought. In his opinion, the body serves an equally important role in poetry as the soul; it is not enough to "look into our hearts and write," according to Eliot, "One must look into the cerebral cortex, the nervous system, and the digestive tracts" (*SE*, 250). On those grounds, Eliot rejects Cowley as a true

metaphysical poet, because "[h]e fails to make the Word Flesh, though he often makes it Bones" (*VMP*, 61). Bones, for Eliot, represent matter without spirit, so Cowley's failure represents a dominance of the body over the soul. Allusions to the story of Ezekiel in the Valley of the Dry Bones (Ezek. 37:1–10) appear frequently in Eliot's work, particularly in *The Waste Land* and in "Ash-Wednesday," and Ezekiel's vision provides an apt metaphor for Eliot's conception of the role of the reader of metaphysical poetry. In the vision, Ezekiel sees before him the dry bones that represent the disunited and scattered House of Israel, which has disintegrated into multiplicity due to its isolation from God. God commands Ezekiel to prophesy to the bones, to announce to them that God "will make them one nation in the land upon the mountains of Israel; and one king shall be king to them all: and they shall be no more two nations, neither shall they be divided . . . any more at all" (Ezek. 37:22). When Ezekiel prophesies to the bones, they acquire first flesh and then spirit (Ezek. 37:4–10); his intention unites them in his mind as long as he concentrates on the unity. Like Ezekiel, the reader of "The Love Song of J. Alfred Prufrock" must hold body and soul together in mind, mentally reassembling bones, fleshing them out and inspiriting them.

91. Eliot's best-known statement of this unifying function of the poet appears in "Tradition and the Individual Talent," where he compares the poet's mind to a catalyst that allows two separate substances to combine into a third. "The poet's mind," he claims, "is in fact a receptacle for seizing and storing up numberless feelings, phrases, images, which remain there until all the particles which can unite to form a new compound are present together" (*SE*, 8). In this essay, he identifies the two substances that unite in the poet's mind to form poetry as emotions and feelings. He associates "emotion" with the individual—"It is not in his personal emotions, the emotions provoked by particular events in his life, that the poet is in any way remarkable or interesting"—and implies that emotion is transcended by "floating feelings" (10). These transcendent feelings are connected in some way to the individual emotions, through an "affinity . . . by no means superficially evident" (10), much as the soul is connected to the body. To "escape from emotion," therefore, implies a mystical leap toward the One. This process occurs best where the soul can achieve the greatest distance from the body: "[T]he more perfect the artist, the more completely separate in him will be the man who suffers and the mind which creates; the more perfectly will the mind digest and transmute the passions which are its material" (7–8).

92. Surette, *Birth of Modernism*, 288.

93. See, for instance, Eliot's 1940 lecture to the Friends of the Irish Academy, published as "Yeats" in *The Selected Prose of T. S. Eliot* (New York: Harcourt, Brace, Jovanovich, 1975), 248. Eliot's early lack of interest in Yeats is belied by a 1914 letter in which he talks of postponing a trip for the chance at a meal with Yeats and Ezra Pound at a Chinese restaurant. Eliot to Conrad Aiken, September 30, 1914, in *Letters*, p. 58.

94. *Letters*, 611.

95. Ibid.

96. Eliot, *Selected Prose*, 257.

CHAPTER 4. "ACROSS THE SOUL . . ."

1. Quoted in Lisa Seale, "Original Originality: Robert Frost's Talks," in *Roads Not Taken: Rereading Robert Frost*, ed. Earl J. Wilcox and Jonathan N. Barron (Columbia: University of Missouri Press, 2000), 105–20, 110.

2. Quoted in John Evangelist Walsh, *Into My Own: The English Years of Robert Frost, 1912–1915* (New York: Grove Press, 1988), 225. Robert Faggen informs me that the parenthetical comments actually read "idealism" and "realism," not "cohesion" and "reaction."

3. Lawrance Thompson, *Robert Frost: The Early Years, 1874–1915* (New York: Holt, Rinehart and Winston, 1966), 70.

4. Ibid., 120.

5. Ibid., 381.

6. Ibid., 382.

7. Parini, 61.

8. James was on sabbatical during Frost's time in Cambridge.

9. Frank Lentricchia, *Robert Frost: Modern Poetics and the Landscapes of Self* (Durham, NC: Duke University Press, 1975), 177. Although he credits James as the major influence, Jay Parini cites Royce as the initiator of the drive in Frost to unite idealism and naturalism (*Robert Frost*, 63).

10. William James, *Psychology: Briefer Course* (Cambridge, MA: Harvard University Press, 1984), 11.

11. Ibid. Cf. Wordsworth, "Prospectus to *The Recluse*":

> How exquisitely the individual Mind
> (And the progressive powers perhaps no less
> Of the whole species) to the external World
> Is fitted:—and how exquisitely, too—
> Theme this but little heard of among men—
> The external World is fitted to the Mind

(ll. 63–68)

12. Ibid., 179.

13. Ibid., 166, 167.

14. Ibid., 163.

15. Robert Frost, *Prose Jottings of Robert Frost: Selections from His Notebooks and Miscellaneous Manuscripts*, ed. Edward Connery Lathem and Hyde Cox (Lunenburg, VT: Northeast-Kingdom Publishers, 1982), 29.

16. James, *Pragmatism: A New Name for Some Old Ways of Thinking*, (New York: Longman Green, 1907), 62.

17. James, *Psychology*, 141.

18. James, *Pragmatism*, 60.

19. Ibid., 52.

20. When Frost asks, "How do I know whether a man has come close to Keats in reading Keats?" ("Education by Poetry," 43), we know how close he has come by "wild surmise."

21. Quoted in Reginald Cook, *Robert Frost: A Living Voice* (Amherst: University of Massachusetts Press, 1974), 295.

22. Edward Connery Lathem, *Interviews with Robert Frost* (1966; repr., Guilford, CT: Jeffrey Norton Publishers, 1997), 208.

23. Ibid., 146.

24. Ibid., 179.

25. Ibid., 245.

26. Robert Frost, *Collected Poems, Prose, & Plays*, Library of America Edition, ed. Richard Poirier and Mark Richardson (New York: Literary Classics of the United States, 1995), 712.

27. Cook, *Living Voice*, 107–8.

28. Lathem, *Interviews*, 176.

29. All quotations from Frost's poetry are from the *Collected Poems, Prose, & Plays*. This extract is lines 40–41, and 45–53.

30. Robert Faggen, *Robert Frost and the Challenge of Darwin* (Ann Arbor: University of Michigan Press, 1997), 139.

31. Although the Big Bang Theory had not yet been introduced, a simultaneity of One and Many as origin of the universe is common to gnostic sects, and Frost, having been raised by a Swedenborgian would have been familiar with this concept. In a 1923 interview, Frost said, "I was brought up a Swedenborgian. I am not a Swedenborgian now. But there's a good deal of it that's left with me" (qtd. in Lathem, *Interviews*, 49). Emerson quotes Swedenborg in *Representative Men*: "Man is a kind of very minute heaven, corresponding to the world of spirits and to heaven. Every particular idea of man, and every affection, yea, every smallest part of his affection, is an image and effigy of him. A spirit may be known from only a single thought."

32. Frost is not alone in this association. Auden explains the vision/voices dichotomy as follows: "Since the eye contains the way of gratification and refusal (the eyelid), this sense is pretty much under control of the will which makes bad use of it more reprehensible. Hearing represents the spiritual sense. Christ spread his doctrine by the spoken word, as did most prophets and leaders. One finds the ear-eye dichotomy illustrated by the conflict between John the Baptist and Salome, Socrates and Alcibiades, and Christ and Mary Magdalene." Quoted in Howard Griffin, *Conversations with Auden*, ed. Donald Allen (San Francisco: Grey Fox Press, 1981), 97.

33. Mark Richardson, *The Ordeal of Robert Frost: The Poet and His Poetics* (Urbana: University of Illinois Press, 1997), 166.

34. Parini, *A Life*, 15.

35. Robert Bernard Hass, *Going by Contraries: Robert Frost's Conflict with Science* (Charlottesville: University Press of Virginia, 2002), 143.

36. Thompson, *Robert Frost: The Years of Triumph, 1915–1938* (New York: Holt, Rinehart and Winston, 1970), 456.

37. Ibid., 460.

38. Ibid., 460–61.

39. To Thomas B. Mosher, July 17, 1913: "What I *can* do next is bring out a volume of blank verse that I have already well in hand and won't have to feel I am writing to order. I had some character strokes I had to get in somewhere

and I chose a sort of eclogue form for them;" To John T. Bartlett, Aug. 7, 1913: "You will gather from the Bookman article . . . what my next book is to be like. . . . I may decide to call it New England Eclogues" (*SL*, 83, 89).

40. Robert Faggen, "Frost and the Questions of Pastoral," in *The Cambridge Companion to Robert Frost*, ed. Robert Faggen (Cambridge: Cambridge University Press, 2001), 50.

41. Brogan, "Ballad," 116–18.

42. Robert Frost, "The Hear-Say Ballad," foreword to *Ballads Migrant in New England*, by Helen Hartness Flanders and Marguerite Olney (Miami, FL: Granger Books, 1953), xii–xiii.

43. Ibid.

44. Victor E. Vogt, "Narrative and Drama in the Lyric: Robert Frost's Strategic Withdrawal," *Critical Inquiry* 5, no. 3 (Spring 1979): 537.

45. Louis Untermeyer, ed., *The Letters of Robert Frost to Louis Untermeyer* (New York: Holt, Rinehart and Winston, 1963), 359.

46. Thompson, *Early Years*, 246.

47. Bergson, *Creative Evolution*, 269.

48. Thompson, *Years of Triumph*, 300.

49. Bergson, *Creative Evolution*, 269.

50. Parini, *A Life*, 240.

51. Tyler Hoffman, *Robert Frost and the Politics of Poetry* (Hanover, NH: Middlebury College Press, University Press of New England, 2001), 185.

52. Lathem, *Interviews*, 19.

53. Affectation has disqualified a number of critics from the appreciation of the speech in Frost's dialogues; Allen Ginsberg once denounced "Home Burial" as a "Coupla squares yakking." Randall Jarrell, *Randall Jarrell's Letters: An Autobiographical and Literary Selection*, ed. Mary Jarrell (Boston: Houghton Mifflin Co., 1985), 418. Another critic denigrates the poems as being "characterized by an aphoristic dialogue long staled by rehearsal" and submits that the only readers likely to enjoy such works "would be the prosperous academic weekenders who have notoriously laid claim to southern New Hampshire." Richard Poirier, *Robert Frost: The Work of Knowing* (New York: Oxford UP, 1977), 108–9.

54. Lathem, *Interviews*, 76.

55. Ibid., 77.

56. Frost, *Prose Jottings*, 40.

57. Ibid., 7–8.

58. Ibid., 6.

59. Untermeyer, *Letters*, 166.

60. Faggen, *Challenge of Darwin*, 104.

61. Hecht, *Hidden Law*, 450.

62. Ibid.

63. Lathem, *Interviews*, 249.

64. Parini, *A Life*, 9.

65. quoted in Parini, *A Life*, 338.

66. Lathem, *Interviews*, 233.

67. Parini, *A Life*, 359.

68. Cook, *Living Voice*, 168.
69. Parini, *A Life*, 124.
70. Cook, *Living Voice*, 267.
71. Lathem, *Interviews*, 94.
72. Cook, *Living Voice*, 276.

CHAPTER 5. "LET EVERYTHING BE VANITY OR ONE"

1. Peter McDonald, *Louis MacNeice: The Poet in His Contexts* (Oxford: Clarendon Press, 1991), 10.
2. Edna Longley, "Louis MacNeice: Aspects of His Aesthetic Theory and Practice," in *Studies on Louis MacNeice*. ed. Jacqueline Genet and Wynne Hellegouarc'h (Caen: Société Française d'Études Irlandaises, Centre de Publications de l'Université de Caen, 1988), 51.
3. Terence Brown, *Louis MacNeice: Sceptical Vision* (Dublin: Gill and MacMillan, 1975), 2–3.
4. Louis MacNeice, *Selected Prose of Louis MacNeice*, ed. Alan Heuser (Oxford: Clarendon Press, 1990), 224–25.
5. Ibid.
6. Edna Longley, *Louis MacNeice: A Study*, (London: Faber and Faber, 1988), 44.
7. Quoted in McDonald, *Poet in His Contexts*, 59. "Neurospastoumenos," originally published in the *Oxford Outlook*, February 1930, is not included in any of MacNeice's books. All other poems quoted are found in *The Collected Poems*.
8. MacNeice, *Collected Poems*, ed. E. R. Dodds (New York: Oxford University Press, 1967), 101.
9. McDonald, *Poet in His Contexts*, 65.
10. Peter Dronke, *Verse with Prose from Petronius to Dante: The Art and Scope of the Mixed Form* (Cambridge, MA: Harvard University Press, 1994), 8.
11. W. H. Auden, *Prose: And Travel Books in Prose and Verse*, volume 1, 1926–1938, ed. Edward Mendelson (Princeton: Princeton University Press, 1996), 6.
12. James, *Pragmatism*, 52.
13. McDonald, *Poet in His Contexts*, 83.
14. James, *Pragmatism*, 52.
15. MacNeice, *Autumn Journal*, Canto II), p. 104.
16. Brown, *Sceptical Vision*, 17.
17. MacNeice married Mary (Mariette) Beazley in 1930 while still at Oxford, despite serious objections from both sets of parents. According to John Hilton's "Louis MacNeice at Marlborough and Oxford," an appendix to *The Strings Are False*, MacNeice's argument with his parents disintegrated into farce when, "not content with Mariette and his drunkenness, Louis seems to have chosen the moment, perhaps unavoidably, for revealing that he cannot really call himself a Christian" (277). See Hilton's account in *The Strings Are False*, 273–80 and in Stallworthy, *Louis MacNeice* (New York: W. W. Norton, 1995), 137–43.

18. Michael O'Neill and Gareth Reeves, *Auden, MacNeice, Spender: The Thirties Poetry* (New York: St. Martin's Press, 1992), 78.

19. Robyn Marsack, *The Cave of Making: The Poetry of Louis MacNeice* (Oxford: Clarendon Press, 1982), 27.

20. Greg, *Pastoral Poetry*, 10.

21. Ibid., 410.

22. McDonald, *Poet in His Contexts*, 57.

23. Ibid., 23.

24. Brown, *Sceptical Vision*, 89.

25. McDonald, *Poet in His Contexts*, 22.

26. Marsack, *Care of Making*, 31.

27. Jon Stallworthy points out that Craven's description of this trip actually represents MacNeice's own experiences of his trip the previous spring. *Louis MacNeice*, 198–99.

28. Marsack, *Cave of Making*, 29.

29. Blunt was certainly no expert on relationships with women, but he and MacNeice were close friends despite the difference in their sexual orientations; Blunt once affirmed, perhaps wistfully, that MacNeice was "irredeemably heterosexual." Quoted in Stallworthy, *Louis MacNeice*, 104.

30. Stallworthy, *Louis MacNeice*, 172.

31. Ibid., 47, 53.

32. O'Neill and Reeves, *Auden, MacNeice, founder*, 66.

33. Marsack, *Cave of Making*, 25.

34. McDonald, *Poet in His Contexts*, 20.

35. Ibid., 21

36. Ibid.

37. MacNeice to ?, November 22, 1938, quoted in Stallworthy, *Louis MacNeice*, 233.

38. Auden, *CW*, 385.

39. Babbitt, *Masters*, viii.

40. Auden, *CW* 386.

41. Ibid.

42. Ibid.

Works Cited

Ackroyd, Peter. *T. S. Eliot: A Life.* New York: Simon and Schuster, 1984.

Auden, W. H. *The Age of Anxiety: A Baroque Eclogue.* New York: Random House, 1947.

———. *Collected Poems.* Edited by Edward Mendelson. New York: Random House, 1976.

———. *The Dyer's Hand and Other Essays.* New York: Random House, 1962.

———. *For the Time Being.* In *Collected Poems*, edited by Edward Mendelson, 269–308. New York: Random House, 1976.

———. *Forewords and Afterwords by Auden.* Edited by Edward Mendelson. New York: Random House, 1973.

———. "A Literary Transference." *Southern Review* 6 (1940–41): 78–86.

———. "Practiced Topophile." *Town and Country* (July 1947): 64, 101.

———. *Prose: And Travel Books in Prose and Verse.* Volume 1. 1926–1938. Edited by Edward Mendelson. Princeton: Princeton University Press, 1996.

Babbitt, Irving. *The Masters of Modern French Criticism.* Boston: Houghton Mifflin, 1912.

Bahktin, M. M. *The Dialogic Imagination.* Edited by Michael Holquist. Translated by Caryl Emerson and Michael Holquist. Austin: University of Texas Press, 1981.

"A 'Ballad Epic' of the Boer War." Review of *The Burden of Engela* by A. M.Buckton. *Times Literary Supplement.* January 15, 1904, 13.

Banfield, Ann. *The Phantom Table: Woolf, Fry, Russell and the Epistemology of Modernism.* Cambridge: Cambridge University Press, 2000.

Bergson, Henri. *Creative Evolution.* Translated by Arthur Mitchell. New York: Henry Holt, 1911.

———. "Laughter." 1900. Translater Unknown. In *Comedy*, edited by Wylie Sypher, 61–190. New York: Doubleday Anchor Books, 1956.

———. *Matter and Memory.* 1908. Translated by Nancy Margaret Paul and W. Scott Palmer. New York: Zone Books, 1988.

———. *Time and Free Will: An Essay on the Immediate Data of Consciousness.* Translated by F. L. Pogson. London: George Allen and Unwin, 1910.

Bloom, Harold. *Yeats.* New York: Oxford University Press, 1970.

Bornstein, George. *Yeats and Shelley.* Chicago: University of Chicago Press, 1970.

Bradley, F. H. *Essays on Truth and Reality.* Oxford: Clarendon Press, 1914.

Brogan, T. V. F. "Ballad." In *The New Princeton Encyclopedia of Poetry and*

Poetics, edited by Alex Preminger and T. V. F. Brogan, 116–18. Princeton: Princeton University Press, 1993.

Brooker, Jewel Spears. *Mastery and Escape: T. S. Eliot and the Dialectic of Modernism*. Amherst: University of Massachusetts Press, 1994.

Brown, Terence. *Louis MacNeice: Sceptical Vision*. Dublin: Gill and MacMillan, 1975.

Childs, Donald J. *From Philosophy to Poetry: T. S. Eliot's Study of Knowledge and Experience* New York: Palgrave, 2001.

Coleridge, S. T. *Biographia Literaria. The Collected Works of Samuel Taylor Coleridge*. vol. 7. Edited by James Engell and W. Jackson Bate. Princeton: Princeton University Press, 1983.

Cook, Reginald. *Robert Frost: A Living Voice*. Amherst: University of Massachusetts Press, 1974.

Craig, H. A. L. "Poetry." Review of *The Age of Anxiety. Spectator*, December 1948: 774, 776.

Dean, Susan. *Hardy's Poetic Vision in "The Dynasts": The Diorama of a Dream*. Princeton: Princeton University Press, 1977.

Dobrée, Bonamy. "The Dynasts." *Southern Review* 6 (1940–41): 109–24.

Douglass, Paul. *Bergson, Eliot, and American Literature*. Lexington: University Press of Kentucky, 1986.

Dronke, Peter. *Verse with Prose from Petronius to Dante: The Art and Scope of the Mixed Form*. Cambridge, MA: Harvard University Press, 1994.

Eliot, T. S. *The Complete Poems and Plays, 1909–1950*. San Diego: Harcourt Brace Jovanovich, 1980.

——. *Inventions of the March Hare*. Edited by Christopher Ricks. London: Faber and Faber, 1996.

——. *Knowledge and Experience in the Philosophy of F. H. Bradley*. New York: Farrar, Straus, 1964.

——. *The Letters of T. S. Eliot*. Volume 1. Edited by Valerie Eliot. San Diego: Harcourt, Brace, Jovanovich, 1988.

——. *Selected Essays: 1917–1932*. New York: Harcourt, Brace, 1932.

——. *The Selected Prose of T. S. Eliot*. New York: Harcourt, Brace, Jovanovich, 1975.

——. *The Varieties of Metaphysical Poetry*. Edited by Ronald Schuchard. New York: Harcourt, Brace, 1993.

Emig, Rainer. *W. H. Auden: Towards a Postmodern Poetics*. New York: St. Martin's Press, 2000.

Frost, Robert. *Collected Poems, Prose, & Plays*. Library of America Edition. Edited by Richard Poirier and Mark Richardson. New York: Literary Classics of the United States, 1995.

——. "The Hear-Say Ballad." Foreword to *Ballads Migrant in New England*, by Helen Hartness Flanders and Marguerite Olney, xii–xiii. Miami, FL: Granger Books, 1953.

——. *The Letters of Robert Frost to Louis Untermeyer*. Edited by Louis Untermeyer. New York: Holt, Rinehart and Winston, 1963.

———. *Prose Jottings of Robert Frost: Selections from His Notebooks and Miscellaneous Manuscripts.* Edited by Edward Connery Lathem and Hyde Cox. Lunenburg, VT: Northeast-Kingdom Publishers, 1982.

———. *Selected Letters of Robert Frost.* Edited by Lawrance Thompson. New York: Holt, Rinehart and Winston, 1964.

———. *Selected Prose of Robert Frost.* Edited by Hyde Cox and Edward Connery Latham. New York: Holt, Rinehart and Winston, 1966.

Fuller, John. *W. H. Auden: A Commentary.* Princeton: Princeton University Press, 1998.

Gillies, Mary Ann. *Henri Bergson and British Modernism.* Montreal: McGill-Queen's University Press, 1996.

Gordon, Lyndall. *Eliot's Early Years.* Oxford: Oxford University Press, 1977.

———. *T. S. Eliot: An Imperfect Life.* New York: W. W. Norton, 1999.

Gray, Piers. *T. S. Eliot's Intellectual and Poetic Development, 1909–1922.* Sussex: Harvester Press, 1982.

Greenberg, Herbert. *Quest for the Necessary: W. H. Auden and the Dilemma of Divided Consciousness.* Cambridge, MA: Harvard University Press, 1968.

Greg, Walter W. *Pastoral Poetry and Pastoral Drama: A Literary Inquiry, with Special Reference to the Pre-Restoration Stage in England.* 1906. New York: Russell & Russell, 1959.

Griffin, Howard. *Conversations with Auden.* Edited by Donald Allen. San Francisco: Grey Fox Press, 1981.

Habib, M. A. R. *The Early T. S. Eliot and Western Philosophy.* Cambridge: Cambridge University Press, 1999.

Hall, Dorothy Judd. *Robert Frost: Contours of Belief.* Athens: Ohio University Press, 1984.

Halper, Edward C. "One-many Problem." In *The Cambridge Dictionary of Philosophy*, edited by Robert Audi, 546–47. Cambridge: Cambridge University Press, 1995.

Hardy, Thomas. *The Collected Letters of Thomas Hardy.* Volume 1: 1840–1892. Edited by Richard Little Purdy and Michael Millgate. Oxford: Clarendon Press, 1978.

———. *The Collected Letters of Thomas Hardy.* Volume 3: 1902–1908. Edited by Richard Little Purdy and Michael Millgate. Oxford: Clarendon Press, 1982.

———. *The Collected Letters of Thomas Hardy.* Volume 4: 1909–1913. Edited by Richard Little Purdy and Michael Millgate. Oxford: Clarendon Press, 1984.

———. *The Complete Poems of Thomas Hardy.* Edited by James Gibson. New York: MacMillan, 1976.

———. *The Dynasts: An Epic-Drama of the War with Napoleon, In Three Parts, Nineteen Acts, and One Hundred and Thirty-one Scenes, the Time Covered by the Action Being About Ten Years.* Parts I and II. In *The Complete Poetical Works of Thomas Hardy*, volume 4, edited by Samuel Hynes. Oxford: Clarendon Press, 1995.

———. *The Dynasts: An Epic-Drama of the War with Napoleon, In Three*

Parts, Nineteen Acts, and One Hundred and Thirty-one Scenes, the Time Covered by the Action Being About Ten Years. Part III. In *The Complete Poetical Works of Thomas Hardy,* volume 5, edited by Samuel Hynes. Oxford: Clarendon Press, 1995.

———. "'The Dynasts': A Postscript." *Times Literary Supplement,* Feb 19, 1904, 53. In appendix E, *The Complete Poetical Works of Thomas Hardy,* Volume 5, edited by Samuel Hynes, 5 vols, 395–96. Oxford: Clarendon Press, 1995.

———. *The Life and Work of Thomas Hardy.* Edited by Michael Millgate. Athens: The University of Georgia Press, 1985.

———. *Thomas Hardy's Personal Writings.* Edited by Harold Orel. London: MacMillan, 1967.

Hass, Robert Bernard. *Going by Contraries: Robert Frost's Conflict with Science.* Charlottesville: University Press of Virginia, 2002.

Hecht, Anthony. *The Hidden Law: The Poetry of W. H. Auden.* Cambridge, MA: Harvard University Press, 1993.

Hoffman, Tyler. *Robert Frost and the Politics of Poetry.* Hanover, NH: Middlebury College Press, University Press of New England, 2001.

Hoggart, Richard. *Auden: An Introductory Essay.* New Haven: Yale University Press, 1951.

Hulme, T. E. *The Collected Writings of T. E. Hulme.* Edited by Karen Csengeri. Oxford: Clarendon Press, 1994.

Issarachoff, Michael. *Discourse as Performance.* Stanford, CA: Stanford University Press, 1989.

Jain, Manju. *T. S. Eliot and American Philosophy: The Harvard Years.* Cambridge: Cambridge University Press, 1992.

James, William. *Pragmatism: A New Name for Some Old Ways of Thinking.* New York: Longman Green, 1907.

———. *Psychology: Briefer Course.* Cambridge, MA: Harvard University Press, 1984.

Jarrell, Randall. *Randall Jarrell's Letters: An Autobiographical and Literary Selection.* Edited by Mary Jarrell. Boston: Houghton Mifflin Co., 1985.

———. "Verse Chronicle." Review of *The Age of Anxiety. Nation* Oct. 18, 1947, 424–25.

Jeffares, Norman A. *W. B. Yeats: Man and Poet.* 1962. New York: St. Martin's Press, 1996.

Jost, Walter. "Lessons in the Conversation That We Are: Robert Frost's 'Death of the Hired Man.'" *College English* 58, no. 4 (April 1996): 397–422.

Lathem, Edward Connery. *Interviews with Robert Frost.* 1966. Guilford, CT: Jeffrey Norton Publishers, 1997.

Lentricchia, Frank. *Robert Frost: Modern Poetics and the Landscapes of Self.* Durham, NC: Duke University Press, 1975.

Levenson, Michael H. *A Genealogy of Modernism: A Study of English Literary Doctrine, 1908–1922.* Cambridge: Cambridge University Press, 1984.

Lockerd, Benjamin. *Aethereal Rumours: T. S. Eliot's Physics and Poetics.* Lewisburg, PA: Bucknell University Press, 1998.

Longley, Edna. "Louis MacNeice: Aspects of His Aesthetic Theory and Practice." In *Studies on Louis MacNeice,* edited by Jacqueline Genet and Wynne Hellegouarc'h, 51–62. Caen: Société Française d'Études Irlandaises, Centre de Publications de l'Université de Caen, 1988.

———. *Louis MacNeice: A Study.* London: Faber and Faber, 1988.

MacNeice, Louis. *The Collected Poems of Louis MacNeice.* Edited by E. R. Dodds. New York: Oxford University Press, 1967.

———. *Modern Poetry: A Personal Essay.* 1938. New York: Haskell House Publishers, 1969.

———. *The Poetry of W. B. Yeats.* London: Oxford University Press, 1940.

———. *Selected Literary Criticism of Louis MacNeice.* Edited by Alan Heuser. Oxford: Clarendon Press, 1987.

———. *Selected Prose of Louis MacNeice.* Edited by Alan Heuser. Oxford: Clarendon Press, 1990.

———. *The Strings Are False: An Unfinished Autobiography.* Edited by E. R. Dodds. London: Faber and Faber, 1965.

Marsack, Robyn. *The Cave of Making: The Poetry of Louis MacNeice.* Oxford: Clarendon Press, 1982.

Mayer, John T. *T. S. Eliot's Silent Voices.* New York: Oxford University Press, 1989.

Maynard, Katherine Kearney. *Thomas Hardy's Tragic Poetry: The Lyrics and "The Dynasts."* Iowa City: University of Iowa Press, 1991.

McDonald, Peter. *Louis MacNeice: The Poet in His Contexts.* Oxford: Clarendon Press, 1991.

Mendelson, Edward. *Early Auden.* 1981. New York: Farrar, Strauss and Giroux, 2000.

———. *Later Auden.* New York: Farrar, Straus and Giroux, 1999.

Meyers, Jeffrey. *Robert Frost: A Biography.* Boston: Houghton Mifflin, 1996.

Millard, Kenneth. "Hardy's *The Dynasts:* 'words . . . to hold the imagination.'" Reprinted from *Edwardian Poetry,* Oxford: Clarendon Press, 1991, 59–79. *Critical Essays on Thomas Hardy's Poetry,* edited by Harold Orel, 165–83. New York: G. K. Hall, 1995.

Miller, J. Hillis. *Thomas Hardy: Distance and Desire.* Cambridge, MA: Belknap Press of Harvard University Press, 1970.

"Mr. Hardy's Drama." Review of *The Dynasts: A Drama,* Part I, by Thomas Hardy. *Times Literary Supplement,* January 15, 1904, 11–12.

O'Neill, Michael, and Gareth Reeves. *Auden, MacNeice, Spender: The Thirties Poetry.* New York: St. Martin's Press, 1992.

Osmond, Rosalie. *Mutual Accusation: Seventeenth-Century Body and Soul Dialogues in Their Literary and Theological Context.* Toronto: University of Toronto Press, 1990.

Parini, Jay. *Robert Frost: A Life.* New York: Henry Holt, 1999.

Poirier, Richard. *Robert Frost: The Work of Knowing.* New York: Oxford University Press, 1977.

Prince, Michael. *Philosophical Dialogue in the British Enlightenment: Theol-*

ogy, *Aesthetics, and the Novel.* Cambridge: Cambridge University Press, 1996.

ae, Patricia. *The Practical Muse : Pragmatist Poetics in Hulme, Pound, and Stevens.* Lewisburg, PA: Bucknell University Press, 1997.

eview of *The Age of Anxiety. Times Literary Supplement,* October 23, 1948, 596.

ichardson, Alan. *A Mental Theater: Poetic Drama and Consciousness in the Romantic Age.* University Park: The Pennsylvania State University Press, 1988.

ichardson, Mark. "Robert Frost and the Motives of Poetry." *Essays in Literature* 20, no. 2 (Fall 1993): 273–91.

iquelme, John Paul. *Harmony of Dissonances: T. S. Eliot, Romanticism, and Imagination.* Baltimore: Johns Hopkins University Press, 1991.

oyce, Josiah. "The One, the Many, and the Infinite." Supplementary Essay to *The World and the Individual. First Series: The Four Historical Conceptions of Being,* 473–588. 1900. New York: Dover Publications, 1959.

ussell, Bertrand. *The Problems of Philosophy.* 1912. London: Oxford University Press, 1977.

antayana, George. *Three Philosophical Poets: Lucretius, Dante, and Goethe.* 1910. Harvard Studies in Comparative Literature. Volume 1. New York: Cooper Square Publishers, 1970.

cholem, Gershom. *Kabbalah.* New York: Meridian, 1978.

chuchard, Ronald. *Eliot's Dark Angel: Intersections of Life and Art.* New York: Oxford University Press, 1999.

chwartz, Delmore. "Delmore Schwartz on Auden's 'Most Self-Indulgent Book.'" *Partisan Review* 14 (September–October 1947): 528–31. Reprinted in *W. H. Auden: The Critical Heritage,* edited by John Haffenden, 368–71. London: Routledge & Kegan Paul, 1983.

eale, Lisa. "Original Originality: Robert Frost's Talks." in *Roads Not Taken: Rereading Robert Frost,* edited by Earl J. Wilcox and Jonathan N. Barron, 105–20. Columbia: University of Missouri Press, 2000.

igg, Eric. *The American T. S. Eliot: A Study of the Early Writings.* Cambridge: Cambridge University Press, 1989.

imon, Linda. *Genuine Reality: A Life of William James.* New York: Harcourt Brace, 1998.

mith, James. "On Metaphysical Poetry." *Scrutiny* 2 (1933): 222–39.

tallworthy, Jon. *Louis MacNeice.* New York: W.W. Norton, 1995.

urette, Leon. *The Birth of Modernism.* Montreal: McGill-Queen's University Press, 1994.

hompson, Lawrance. *Robert Frost: The Early Years, 1874–1915.* New York: Holt, Rinehart and Winston, 1966.

———. *Robert Frost: The Years of Triumph, 1915–1938.* New York: Holt, Rinehart and Winston, 1970.

ntermeyer, Louis, ed. *The Letters of Robert Frost to Louis Untermeyer.* New York: Holt, Rinehart and Winston, 1963.

Veltruský, Jirí. *Drama as Literature*. Lisse: Peter de Ridder Press, 1977.

Vogt, Victor E. "Narrative and Drama in the Lyric: Robert Frost's Strategi Withdrawal." *Critical Inquiry* 5, no. 3 (Spring 1979): 529–51.

Walkley, A. B. " 'The Dynasts': A Suggestion." *Times Literary Supplement* Jan uary 29, 1904, 30. In appendix E, *The Complete Poetical Works of Thoma Hardy*, volume 5, edited by Samuel Hynes, 386–88. Oxford: Clarendo Press, 1995.

Walsh, John Evangelist. *Into My Own: The English Years of Robert Fros. 1912–1915*. New York: Grove Press, 1988.

Wells, Robert. Introduction to *The Idylls of Theocritus*. New York: Carcane 1988.

Whitaker, Thomas R. *Swan and Shadow: Yeats's Dialogue with History* Chapel Hill: University of North Carolina Press, 1964.

Wickens, C. Glen. *Thomas Hardy, Monism, and the Carnival Tradition: Th One and the Many in "The Dynasts."* Toronto: University of Toronto Pres 2002.

Witt, Mary Ann Frese. "Reading Modern Drama: Voice in the Didascaliae. *Studies in the Literary Imagination* 25 (Spring 1992): 1, 103–11.

Wright, Walter F. *The Shaping of "The Dynasts": A Study in Thomas Hardy* Lincoln: University of Nebraska Press, 1967.

Yeats, W. B. *The Autobiography of William Butler Yeats*. Garden City, NY Doubleday Anchor Books, 1958.

———. *Essays*. New York: MacMillan, 1924.

———. *Essays and Introductions*. New York: MacMillan, 1961.

———. *Memoirs*. Edited by Denis Donoghue. New York: MacMillan, 1972.

Index

Abercrombie, Lascelles, 172 n. 28
Addison, Joseph, 131
Alighieri, Dante, 88, 93, 96, 104–5
allo-repetition, 102–4
Auden, W. H., 23, 30, 31–32, 79, 139,
141, 155, 157, 169, 170, 183 n. 41,
188 n. 32; the baroque, 49–50, 65–
66, 70–71; and the critics, 34, 45,
77; and drugs, 173 n. 3; influenced
by Hardy, 21, 30, 35–36; and Judaism, 53–55, 76, 178 n. 61; lecture at
Swarthmore, 40, 41, 49–50, 175 n.
30; philosophy, 39–41; on unity and
civilization, 173 n. 40; on war,
174 n. 15, 176 n. 46.
—Works of: *The Age of Anxiety*, 21,
31–32, 34, 35–37, 41, 42–46, 49–56,
57–58, 62–63, 64–69, 70–71, 74–76,
77, 155; *The Ascent of F6*, 51; "The
Dance of Death," 34; *The Dyer's
Hand*, 36, 45, 75, 77; *For the Time
Being*, 21, 35, 39, 51; *Letters from
Iceland*, 157; *The Orators*, 51; *Paid
on Both Sides*, 35; "Practiced Topophile," 64; *The Prolific and the
Devourer*, 40; *The Sea and the Mirror*, 21, 35; "The Virgin and the Dynamo," 177 n. 53

Babbitt, Irving, 13, 83–84
Bakhtin, Mikhail, 68
ballad form, 27–28, 78, 124–25, 131
Barnes, Djuna, 172 n. 28
Bergson, Henri, 17–18, 20, 32, 38, 82,
84, 89, 90–91, 92–93, 94–95, 98,
100–101, 103, 109, 119, 128, 130,
156, 185 n. 86.
—Works of: *Creative Evolution*, 17,
84, 91, 109, 128; "Laughter," 100;

Matter and Memory, 84, 103; *Time
and Free Will*, 185 n. 86
Blake, William, 79, 95–96, 137
Blavatsky, Helena (Madame), 100
Blunt, Anthony, 147, 163, 191 n. 29
body/soul relationship, 14, 16, 25, 38–
39, 49, 52, 79, 80–81, 84, 85, 86, 90,
98–100, 110, 144, 175 n. 27, 186 n.
91
Bottomly, Gordon, 172 n. 28
Bradley, F. H., 14, 32, 82, 85, 140
Byron, George Gordon (Lord Byron),
28

Coleridge, S. T., 28, 83
Crowley, Aleister, 97

Day Lewis, Cecil, 114, 166
debate of body and soul. *See* dialogue
of body and soul
Democritus, 16
dialogue form, 22–25; relationship between poet and reader in, 31, 36–
37, 71–72
dialogue of body and soul, 22, 25–26,
32, 86–88, 90, 92–94, 98, 144
didascalia, 57–60, 66–71, 76–78
Donne, John, 79, 81–82, 106
Driscoll, Louise, 172 n. 27
dualism, 15, 16, 26, 38–39, 46–47, 79,
109, 171 n. 11, 175 n. 21

eavesdropping effect, 23–24, 126–27,
167
eclogue form, 26–27, 124–25, 146,
151–52, 161, 165, 166
ecstasis, 32, 93, 96–97, 98–100
Eliot, T. S., 18, 19, 21, 22, 30, 108,
109, 137, 139, 140, 169; influence of

199